D0622599

Law, Economics and Cyberspace

NEW HORIZONS IN LAW AND ECONOMICS

Series editors: Gerrit De Geest, *University of Ghent and University of Antwerp, Belgium and University of Utrecht, The Netherlands*; Roger Van den Bergh, *University of Rotterdam and University of Utrecht, The Netherlands*; and Thomas S. Ulen, *University of Illinois at Urbana-Champaign, USA.*

The application of economic ideas and theories to the law and the explanation of markets and public economics from a legal point of view is recognized as one of the most exciting developments in both economics and the law. This important series is designed to make a significant contribution to the development of law and economics.

The main emphasis is on the development and application of new ideas. The series provides a forum for original research in areas such as criminal law, civil law, labour law, corporate law, family law, regulation and privatization, tax, risk and insurance and competition law. International in its approach it includes some of the best theoretical and empirical work from both well-established researchers and the new generation of scholars.

Titles in the series include:

Law, Economics and Cyberspace

The Effects of Cyberspace on the Economic Analysis of Law

Niva Elkin-Koren

Professor of Law, University of Haifa, Israel

Eli M. Salzberger

Professor of Law, University of Haifa, Israel

NEW HORIZONS IN LAW AND ECONOMICS

Edward Elgar

Cheltenham, UK • Northampton, MA, USA

© Niva Elkin-Koren, Eli M. Salzberger 2004

All rights reserved. No part of this publication may be reproduced, stored in a retrieval system or transmitted in any form or by any means, electronic, mechanical or photocopying, recording, or otherwise without the prior permission of the publisher.

Published by
Edward Elgar Publishing Limited
Glensanda House
Montpellier Parade
Cheltenham
Glos GL50 1UA
UK

Edward Elgar Publishing, Inc.
136 West Street
Suite 202
Northampton
Massachusetts 01060
USA

A catalogue record for this book
is available from the British Library

ISBN 1 84064 669 1

Printed and bound in Great Britain by MPG Books Ltd, Bodmin, Cornwall

Contents

Preface and Acknowledgments

This book originates from a paper delivered in Utrecht at the 1999 conference of the European Association of Law and Economics, which was subsequently published in the International Review of Law and Economics (Elkin-Koren and Salzberger 1999). We were encouraged by the Edward Elgar publishing staff to expand the article and transform it into a book. Whether this encouragement paid off is for our readers to judge.

Since 1999 Cyberspace has been constantly changing, giving rise to a vast body of fresh literature, new laws and court decisions. The pace of these changes was so intensive that the mere velocity of technological development became one of the major themes of our book. Although the book is very different from our original paper, its main thrust has not changed; nor has its central conclusion. The book revisits the analytical framework of economic analysis of law and examines its applicability to the new information environment. It concludes that the existing paradigms of law and economics are ill equipped to analyze the new economic and non-economic markets formed and affected by Cyberspace, mainly because the conventional analysis can no longer rely on the presuppositions held by the law and economics approach, in its positive and normative analyses. Our book offers, alongside the basic economic market analysis, an extensive treatment of non-market activities, notably an elaborate discussion of the theory of the State in the age of Cyberspace.

This book is a joint effort of two authors. We come from very different traditions: Eli Salzberger hails from the world of legal philosophy and law and economics, and Niva Elkin-Koren originates from the world of information law and intellectual property. Writing this book together created a rare opportunity for testing our presuppositions and challenging our conceptual frameworks. Nothing was self-evident, and recurrently we encountered the limits of our own intellectual traditions. This turned our writing process into a self-reflecting, fascinating dialogue among discourses, disciplines and ideologies. The manuscript often bridges some of the differences, but at the same time seeks to retain the distinctiveness of voices. We hope that the often dialectic nature of the outcome will stimulate further challenges to the current analytical framework.

Of the many people who provided us with assistance and support in this project, a few deserve special mention. First and foremost is our chief research assistant, Rachel Aridor, whose dedication, talent and creative insights made a vital contribution to the final product. Shay Gimelstein and Nowam Kleiner conducted valuable research and bibliographic work. We are grateful to our colleagues Michael Birnhack, Fania Oz-Salzberger, Bernt Hugenholtz, Lodewijk Asscher and Jurian Langer who read parts of the manuscript and provided enlightening comments and feedback. Parts of the book were also presented at various conferences, among which were the EALE conference in Vienna, the Corsica workshop in Law and Economics held in Reims, and colloquiums at the Institute for Information Law at the University of Amsterdam, at the Faculties of Law at the University of Haifa and Tel Aviv University and at the Interdisciplinary Center in Hertzelia. We wish to thank their participants for valuable remarks. We thank Roberta Neiger who did an excellent job of editing and bringing the manuscript to a publishable state. The final camera copy was prepared by David Gottesmann of Pardes Publishing House. We wish to thank Dymphna Evans and the other members of Edward Elgar Publishing Limited for their encouragement, patience and faith in the manuscript, which was long overdue.

Finally we wish to thank our family members: Fania Oz-Salzberger and Dean, Nadav and Kitzi Salzberger; Omer, Uri and Danny Koren. Thank you all for sharing the writing process with us, endorsing us with stimulating ideas, love and support.

Part One

SETTING THE GROUNDS

1. Introduction

'If you torture the data enough, nature will always confess.' R. Coase, 1981

1. PHRASING THE QUESTIONS

Information technologies have dramatically altered many aspects of our everyday life. They change the way we communicate with one another, the way we purchase, entertain, interact, learn, research, deliberate, do business, and indeed, think. The invention of the printing press in the fifteenth century can be seen as the major catalyst for the Industrial Revolution and for major changes in political thought, as well as the gateway to the Enlightenment. During the past two decades it has been the Internet that is revolutionizing economic, communal and political life. This Cyber-revolution is the most significant transformation in the information environment since the invention of printing.

Cyberspace has become an integral part of people's everyday life, and the online information environment constitutes the human condition of our time. People spend a large portion of their time using the Internet for entertainment, business, social relationships and political activities. The increasing human activity in Cyberspace is transforming social and cultural norms, creating a web of new communities, with diverse characteristics – linguistic, cultural and economic. It is beginning to blur some old boundaries across classes and social hierarchies, while at the same time drawing new borders of the digital divide, between the haves and the have nots, between those who are in command of the technology and the technologically illiterate. The new information environment further introduces fresh players and novel market and non-market behaviors that cannot be easily explained by standard sociological, political or economic concepts. Cyberspace can even be thought of as affecting the definition of the self.

Even though Cyberspace and the information environment have received a lot of attention in the literature, many dispute the idea that it is a distinct phenomenon worthy of a special inquiry. This skeptical view holds that the changes introduced by information technologies are only in form, i.e., enabling new actions, modifying the speed or scope of human activities, but do not change the substance. They transform neither fundamental social structures nor the organization of economic behavior (see, for instance, May 2002).

This 'Cyberskepticism' also exists in the economic literature, and consequently in some law and economics writings. A telling example of this

3

approach in the law and economics movement can be found in the speech delivered by Frank Easterbrook at a symposium on intellectual property in the age of Cyberspace, held at the University of Chicago. Judge Easterbrook, a former University of Chicago law professor in law and economics, cooled down the enthusiasm of the conference participants by stating that to talk about the law of and in Cyberspace, or, more particularly, to talk about property in Cyberspace, the topic he was asked to address, is just like talking about the law of the horse. Cyberspace does not, according to Easterbrook, alter the basic tenets of legal theory or of the economic analysis of law. The same old principles can be applied to Cyberspace. So, just as Dean Casper of the University of Chicago Law School refused a century ago to offer a course in 'The Law of the Horse' there was no justification to re-construct legal theory just because we had entered an era of extensive usage in computer networks (Easterbrook 1996).

This book begs to differ. The networked information environment, we argue, should exert a crucial influence on economic thinking, on the perception of law, and, by derivation, on the economic analysis of law. It challenges fundamental concepts, such as the notion of work as linked to a workplace or market exchange, the notion of community as linked to geographical space, the sources of law and its traditional perception as anchored in the state, the concept of knowledge as linked to a particular social situation, the perception of creative output as executed by atomistic individuals motivated to maximize profits, the roles of technology and its interrelation with the law, and the belief that proxies and representatives are indispensable for collective action and public decision-making processes.

Take Linux as an example. GNU/Linux is a peer-produced operating system, jointly developed by hundreds of thousands of minds around the world, and successfully run by approximately eight million users connected to the Web. Are the hordes of Linux developers who engage in an ongoing collaborative effort around the world 'working'? Can we explain their joint effort by resorting to our traditional notion of 'work' as sharply distinguished from leisure? Can interaction and collaboration of programmers in a digitally networked environment be sufficiently understood as market exchange? What counts as market in a virtual global network of communication? Does Linux produce a public good? Can it become a monopoly? Do Linux users and developers constitute a community and, if so, what makes it possible? Should online communities obey the rules that govern the physical residence of their constituents? What is the interface between non-market enterprises, such as Linux, and market mechanisms of production?

Our study explores these questions and others, critically examining the analytical framework offered by law and economics for addressing them. We conclude that there is an imperative need for re-evaluating the analytical tools used for studying the information environment. The traditional analytical concepts, which structure the way we arrange our social reality, are based on various assumptions regarding the world. These assumptions must be examined in the new circumstances created by information technologies. To the extent that these assumptions are no longer consistent with the world today, they must be modified, allowing for the development of new analytical schemes.

This book visits the existing economic paradigms, the prisms through which we observe the online information environment, and attempts to identify their biases and distortions. We elaborate on the limits of the fundamental economic paradigms when applied to Cyberspace, how they construct the reality that is the subject of study, what is left out of sight using these paradigms, and to what extent these paradigms are useful for identifying new phenomena, noting the various factors which affect economic behavior and providing a sufficient explanation. The uncritical use of a conventional analytical framework runs the risk of producing a distorted view on both positive and normative levels. This critical analysis is particularly important when the economic analysis of law is at stake, as it has a significant say in formulating legal policy.

2. CYBERSPACE, PARADIGM SHIFT AND THE EVOLUTION OF THE ECONOMIC ANALYSIS OF LAW

The term 'paradigm shift' was coined by Thomas Kuhn when he put forward a theory about the development of the natural sciences (1962). In ancient times and up to the Middle Ages, science was perceived as a priori, a set of truths resulting not from experiment, but from thought. Scientific discovery or analysis were seen very much as the result of the same sort of argumentation as morals or political philosophy, applying logic or intuition to a given set of observations. Such were the scientific efforts of Aristotle and Ptolemy. It was Francis Bacon who shifted scientific thinking towards an emphasis on facts that can be discovered through experiments and an inductive process. Bacon thus saw scientific inquiry as one of constant and accumulative progress, like a building, which is constructed stone after stone.

Kuhn disputed this description and argued that science develops in leaps. Regular scientific research is conducted within a set of boundaries that are based on presuppositions left unquestioned by the contemporary scientific world. These boundaries were dubbed by Kuhn a 'paradigm'. Scientists in their research (and in their research agenda) are trying to complete a jigsaw puzzle, where the framework of the puzzle is pre-determined by the paradigm. However, in the course of scientific research it turns out that not all pieces fit their spots, and some pieces tend to cross the set boundaries. Scientists try to force the pieces into the slots they think are meant for them. But at one focal point the framework collapses. Doubts bring about rethinking of the pre-set presuppositions; the paradigms shift. A new paradigm is constructed, which sets new presuppositions and a new research agenda. Regular scientific research continues within the new paradigm, until that too is ripe for replacement.

Many scientific disciplines experienced a *paradigm shift* of the kind described by Kuhn. So far, economic theory has gone through very few shifts since Adam Smith's *The Wealth of Nations* ([1776] 1961). The hype of the late 1990s and the rise of the 'new economy' caused some confusion among economists. Yet, this confusion has not yet been translated into an overall scrutiny of the fundamental tenets of economics, and, by derivation, of the economic analysis of law.

The limits of standard economic analysis are evident in explaining the 'high-tech bulb' and the behavior of the NASDAQ during the late 1990s. Economists were puzzled by the rise of startup companies, such as Napster, which do not sustain any business model or prospective profits, but nevertheless managed to attract users and investors in a short period of time. The term 'new economy' was often used to describe the economy of the Cyber-revolution era, but it often reflected no more than a lack of understanding of the emerging circumstances, and a sense of confusion regarding the information environment. In retrospect, what was called the 'new economy' is actually a range of new phenomena brought about by Cyberspace, described and analyzed in the framework of the insights of conventional economic analysis.

We believe that Cyberspace challenges standard economics, and consequently law and economics, on various levels related to the unique nature of its central asset: information. Traditional economic models, for example, prove insufficient for explaining the success of GNU/Linux. What makes the development of Linux, as powerful public domain software, possible? How can such a significant technology that runs on major facilities around the world emerge in the absence of obvious monetary incentives? What makes such innovative technology managed by no central management sustainable against every basic economic intuition? But Linux is by no means a unique case. An example for another phenomenon, which traditional economic models find difficult to explain, is Peer to Peer (P2P) networks. The question of why tens of millions of individuals have chosen to upload free, high-quality sound recordings for their fellow anonymous users, despite the absence of obvious incentives, is puzzling. Although these phenomena and others are extensively discussed in the literature of recent years, there were only few attempts in the economics and law and economics literature (a salient exception is Benkler 2002) to examine critically the tenets of the analytical framework.

An important aspect of the ill-equipped tools of the traditional analysis has to do with technology, a theme discussed in several chapters of this book. Technology was obviously always present in the world and effective in the economic scene. Yet traditional economic models pre-assumed the state of technology to be fixed or exogenous to the analysis. The current pace of technological change makes it impossible to leave it outside the economic calculus. Naturally, technology affects efficiency. However, while under standard economic analysis, technological state of the art is held fixed, it can no longer be considered static when technology reinvents itself every year.

Moreover, technology does not evolve in a vacuum. Technological innovation and utilization occur within a complex web of socio-economic structures. The introduction of new technologies has a dialectic relationship with other processes. Legal rules and market processes may directly affect the types of technologies available by explicitly prohibiting the use of certain technologies by law or by providing incentives to particular technologies and not others. Technology, in turn, affects the law. Information technologies are often functioning as a regulator, thereby substituting law or supplementing its function in directing people's behavior. The information environment thus implies serious ramifications for law – its nature, definition and roles. Technology should, therefore, become endogenous to the analysis, and the economic discourse should be expanded to address it.

3. THREE GENERATIONS OF ECONOMIC ANALYSIS OF LAW

Our study offers a tentative look at the changing world of law with the emergence of Cyberspace from the perspective of the economic approach to law. The economic analysis of law emerged in the second half of the 20th century as the dominant theoretical paradigm for legal academia, and it is gradually capturing various segments of legal practice as well. The economic approach towards law extends the traditional economic models designed to analyze traditional markets and applies them to non-economic markets and non-market human interactions. It also emphasizes the role of law within economic and non-economic markets. In performing these tasks, the economic analysis of law also shifted traditional economic analysis to put more weight on normative analysis, pointing to the desirable legal rules and institutions to achieve economic efficiency.

One can describe the Law and Economics Movement as comprising three generations, which can be perceived as separate paradigms of sorts: the traditional Chicago School Economic Analysis of Law, Transaction Cost Analysis, and Neo-Institutional Economic Analysis of Law and Legal Institutions. The classification to several generations is functional. As some of the roots of the Neo-Institutional law and economics can be traced to the 18th century works of Borda (1781) and Condorcet ([1785] 1955), the term 'generation' is being used here not merely on a chronological basis, but rather as an indicator for the width and complexity of the economic analysis. The science of economics is cornered upon the transformation of real world conditions into a simplified setting. This is the basis for applying rigorous models of analysis. The presuppositions that set the framework for modeling can determine the complexity of analysis, and thus the precision of its results. In this sense, the Chicago School can be labeled first generation law and economics, while Neo-Institutional law and economics can be labeled third generation.

The Chicago School views the micro-economic model as the suitable theoretical framework for the analysis of all legal questions, including those which are not traditional market issues. The tools of micro-economic theory – the curves of supply and demand – can be applied to analyze the market of children for adoption or the market of crimes or the market of laws in general, just as they are applied to the market of apples or cars. The Chicago framework does not distinguish between rational individuals and other, more complex, market players such as firms, governments or agencies. The state, its structure and institutions are perceived as exogenous to the analysis. Markets and states are assumed to correspond to each other.

A transitional generation in the development of the Law and Economics thought is Transaction Cost Analysis. Its starting point is, in effect, an extension of the Chicago School's focus on the basic micro-economic model of markets and especially on market failures that justify central intervention. This extension eventually brought about the third generation of Neo-Institutional Law and Economics. At the heart of Transaction Costs Analysis is the Coase theorem, which undermines the categorization of the traditional market failures and especially the analysis of the remedies to correct them. Coase's analysis points at transaction costs as the focal factor, which determines modes of production (Coase 1937) and diverts the market from efficiency. Thus, it is almost the sole factor to take on board when legal rules are considered (Coase 1960). The concept of transaction costs, originally used to analyze the interaction between individuals in the market, was soon broadened to include the analysis of the emergence of institutions, their internal decision-making process and their external interactions. In doing so, the methodological tools used for the analysis were expanded, and hence the shift towards the third generation.

The third generation of economic analysis of law, which can be associated with the Neo-Institutional paradigm, is the broadest framework of economic analysis insofar as it incorporates institutional structures as endogenous variables within the analysis of law. Thus, Neo-Institutional analysis views the political structure, the bureaucratic structure, the legal institutions, and other commercial and non-commercial entities as affecting each other. Political rules intertwine with economic rules, which intertwine with contracts. The tools that are used in the analyses of the Neo-Institutional law and economics are the traditional micro-economics or welfare economics models, alongside public choice, game theory and institutional economics (Mercuro and Medema 1997).

Although we used the term 'generation' in the description of the three major paradigms of law and economics, we by no means imply that early generations are gone. The first generation – the Chicago School – is very much alive. Significant work in law and economics is being carried out in this framework, and also in the framework of Transaction Costs. These approaches must therefore be taken on board as we apply the law and economics thinking to Cyberspace.

4. SYNOPSIS OF THE BOOK

The book is divided into three parts. Part One is introductory and explicates on the two foundations of the book – the law and economics movement and Cyberspace. In addition to the introduction to the economic analysis of law and its three generations, we elaborate, in Chapter 2, on the Internet, its history, and the key concepts developed around it: the information age, information society and information economy, and the most controversial term – *Cyberspace*. We delve into the politics of names surrounding the term *Cyberspace*, thereby touching upon the wide range of ramifications of the information technology revolution, most of which we do not attempt to cover in this book.

Part Two focuses on Cyberspace as an economic market. It examines the characteristics of online markets, analyzing possible market failures in comparison to those in the non-virtual world, and drawing general descriptive and prescriptive insights as to the appropriate scope of central intervention in the market in the age of Cyberspace. The main thrust of Part Two, however, is an exploration of the viability of the traditional economic models to Cyber-markets and traditional markets affected by Cyberspace. Chapters 3–7 cover the traditional market failures identified by the first generation law and economics – the Chicago School: Monopolies (Chapter 4), Public Goods (Chapter 5), Information (Chapter 6) and Externalities (Chapter 7). Chapter 8 focuses on Transaction Cost economics – the second generation of law and economics.

In each of these chapters we show that applying the traditional economic analysis points to a significant decline of market failures, which indicates less justification for central intervention. Cyberspace is predicted to eliminate or at least notably diminish the traditional failures of public goods (i.e., information), monopolies, lack of information, externalities, and transaction costs. However, new types of market deficiencies arise, which the existing models fail to detect and are ill-equipped to analyze. Technological standards as a source of monopolistic power, the changing nature of information that was traditionally perceived as a public good, the technological race between enforcement measures by the code and counter measures, and the costs involved in verifying information are but a few examples.

Chapter 4 demonstrates that low entry and fixed costs, size of market and scarcity tend to point to a significant decline in the market failure of monopolistic powers. However, new types of monopoly problems emerge, related mainly to technology and standards. The identification of such monopolistic powers is different from identifying monopolies in the non-virtual world, and traditional remedies of price and quantity control, on the one hand, and restrictions on mergers or breaking up firms, on the other hand, may not be efficacious to remedy these new problems.

Likewise, in Chapter 6 we find that lack of information cannot be regarded as a source of market imperfection, and thus as a justification for central intervention by the government in producing information or regulating its disclosure. However, an opposite market failure can be observed – an overflow of information. This overflow triggers the rise of new intermediaries such as search engines, which distort full and symmetric information, create new costs and distinct failures that require innovative solutions. Very similar conclusions are drawn in Chapter 8, which focuses on transaction cost law and economics. Cyberspace, we find, significantly reduces traditional transaction costs, such as negotiating and contracting. This has ramifications for various branches of law, such as contracts and torts. However, new types of transaction costs emerge that are related primarily to technology.

Here we arrive at the second major point of our analysis. Cyberspace undermines many of the underlying assumptions of both Chicago School and Transaction Cost Analysis. In the latter context, the traditional Transaction Cost Analysis assumes a given technology. It does not take into account the possibility of changing technologies as a result of the choice of legal rules. Our discussion demonstrates that technologies should not be taken as a given. The introduction of new technologies has a dialectic relationship with other processes. We therefore conclude that technology should become endogenous to the analysis, and that the economic discourse should be expanded to address it.

Similar conclusions can be drawn from our discussion of the traditional market failures, such as public goods and externalities. The externalities analysis is constructed upon the pre-given factor of communal units and sub-units for which welfare maximization is conducted. Since Cyberspace breaks the territorial boundaries of communities, and enables multiple community membership, the viability of this whole analysis is questioned. In addition, the conventional solution of central intervention to internalize the externalities would prove ineffective.

Technology seems to be the major factor in the new information age. It affects the underlying assumptions of the traditional analysis. This becomes apparent, for example, in our discussion of public goods. The extent to which information in Cyberspace is a public good is not clear-cut. It depends on the technological state of the art. Since the technologies available in Cyberspace are rapidly and constantly changing, the public good analysis may prove inconclusive in determining when government intervention is necessary and by what means.

The conclusion from Part Two, therefore, is that both analytical frameworks – the Chicago School and Transaction Cost law and economics – should go through a paradigmatic shift. This can enable better understanding of the new market environment and provide superior guiding tools for policy-makers and central intervention.

Part Three focuses on Cyberspace as a community, especially as a political community. Chapter 9 dwells on the positive level of analysis, while Chapter 10 constructs a normative argument. Chapter 9 discusses the role and nature of Law and the organization of communities and offers some general thoughts regarding the 'state', or our public sphere, in light of the third generation law and economics – the Neo-Institutional school. The traditional market failure analysis presupposes the organization of markets, their connection with territory-based communities, the nature and hierarchies of central government, and the means by which central government can intervene in market activities. The analysis of Cyberspace can no longer be based on these presuppositions.

Chapter 9 further explores the theory of the firm – another important pillar of the Institutional and Neo-Institutional analyses – and discusses the organization of production in Cyberspace. We pay special attention to the variables held as exogenous in standard market analyses: law, norms, and their enforcement, and explore them in the context of Cyberspace. We examine how Cyberspace affects states as independent identifiable entities; how it affects collective action and rule-making processes; how it affects the law as an institution.

Although in many respects the Neo-Institutional framework seems to capture numerous variables relevant to the understanding of the information environment, applying this paradigm to Cyberspace may seriously shake some of its tenets. We touch upon three of the major features of our organization of life in Cyberspace that significantly differ from their counterparts in the non-virtual world – the firm, the state and the individual. We conclude that the transformation by Cyberspace of the two basic ingredients – the territorial state as the major collective unit of analysis and the individual as the atom of it, together with the transformation of production activity – have bearings on the changing concept of law, and on the whole project of the economic analysis of law.

Chapter 10 is different from all other chapters, as it offers a normative analysis, examining collective action, rule-making processes and the organization of the public sphere. We explore how the new technological frontiers opened by Cyberspace bear upon the liberal theory of the state (and on the economic theory of the state). We conclude that Cyberspace shakes the paradigm of liberal democracy and calls for re-examination of its basic foundations: representative democracy governed by checked and controlled majority decision-making.

A by-product of this argument is an attempt to incorporate republican theories of the state into economic analysis. The focus here is on the presupposition regarding individual preferences—whether they are exogenous, given, or internal to the collective decision-making process.

5. SUMMARY

This book revisits the analytic frameworks of the economic analysis of law and examines their applicability to the information environment. We believe that without better understanding of the nature of Cyberspace, the application of basic concepts, such as monopolies, lack of information, and transaction costs, would not yield accurate prediction of economic consequences, let alone an adequate basis for policy making. We attempt in this book neither to provide an alternative explanation nor to offer a full and comprehensive new modeling. Such an ambitious task would require further investigation and research. Simply examining the tenets of economic analysis in the information environment would help us identify the limits of this analytic framework, and draw attention to its weaknesses, which require further research. This is particularly important for lawyers and policy makers, who believe in using economic analysis of law as a possible basis for reasonable policy making.

2. Cyberspace in Context

This study explores the economic analysis of law in light of the digital-networked information environment. In a nutshell we conclude that the new information environment creates a new reality that challenges the analytical framework of standard law and economics. But before delving into the application of economic analysis to the new information environment we wish, in this chapter, to take a broader view and discuss briefly the various definitions and descriptions of this new environment. We believe that the (semantic) characterization of this new environment and its scope have some implications on its economic analysis. These will become apparent in the following chapters.

The *Internet* is the technical term for a worldwide system of computer networks – a network of networks – in which users at any one computer can get information from any other computer (and sometimes talk directly to users at other computers). *Cyberspace* is the term used to describe the social, cultural or indeed the psychological phenomenon created by the Internet. It is the impression of space and community formed by the Internet and its users; the virtual 'world' that Internet users experience when they are online. The term 'Cyberspace' was coined by William Gibson in his 1984 novel *Neuromancer*, although in this book Gibson more frequently uses the term 'matrix' to describe the same phenomenon. While 'Internet' is a technical term, with a definition almost universally accepted, 'Cyberspace' is a controversial term, which has numerous definitions.

The purpose of this chapter is to place in context the application of the economic analysis of law to Cyberspace. We begin by defining the Internet and briefly describing its history. We then introduce two key concepts in the literature of the information age: information society and information economy. Finally, we delve into the politics of names and metaphors surrounding the term *Cyberspace*, thereby touching upon the wide range of ramifications of the information technology revolution, most of which we do not attempt to cover in this book.

1. THE ONLINE INFORMATION ENVIRONMENT: A BRIEF HISTORY OF THE INTERNET

The Internet is neither the product of an ingenious designer following a master plan, nor the output of individuals' efforts coordinated through market signals.

The Internet resulted from a mixture of both: central design and investment, on the one hand, and the grass-roots efforts of numerous developers using acceptable protocols and standards, on the other hand.

In fact, the Internet was conceived by US Defense Department military strategists, whose aim was to build a decentralized computer network resilient to hostile attacks. The theory was that a distributed network would be more resilient to repeated attacks than a centralized network. A packet switching technology was designed to serve this strategic goal, thus reducing dependency on central control systems, and securing continuous service even in case of major damage resulting from nuclear or other strategic attacks. The first high-speed computer network ARPANET was initiated in the 1960s by the Advanced Research Projects Agency of the United States Defense Department (DARPA). In the beginning of the 1970s, ARPANET grew from four hosts at US campuses into 23 hosts connecting universities and government research centers around the US, and eventually launching an international connection.

While the grass-roots nature of the Net is celebrated, not much attention is given to its military nature in its early days, and to the role played by the state in its initiation. Ironically, the militaristic strategy of decentralization adopted by the users and developers who shaped the information environment in its early days, enabled the celebration of the ethos of a free and voluntary communitarian society.

In these early days and until the beginning of the 1990s, the American government restricted access to ARPANET. However, during that time, other applications such as USENET, and other networks, such as BITNET and CSNET, provided services to universities outside ARPANET (Willmore 2002). Due to restrictions on access to the ARPANET, key Internet applications were designed by non-governmental agents and on non-governmental infrastructure. Thus, alongside the deliberate, centrally planned, decentralized project designed by the government, non-governmental forces worked on independent technological endeavors, developing the Internet as an anarchic sprawl and responding to grass-roots pressure (Hauben and Hauben 1997). These conflicting forces – centralized government control and decentralized private innovation or in Raymond's terms, 'The Cathedral and the Bazaar' (Raymond 1999) – may explain some of the controversies regarding the 'true' nature of the Internet, which are still relevant today (Rosenzweig 1998).

Toward the late 1970s and during the 1980s, ARPANET moved from its military/research roots, and became the Internet as we know it today. Restrictions on traffic on the backbone of the Internet (National Science Foundation's backbone – the 'NSFNET') were lifted in 1991, when the NSF permitted commercial use. This decision cleared the way for the privatization of the Internet and the development of electronic commerce.

Privatization was also technologically driven, and was partly due to the introduction of new technologies, such as TCP/IP (1983), which is a communication standard that allowed the inter-connection of independent and incompatible computers and information systems, followed by the World Wide Web (1990) and Mosaic (1993), the first graphics-based Web browser. These technologies allowed open access in the sense that they were based on standards open and available to all. Connecting to the Internet required merely adopting such standards, which were subject neither to military restrictions, nor to any proprietary rights.

The state's withdrawal, however, was never complete, and governmental sponsorship of research and development related to the Internet was alive and became a controversial issue during the second half of the 1990s, focusing on public investments in the next generation Internet (Next Generation Internet Research Act of 1998). But the process of privatization was stronger, and transformed the Internet from a state-designed and sponsored enterprise, into an anarchic global network-of-networks, sponsored by private entities, and composed of applications designed by a variety of independent parties. In the late 1990s, economic enterprises, old and new, discovered quickly the economic potential of the new medium. Today, not only is the vast majority of traffic in Cyberspace commercial, but private businesses are becoming more and more instrumental in the technological development of the Internet and its architecture (Lessig 1999).

Apart from the shift from central design towards commercial capture, the Internet has undergone unprecedented growth in terms of the number of users and their worldwide spread. From 23 hosts in the 1970s, the Internet grew to 201 in 1981, and then to 130,000 hosts in 1989, 1,776,000 in 1993, more than 19 million hosts in 1998 and 126 million in 2001 (Gromov 2002). In 1995, the number of online users was estimated at 16 million (less than 0.4 percent of the world's population). The estimate for 1998 was 147 million, which increased to more than 600 million in 2002, and is nearing 10 percent of the world's population (Press 2000). The volume of traffic over the Internet is thought to double every 100 days. In the last decade, computer performance has doubled every 21 months (Roberts 1999). These incredible growth rates are related to changing technological frontiers. In the course of this book we will indicate why these unprecedented growth rates are a crucial factor for the economic analysis of the Internet, and why most of the conventional law and economics literature provides inadequate tools to analyze it.

To summarize this brief historical survey, the Internet is a mixture of openness and hierarchy operating in the realms of both community (social, cultural and political life) and commerce. Understanding the conflicting forces that affected the development of the Net may highlight some of the contemporary controversies regarding its nature. Rather than emphasizing a single dominant factor, it would be advisable to acknowledge its complicated nature, as suggested by Rosenzweig (1998, p. 1531):

The rise of the Net needs to be rooted in the 1960s in both the "closed world" of the Cold War and the open and decentralized world of the antiwar movement and the counterculture. Understanding this dual heritage enables us to better understand current controversies over whether the Internet will be "open" or "closed" – over whether the Net will foster democratic dialogue or centralized hierarchy, community or capitalism, or mixture of both.

2. A CONCEPTUAL ROADMAP

The Internet today, as we defined in the introduction to this chapter, is a worldwide system of computer networks in which users at any one computer can get information from any other computer. Despite its changing character, its main feature is still a decentralized exchange of information created and stored on personal computers. This new method of communication and exchange and its rapid growth created a digital networked information environment, which has a significant impact on life also outside the Net. A few key concepts became associated with this new information environment. These concepts encompass several aspects of the information age, and reflect different focuses of scholars from various disciplines who study the Internet's special characteristics.

Two of these concepts that are relevant to our study and became the ruling buzzwords of the late 1990s are the *new economy* and the *information economy*. News headlines reported the financial success of new startup companies that abandoned the restraints of the old economy and joined the winning waves of the new economic post-industrial revolution. The booming of the NASDAQ was conceived as a mystery comprehended only by those who mastered the governing rules of the *new economy*. Soon after, when the NASDAQ dropped and a large number of high tech companies crashed, many defeated converters of the new economy turned back to the good old economic models, seeking a comforting explanation for the major financial losses. The collapse of the financial markets chilled some of the enthusiasm and innovation associated with studying the information age as a distinct phenomenon. Nonetheless, the centrality of information to our economy and society began long before the financial flourishing of high-tech industries in the late '90s, and is bound to remain thereafter. Therefore, the study of this phenomenon and its various socio-economic and political aspects continues to be as vital and relevant today as it was during the '90s.

Indeed, one of the most controversial issues in the literature related to information and communication technologies in the past decade is whether we can justifiably talk about an *information economy* and an *information society*. Does the information environment have any distinctive characteristics that require a special analytical treatment unattained by existing paradigms? Does the central role of information and its changing character constitute a new phenomenon governed by new paradigms or can we explain the apparently new developments with the existing analytical tools?

Some argue that the information age deserves new treatment. Information has become the primary resource in post-industrial economies, superseding physical resources, which were the economic underpinnings of industrial or agrarian economies. The machine tools of the information society are computers and telecommunications, rather than lathes or ploughs. Knowledge has become one of the primary bases of wealth. Occupation is predominated by information-related work and even leisure activities are connected to the information society. The major arenas of economic and non-economic activities are informational goods (Webster 1995, p. 10–13).

The term *information economy* (sometimes referred to as the *new economy*) emerged in the literature during the last decades of the 20th century. It generally refers to the economic situation in which information becomes the major good produced by societies, and on which the wealth of individuals and nations is increasingly dependent. Productivity in the information economy depends on the capacity to generate, process and apply knowledge-based information. Consequently, economic relations are no longer organized on the basis of control over natural resources and physical goods, but on the basis of control over information and knowledge.

Information is different from physical assets in many respects. It is non-tangible and virtual, although it could be manifested in material forms such as books or CDs. The creation of new informational products requires primarily informational resources. We use software – data processing systems – to create other data processing systems. The economic nature of resources in both input and output are very much the same. Information as a means of production is very different from any other tangible resource. It can never be used up, and, in fact, once created, can benefit an unlimited number of users. Yet, another essential resource of production is human capital that is, of course, limited and subject to various constraints. Consequently, productivity in the information economy requires the use of resources that are limited, but non-exhaustible in that they are not consumed by their use.

The various developments in information technology are further considered as evidence of a new type of society, an *information society* (Webster 1995, pp. 7–10). Breakthroughs in information processing, storage and transmission have significant social ramifications. They impinge on the way we communicate with one another: interaction is more rapid, instant, often anonymous, and crosses geographical borders irrespective of distance. The ability to connect instantly to users around the world creates a sense of a 'global village' (McLuhan and Fiore 1967). It affects the way we define and perceive ourselves within a social context. It affects our affiliations with other individuals and with various local and online communities.

We increasingly become dependent upon information, information processing, and communication means for everyday activities. Information technologies transform the way we work and do business. They change the way we research, study and educate. They affect how we create, innovate and interact. Digital networks, which instantly connect individual users in different locations, shape the organization of time and space, changing institutional structures such as firms, and the organization of labor (Webster 1995, pp. 18–21). They further transform communal institutions, and indeed the institution of the state. The notion of Information Society portrays a society in which the creation, distribution, and manipulation of information turn out to be the most significant economic and cultural activity.

While many celebrated the revolutionary nature of the information age, others are more skeptical of the new developments, rejecting the very idea that there is anything distinctively new in the economy of the new information era (Shapiro and Varian 1999). Some even deny that the *information economy* in its various forms and manifestations exists as a distinct phenomenon, which requires special treatment, arguing that it is simply the continuity of standard economic relations (May 2002, pp. 49–80). Furthermore, the skeptics deny any distinctive shifts in social structures and any change in political practices of communities (May 2002, pp. 81–113).

Our study takes a step back and calls for re-evaluation of the analytical tools used for studying the information environment. These analytical concepts, which structure the way we arrange our social reality, embed various assumptions regarding the world. It is our purpose to draw attention to those assumptions that are relevant to information technologies and to the study of the information environment. If these assumptions are inconsistent with the information environment, and are inadequate for understanding how it works, the use of the analytical framework runs the risk of producing a distorted view on both positive and normative levels.

Such a critical examination of the frameworks of analysis could serve as an interesting case study for examining the more general claims often made in the context of this debate. Viewing the world through an old pair of glasses may impose significant constraints on our ability to notice new phenomena. Without examining the limits of the old paradigm, one cannot seriously argue that much about the world has not changed. This critical analysis is particularly important when the economic analysis of law is at stake, as it has a significant say in formulating legal policy. It is necessary to first appreciate the various aspects of the information environment, in order to define the possible role of law in regulating it.

3. THE POLITICS OF NAMES: CYBERSPACE, INTERNET AND THE INFORMATION ENVIRONMENT

While the term *Internet* is merely the technological terminology for computer networks, *information economy* and *information society* are more loaded terms. The former describes the branch of the science of economics dedicated to the analysis of the economic players and interactions in the new information age and society. It is controversial because, as we explained above, economists debate whether there is a need for a new sub-field of economics, or indeed a new paradigm, to analyze the Internet and its effects on the world outside it. The latter describes the effects of the gigantic computer network on our societies, when they exist in the traditional, physical space. *Cyberspace* is the most controversial term among the four, as it is used to describe the social, cultural and psychological phenomena created by the Internet – its metaphysical facets.

Cyberspace is a term loaded with spatial meanings (Hunter 2002). While some people regard Cyberspace as the total interconnectedness of human beings through computers and telecommunication without regard to physical geography, others believe that the network created by the Internet is indeed a place, a new space, and that its users not only connect through it, but also surf and even reside in it. This metaphor is very powerful in shaping the relations among different users of the Net and it is highly significant for the analysis of the ramifications of the Internet in terms of sociology, psychology, political theory, moral theory and indeed, law and economics.

In the late 1980s when people, mainly computer professionals, first connected their home computers to the Internet, the Net was a lot harder to navigate. To go from one computer to another, one had to use what is known as a command line interface. All interactions between a person and a remote computer took place by typing a long string of alphanumeric commands and then reading a textual response sent back from a distant computer. There were no pretty pictures, no mouse and no pointing and clicking (Hagerty 2000, Ch. 1).

In the early 1990s, the technology we call the World Wide Web was introduced. The Net was no longer the exclusive domain of specialists. Text-based interfaces were almost gone and graphical interfaces with a simple point-and-click method were introduced. The Net was experienced by many as a place, a new area, in which one can navigate or surf. This new world was formed by the display of data as an artificial three-dimensional space, which the user can manipulate and move through by issuing computer commands. The language used by users to describe their operation of the Internet reflects the experience of it as a location. People *surf* or *navigate* the Net, *move* from one site to another, *entering* or *visiting locations, addresses* or *chat-rooms,* software operates *spiders* that *crawl* over Websites, *entry* or *access* may be denied or limited without the right *key* (Hunter 2002). Indeed, today, when one opens the TELNET software, on the background pages of the Web, one can almost sense a switch from a real place to two-dimensional computer interface. The contrast between the black and white, plainly textual basic environment of TELNET, and the colorful, visually rich and illusionary environment of the WWW emphasize the experience of the Internet as a new space.

The notion of Cyberspace as a place has significant practical legal consequences. If we perceive Cyberspace as a place, and treat it as we treat other physical spaces, we can more easily assign property rights to its inhabitants in their respective properties. The perception of Cyberspace as a place led some courts to perceive Web sites or email systems as physical places, thus providing legal remedies against trespassers, equivalent to the protection granted in the physical world (Elkin-Koren 2003). A good example is the case of eBay, the largest online person-to-person auction site. eBay objected to the unauthorized use of its database by Metacrawlers and data aggregators like Bidder's Edge, which facilitated a single search for items across numerous online auctions. eBay filed a suit against Bidder's Edge, claiming that the defendant trespassed its auction Web site.

The Court granted eBay a preliminary injunction enjoining Bidder's Edge from accessing eBay's systems by use of any automated querying program without eBay's written authorization. The eBay decision established a newly created right to exclude indexers, based on the highly controversial doctrine of *trespass to chattel*. Perceiving Cyberspace as a 'place', the Court held that eBay's servers and their capacity are private property, and therefore access is conditioned upon the owner's permission. The Court ruled that Bidder's Edge searches constituted an unauthorized use of eBay's property, depriving eBay of the ability to use the occupied portions of its personal property for its own purpose (*eBay Inc.*, 100 F.Supp.2d 1058). The court's analysis applies perceptions taken from the physical space (such as entering and possession) to describe virtual activities such as data processing and data communication. Data mining of the type exercised by Bidder's Edge, or any other search engine for that purpose, does not involve physical entry to any Website or computer server. It is a communicative action of exchanging signals among computer applications. The use of the physical metaphor of space is constitutive. It creates (legal) borders in the online environment, the functionality of which is highly dependent on connectivity and interoperability.

The eBay ruling exemplifies how the term Cyberspace expanded the meaning of the Internet, by ascribing a notion of physical place to it. But what kind of place is it? In the early days of the WWW, this 'place' was often understood as an unexplored territory similar to other new frontiers in American history, the modern equivalent of the American West. Similar to the Western frontiers, Cyberspace was perceived as a no-mans-land subject to no laws; a refuge safe from real-world constraints, and associated with freedom and liberty (Yen 2003). With the growing role of commercial entities in the

Net, some scholars switched from the romantic Western Frontiers analogy to a darker Feudal Society analogy, where the 'lords' of Cyberspace – ICANN, for example – assign and allocate domain names, like the lease of lands by lords in Middle Ages Europe. Similarly, others point at a new (unholy) alliance between online market players, such as Internet Service Providers, search engines, content producers, and application designers, who function as private nodes of power, and are recruited by territorial states for implementing government power in the online environment (Birnhack and Elkin-Koren 2003).

The notion of Cyberspace as a place, together with its perception as free and liberal, opened the door to innovative ideas regarding the role of law in the new virtual environment. For example, Post and Johnson (1996) argued that global computer-based communications cut across territorial borders, and created new boundaries, which defined a distinct Cyberspace. This distinct Cyberspace deserves laws and legal institutions of its own, and will defeat the territorially based law-making and law-enforcing authorities from the 'real world'. In the distinct Cyberspace, new rules will emerge in order to govern a wide range of new phenomena that have no clear parallel in the non-virtual world. While the post-national situation described by Post and Johnson left the national state outside the scene, the description of the Net as a feudal society carries with it very different consequences as to its self-rule and the need for external intervention. The latter characterization implies more desirable intervention by the traditional liberal democracy central control (i.e. the national state), to prevent or curtail the feudal society attributes of Cyberspace.

The term Cyberspace is not only used to describe the Internet as a place. It is also being used to describe the world of interconnected minds. Regardless of whether places visited through a computer network have a physical existence, many Net users and researchers have ascertain that Cyberspace exists at least in the same way that literary and mythological places and characters live in the domain of the human collective consciousness (Hagerty 2000, Ch. 1).

Although most people physically sit alone in front of their computers when connecting to the Internet, they seldom feel alone when they are in Cyberspace. Even when not using an interactive environment, such as a chat room, people often report a sense of being in the midst of a large crowd in some public space. Many people noted that this large, invisible crowd of strangers feels like a friendly group. Perhaps this is because the majority of people in Cyberspace are there voluntarily (Hagerty 2000, Ch. 1). Again, this feeling is not shared when people use the old interface of computers, such as the use of TELNET mentioned above.

Cyberspace is not just a place of interconnected minds. It has largely come to represent a synergistic collection of concepts about where one's mind is when involved in mental activities that are leveraged by technology. Being in Cyberspace is comparable to an out-of-body experience that has been activated by some form of technology. Cyberspace affects human minds. In Cyberspace our personality changes. Our minds are more willing to explore new ideas, taste forbidden delights, and meet some very interesting people (Hagerty 2000, Ch. 1).

Not all the scholars subscribe to the metaphysical descriptions of Cyberspace, and thus to their ramifications for traditional institutions. Many argue that the idea that Internet is a place is a ridiculous one, because there is no one 'in' Cyberspace (Lemley 2003). The Internet is simply a bundle of computer protocols that permit computer users to transmit data between their computers using various communication networks (Moglen 2000).

In this book we use the term Cyberspace as it is probably the most influential Internet metaphor, narrative or scientific description – depending on one's point of view. We believe that this term encompasses not only the technological significance of the new information revolution, but also its economic, social and political significance. Language affects legal concepts and practices, and if the Internet created new linguistic realities, the conceptual effects of it on the law cannot be ignored. We use this term, however, without ascribing to it any particular political meaning. It will be left to the reader to decide, after comprehending our law and economic analysis, which of our insights are constructed upon the new phenomena directly related to the new technological environment and which are based on popular or linguistic representations of the new phenomena. It will be left to the reader to choose which term to adopt, and to which meanings to subscribe.

Part Two

CYBERSPACE AS A MARKET
AND ITS FAILURES

3. Introduction to Part Two

The most important general premise of the economic theory is that open competition within a perfect market will lead to efficiency, which is the most desirable social outcome. The concept of efficiency in economic theory relates to both the production of goods and their allocation. Efficiency in production means that it is impossible to produce more goods using the available resources. Efficiency in allocation means that it is impossible to transfer goods among individuals in a way that makes one individual better off without making the others worse off, or alternatively that it is impossible to enhance the total welfare of society by further transfers of goods or services. Yet, the term efficiency can be defined in a broader way. It can encompass both Thomas Hobbes' analysis of the creation of the state as an efficient solution to the problems of the state of nature, as well as Adam Smith's analysis of the invisible hand as the balancing factor of human markets.

The premise that open competition within a perfect market will lead to efficiency contains a positive component (open competition will lead to efficiency) and a normative component (efficiency is the desirable social outcome). This general premise was advanced by the economic approach to law in several directions, the two most important being the economic theory of the state and the limits of free markets justifying central intervention. The economic theory of the state analyzes the emergence of the state, its central government, and its institutional structure as derived from problems of collective action that are market failures of sorts. Studies of the limits of the free market seek to identify the circumstances in which central government is justified, or should intervene in shifting the market (imperfect) solution. Only in such circumstances should government intervene. Such circumstances are once again related to market failures.

Part Three of the book elaborates on the economic approach and the theory of the state in the era of Cyberspace. Subsequent chapters in this part focus on the traditional market aspects of Cyberspace.

Cyberspace increasingly resembles an economic market – a traditional outlet for goods and services. It was not originally conceived as such. The Internet was perceived as a new forum for exchanges of views, information and research, a new community and a multi-cultural sphere, which enables direct communication among users around the world. When the US National Science Foundation decided in 1991 to lift restrictions regarding traffic on the backbone of the Internet, it cleared the way for commercial use and the development of electronic commerce. Economic enterprises, old and new, discovered very quickly the economic potential of the new medium. Today, not only is the vast majority of Cyberspace traffic commercial, but private businesses are becoming more and more instrumental in the technological developments of the Internet (Lessig 1999). Thus, only in the last decade has Cyberspace been captured by traditional and new market players whose primary interest is economic profit.

Cyberspace constitutes today a concrete marketplace where goods and services are traded. Individuals are using the Internet to offer their personal belongings for sale, such as their paintings or used books. Corporations are using the Net for marketing to potential consumers on and offline. Potential buyers surf the Internet for bargains, visiting corporate sites or using various search tools to identify potential sales. By establishing direct electronic contact between buyers and sellers, Cyberspace creates a global marketplace, where commodities can be traded worldwide. It is a market in a functional sense, in that it brings buyers and sellers in contact with each other and enables an exchange of goods and services where prices are determined by the combined actions of all players (Hanson 1986).

Cybermarkets do not entirely replace traditional offline markets. The interface between Cyberspace and physical economic markets is multifarious. One can identify three possible categories of this interface: (1) Cyberspace completely substitutes for physical markets (2) Cyberspace partially substitutes for physical markets, and (3) Cyberspace indirectly affects transactions, which are negotiated and concluded in traditional physical markets.

The first category, where Electronic-Commerce can fully substitute for more traditional commercial practices, includes entire transactions that are negotiated, concluded and carried out online. This is the case when informational goods and services are traded, such as software, music, news, e-books, and related services. Thus, a Web site from which a user can directly download music files or software, may substitute for record stores. Online distribution of news may substitute for printed newspapers or broadcasted radio news. Transfer of money may also be processed online, using credit cards, e-cash or payment processing services provided by intermediaries such as PayPal or SafetyPass.

In a second category of e-commerce, Cyberspace partially substitutes for the physical market. In this category we find transactions that are negotiated and concluded in Cyberspace, using various techniques of online contracting. Yet, the actual execution of the transaction is made in the physical world. This applies to both products – the purchase of various material goods through the Internet, and services, e.g. booking a hotel room by Internet or making online reservations for airline tickets that replace travel agents. When actual delivery of physical artifacts is necessary, many ingredients of traditional market analysis will apply.

A third category covers all cases in which Cyberspace is being used merely as an additional marketing platform for suppliers, and enhances search capabilities of consumers who are searching for bargains. Thus Cyberspace may also affect transactions, which are both carried out and concluded in the physical world. In the analysis of market failures that follows, we consider these three categories, as they might be relevant in different ways to the effects of Cyberspace on the traditional market analysis.

Cyberspace could also be treated as a market in a more abstract way: as 'the paradigm of human interaction, whether the subject of exchange is goods and services or it is a public action' (Bouckaert and Geest 2000, pp. 1043–1044). In this sense, Cyberspace as a type of human interaction should be evaluated not only like any other market by the criterion of efficiency, but also as a public sphere, commons or mechanism for private and collective actions. In this part of the book, however, we will treat the economic market facet of Cyberspace.

There is a remarkable consensus within the economic approach with regard to the intellectual framework for analyzing and justifying state regulation of the economy. Since Adam Smith's *Wealth of Nations* (Smith [1776] 1961), economic theory had always been skeptical of government intervention in the market. Free and open markets, it was thought, would function efficiently if not interrupted by government actions. Therefore, a *prima facie* case for central or public intervention requires a demonstration of the failure of a free market (Cooter 1997, Breyer 1982). In this matter, the Chicago school adopts the traditional welfare economics identification of market failures. A market failure exists when there are no multiple players on both sides of the market (the problem of monopolies), when these players do not have the same full information relevant to their market activities (imperfect information), when any of the players bypass the market through involuntary actions (the problem of externalities), or when the traded commodity is a public good.

Later in the development of the market approach, and following Ronald Coase's groundbreaking article, *The Problem of Social Cost* (1960), the framework of these market failures shifted to a more general setting of transaction costs. It is important to note that these four (or five) categories of market failures are not mutually exclusive; particular issues can be analyzed in more than one framework. For instance, some phenomena can be analyzed either as an externality or as a public good.

Examining Cyberspace by simply applying the neoclassic microeconomics paradigm might prove to be unproductive and even misleading. That is because some of the presumptions and modes of analysis are simply inadequate for the new network information environment. Applying these analytical tools intact may produce a distorted picture of the information environment and indeed screens deficient pictures of traditional markets. It may cause us to focus on market failures that are no longer pertinent, such as the public good nature of informational goods, while failing to identify new modes of production that do not easily fit the traditional paradigm, such as peer-produced content (Benkler 2002). Such phenomena, that do not obey the modes of standard market analysis, require a fresh look. Their existence further calls for a better understanding of the interface between market and non-market modes of human interaction and activities in the information environment. The primary goal of this part is to highlight the shortcomings of traditional market analysis in the context of Cyberspace.

The following discussion, however, traces the traditional doctrinal analysis, and examines separately the traditional market failures, as applied to Cyberspace. In the following chapters we focus on the market as an organizing theme in the three generations of law and economic literature, examining their analysis in light of the emerging Cybermarkets. We begin with the traditional welfare economic analysis of the market, which focuses on the four traditional market failures: monopolies (Chapter 4) public goods (Chapter 5), Imperfect Information (Chapter 6) and externalities (Chapter 7), followed by transaction costs analysis (Chapter 8). Each of these chapters will show how the new digitally networked information environment has significant bearing on the pre-Cyberspace and post-Cyberspace analyses. We included the discussion on Neo-Institutional law and economics in the third part of the book, which is dedicated to the theory of the state, as it incorporates traditional market analysis with political markets.

4. Monopolies

A monopoly is one of the classic market failures. While under conditions of perfect competition, producers and consumers see the price as fixed, and therefore set their quantity of output or input on a level at which their marginal costs or benefits equal the price, a single producer (monopoly) or a single consumer (monopsony), sees a changing price curve, and therefore sets its output or input in a way that maximizes its profits, leading to an inefficient level of production or an inadequate market solution. The same premise applies to a situation in which a small number of producers (cartel) or consumers coordinate their market actions.

Under traditional micro-economic analysis, any non-price-taking behavior implies a violation of the efficiency conditions. Antitrust laws seek to guarantee competition by prohibiting certain anticompetitive behaviors (such as price coordination) or by preventing the accumulation of monopolistic power (for example, by prohibiting mergers). When a monopoly is a natural situation due, for instance, to economies of scale (the scale of the market), or to an exceptional ratio between fixed costs and marginal costs (in the case, for example, of public utilities), the monopoly is allowed to continue to exist but is closely regulated by the government.

Sometimes monopolies are even created by the government to remedy other market imperfections. This is the case, for instance, with a patent system. Patents are limited monopolies in innovations, created by governments to remedy the market failure of public good. Innovations, like other informational products, are non-excludable. Namely, they are often easily copied, thereby diminishing incentives for investing in new inventions. The patent systems seek to remedy this market imperfection by granting a monopoly to the patentee over his or her innovation for a limited time.

Cyberspace has several features that are likely to decrease monopoly problems, hence reducing the legitimacy of central intervention in the market. On the other hand, the information environment creates new types of monopoly-related problems. These impediments on competition are idiosyncratic, and could become invisible to traditional micro-economic analysis. Some of these features call for innovative solutions, which are described next.

1. DIMINISHING TRADITIONAL MONOPOLISTIC EFFECTS

There are several features of Cybermarkets that are likely to reduce monopolistic powers:

1.1 Entry Costs and Fixed Costs

One of the important sources for monopolies in the non-virtual world is high entry costs and the need for a substantial initial investment to establish a viable business in the market. These features can characterize a natural monopoly, a condition in which the fixed production costs are so high that it is more efficient for a single provider to serve the market. Some public utilities such as electricity and gas are typical examples. High entry costs, however, also characterize some unnatural monopolies. Entry barriers and high fixed prices, as opposed to changing costs, are often combined by existing market players with tactics of short-run price cuts to prevent new entries. Such tactics are aimed at maintaining existing monopolistic powers.

When we look at products and services for which Cyberspace completely replaces the physical market, i.e. products and services that are supplied online, the entry cost is significantly lower than the cost incurred when seeking entry to non-virtual markets. Those transactions that can be fully executed online are information related, including financial services, data services or the sale of informational products such as software, text, music and videos that can be downloaded as files directly to end-users' hardware.

Consider, for instance, the publishing business. In the non-virtual world, entering such an industry requires major investments, such as purchasing and operating a printing press, buying paper, and paying distributors for shipment and handling. In Cyberspace, any 10-year-old can become an independent publisher. With the click of a mouse he or she can distribute text to millions of Internet subscribers. News forums can be easily established allowing every user to become a news source. The use of software allows online communities to measure, and make visible, the rating of such reports among users, thus establishing their reliability.

The reduced entry cost opens the online publishing market to competition, and leads to the prosperity of many small online distributors of academic papers, news, professional information on newsgroups and forums, and Weblogs. The lower level of entry cost associated with online publishing further reduces the effectiveness of short-term tactics used to prevent new entries into the market. This, in turn, affects dominance and control in the relevant markets. The proliferation of online news Web sites weakens the dominant powers of the mass media. When news can be obtained not only from CNN, but also from new online papers such as Debkafiles.com, or from newsgroups, the major news companies are faced with competition. As we discuss below, the significance of the monopoly-like nature of the mass media goes beyond the media industry. It also affects concentration in retail markets.

Similar, though muted, effects can be attributed to products and services for which Cyberspace is only a platform for negotiating a bargain that is then performed in the physical world. Here too, the entry costs or fixed cost (in contrast to the marginal cost of production) can be reduced significantly. Consider, for instance, the cost associated with opening and running a non-virtual bookstore: One has to rent or buy real estate in a strategic location, decorate it, arrange for storage, and hire a relatively large staff. An online business cuts the cost of operating a physical commercial space.

Furthermore, since the purchasing process is entirely virtual, allowing the customer to surf through Web sites offering new and old titles, there is no need to maintain an inventory. Delivery, and often production, is made only upon demand. Internet retailers have nearly unlimited 'virtual inventory' as they keep centralized warehouses and shipping agreements with distributors. While the average book may sit on a brick-and-mortar shelf for six to twelve months before it is bought, and the cost of this inventory in a chain of hundreds of stores is huge, virtual stores such as Amazon.com can keep only few copies in their warehouses and restock only when customers buy the titles. While typical large stores have 40,000 – 100,000 books on their shelves, Amazon.com provides easy access to 2,300,000 books (Brynjolfsson, Smith and Hu 2003, pp. 1–5). Therefore, online retailers can offer convenient access to a larger selection of products at lower cost.

Furthermore, the large (virtual) inventory allows online consumers to search through a large collection to find the book of their choice. Online search applications and personalized feedback features enable consumers to locate, evaluate, and order books. Purchasing a book from an online bookstore generally involves lower transaction costs, such as the cost of searching for books and prices (Brynjolfsson, Smith and Hu 2003, pp. 1–5). The relatively low cost of entry would stimulate competition.

The same analysis may apply to any other online business selling products or providing services. The muted monopolistic problems of entry and fixed costs are also related to the boundaries and size of the market, on which we will elaborate below. First, let us add a few words on advertising and marketing, which constitute significant costs in the physical business world and reduced costs online.

1.2 Cyberspace, Advertising and the Monopoly Problem

Advertising aims to introduce the manufacturer or supplier as a serious player in the market, and to create demand for certain products. Traditional advertising tactics rely heavily on use of the mass media, such as television, radio, and newspapers. As media use is very expensive, only large suppliers of products and services can advertise, thus acquiring a significant advantage in the market. The debate that emerged in recent years regarding lawyers' advertisements is an interesting example.

Traditionally lawyers' advertising was prohibited due to the 'moral' character of advertising, which was deemed unrespectable for the legal profession. This practice was ruled illegal on the basis of anti-competitive policies, first in the USA in *Bates v. State Bar of Arizona* (433 U.S. 350) and subsequently in other countries. But advertising was not fully permitted, and today the debate has shifted from the traditional moral reasons against advertising to equality issues associated with the market advantage that advertising creates for the big law firms. Easy and relatively cheap online advertising options can weaken the traditional monopolistic position of businesses operating in the non-virtual world.

Indeed, virtual advertising is much less costly than its traditional counterparts and far more accessible to smaller businesses. While the cost of traditional advertising is $120,000–130,000 for 30 seconds on network television, $4,000–40,000 for 30 seconds on local television, $5,000–80,000 for 30 seconds on cable television, $200–1,000 for 60 seconds on the radio, and $120 (full page) per thousand circulation in the newspaper (all prices are in the US), the cost of Internet advertising is much cheaper. The cost of direct mail advertising is $15–20 per thousand for coupons; $25–40 per thousand for newspaper inserts, and $5,000–25,000 for a one to three month rental of billboard space (Mishra 2002).

Advertising in the online environment is guided by a different set of rules. Online distribution differs from the one-to-many distribution of newspapers, radio, and television. Distribution online allows one-to-one direct communication, and many-to-many mass communication among masses of users. The low cost of online distribution allows businesses that sell online to compete with multinational corporations. Advertising no longer requires the distribution of copies or broadcasting to the widest audience possible; rather, it provides access to information posted online.

Operating a Web site that is listed by leading search engines involves a lower entry cost than paying for primetime commercials or for a single ad at a major newspaper. When distribution is made cheaper, small businesses can still afford to advertise to their local communities or potential niche buyers. Furthermore, new advertising models no longer seek to capture the masses, but try to target individual consumers, and tailor advertising to their interests and needs. Such individualized advertising may prove more effective than mass advertising, which is designed to reach as many people as possible. Having said that, online advertising may involve aggregating information on consumers' interests, buying habits, and preferences, and may raise serious privacy concerns.

The systematically lower cost of online advertising has an equalizing effect that is lowering entry barriers and fueling competition. But the weakening of monopolistic powers vis-à-vis advertising has another, less obvious, aspect. It is connected to the business model of the mass media, which is based on creating and distributing attractive content for free, thereby pulling together a large audience, then selling that audience's eyeballs to advertisers. The costs of producing content, such as a television series, or gathering and processing news, are fixed. They are not dependent on the number of consumers. The marginal cost of producing additional copies is relatively low. Economies of scale related to the large expenses of producing content, and its mass distribution, led to the growth of concentrated corporate control of the mass media.

This process of media concentration was strengthened by the consolidation of advertising agencies into a few worldwide operators. Advertisers would prefer to place their ads with the media that have the widest circulation, thereby increasing their revenues and facilitating further investments in widening the media's reach. This circulative impact, as Bagdikian (1997, pp. 122–133) argues, eliminated competition among newspapers in the US in the second half of the 20th century and led to a monopoly in daily newspapers. The anticompetitive effect was even stronger in the television industry, which broadcasts free programming and is often exclusively sponsored by advertisers.

The resulting economic structure, in which advertisers had fewer outlets for distributing their ads, further increased the costs of advertising. It also made it harder for small business to penetrate public awareness and compete with large conglomerates. Consequently, the integration of worldwide mass media with worldwide mass advertising significantly reduced competition. As argued by Bagdikian (1997, p. 121): '[M]ass advertising has been a major contributor to the drastic shrinkage in shares of sales by small, local businesses and has helped large national and multinational corporations achieve market control and political power.'

The information age enhances the significance of advertising. This has to do with the fact that information is the primary asset in the information economy. Consequently, many of the goods and services for which we bargain have no fixed demand. Indeed, informational goods include functional products such as computer programs that could prove necessary to increase efficiency. Yet, informational goods also include entertainment, technological gadgets, images, and lifestyles encoded in brand names such as Barbie and Coke. 'Merchandising', Barber (1995, p. 60) argues, 'is as much about symbols as about goods and sells not life's necessities but life's styles – which is the modern pathway that takes us from the body to soul.' Advertising is crucial for creating a demand for such informational goods, and without it such demand would not necessarily exist.

This rather ideal picture of online advertising is subject to an important reservation. Online access is only partly direct and decentralized. In many cases it is mediated by search engines. There is no useful way to find the 'information needle' in the stacks of online 'information hay' without the aid of search engines. Search engines are intermediaries that potentially suffer from many of the illnesses associated with the old media. The attributes of this new type of intermediary are further discussed in Chapter 6.

1.3 The Size of the Market

The emergence of many non-virtual monopolies is related to market scale. A very small market may not justify more than one provider of any particular product. Cyberspace creates a large-scale cross-national marketplace. The e-commerce market presents potential benefits for sellers and buyers alike. Online vendors can compete with other vendors outside their geographical location and across national borders. Potential buyers of a popular computer program may purchase a copy from their official local vendor, who is often licensed exclusively to distribute the software in a particular territory. Online purchasers may also obtain the program from numerous other locations by downloading it directly from the Net.

Cyberspace has no fixed borders. It is certainly not a defined territorial unit and the use and movement of resources are not restricted to any particular territory. National boundaries cannot easily apply to Cyberspace, and protective policies such as customs and other trade barriers become less feasible. In addition, taxing online transactions may involve an increasingly higher level of control over online transmission, requiring tax collectors to monitor the Net constantly to identify transactions in virtual goods (such as computer program or news articles) among the mass volume of communication and information exchanges. Though such actions may be technically feasible they may involve undue invasions of privacy. Furthermore, such barriers can be easily bypassed in Cyberspace by shifting the 'location' of the transacting parties. What is complicated and costly in the non-virtual world can be achieved by pressing a button on the computer.

It is noteworthy that in this context of diminishing monopoly market failures, Cybermarkets will also project on businesses that operate in traditional markets only, and do not run an online business. The relatively low cost access to masses of potential consumers around the world may affect the market power of vendors outside Cyberspace. Thus, for example, a monopolistic bookstore chain will face competition from Cyberian-bookstores, which might encourage the traditional industry to enter the Cyber-market. Monopolies, which in the non-virtual world result from the size of the local market, are likely to disappear.

In this respect the feasibility of online business may affect also monopolies that currently operate in the non-virtual world. For instance, virtual bookstores like Amazon.com push non-virtual book chains such as Blackwell, Dillons, and Barnes & Noble into the Cyber-market. This, in turn, may further weaken the monopolistic powers of local bookstore chains that do not step into Cyberspace. Thus, economies of scale are likely to scale down significantly, diminishing monopolistic powers.

The story of Amazon.com and the book market is a significant example of Cyber-revolution in this respect. Amazon.com was launched in July 1995, in Seattle, by Jeff Bezos. At that time Bezos was thirty years old. He wrote the business plan on his laptop, while his wife drove him cross-country. He chose the book industry because it was large, fragmented and had an already well-established distribution system. In its first week, Amazon.com took more than $12,000 worth of orders. By the end of 1996, Amazon.com had spent over $6 million on advertising and had leaped ahead of its high street rival, Barnes & Noble, with $16 million in online book sales.

Bezos was described as 'one of a few young entrepreneurs using Cyberspace technology to steal real world customers from traditional businesses' (Martin 1996). Within three years, Amazon.com was worth hundreds of millions, and later billions of dollars. In January 1999, Amazon.com had sold more than $250 million worth of books. Its share price topped $400, bringing the company's value to $22.1 billion, exceeding the combined value of Kmart and JCPenney (Wishart and Bochsler 2003).

In response to Amazon.com successes, actual book retailers have been working to build up their own loyal online customers. By the spring of 1997 Barnes & Noble, the largest retail book chain in the world, had launched its own virtual store, in order to protect its market dominance in the physical world. It had a total of $2.8 billion in sales in 1997, of which $14 million had been sold online through its Internet site. Following Barnes & Noble, Borders Group, which operates the Borders Books and Waldenbooks chains, built the largest mail-order warehouse in the world to accommodate online sales. Subsequently Bertelsmann, a German media company, bought half of Barnes & Noble's online operation for $200 million. Both companies agreed to inject another $100 million into the electronic business in order to rough up Amazon.com (Cairney 1998).

Cyberspace, as we have noted before, may play various roles in e-commerce. It may merely provide a platform for marketing efforts of vendors (advertising, contacting actual and potential users, distributing information and coupons). It can serve, as it increasingly does, to facilitate the transactions by allowing customers to place an order, which is later delivered by vendors via mail. Cyberspace may also allow the execution of the entire transaction. Informational goods (computer programs, music, video clips, text and data) may be delivered online.

When parties use Cyberspace merely to process orders, the effects of Cyberspace are muted, as mail order performance of vendors may still depend on the real-world infrastructure that allows prompt distribution at low cost. Cyberspace, however, expands the variety from which customers may choose, and therefore enhances competition, as it reduces costs in comparison to mail orders. In addition, such Cyberspace transactions do not allow effective protective measures of national governments. Yet, when an entire transaction is performed in Cyberspace, as is the case with informational goods and services, the advantage of such local infrastructure is significantly lower, so monopolistic effects may be further reduced.

1.4 Monopolies Resulted from Scarcity

Scarcity is another dominant explanation for the emergence of monopolies, and is also a source for other market imperfections, for which the deliberate creation of monopolistic powers is a solution. Some scarce resources require central control and management to render their use efficient. Land is probably the oldest and most obvious example. The predominant economic justification for assigning property rights in land in the first place is the 'tragedy of the commons'. When too many people can legally use a resource, such as a lake, or land, they will over-consume that resource (Hardin 1968). Assigning private property rights, which are a set of exclusive rights to control the use of a resource, i.e. monopolistic powers, is viewed as a remedy to the threat of collective over-consumption by individuals acting separately. Thus, in such cases monopolistic powers are created as an intentional solution to other market failures.

Scarcity characterized the pre-Cyberspace communication industry. Take, for example, broadcasting. Its monopolistic character has partly to do with the scarcity of the electro-magnetic spectrum available for television and radio broadcasting, or, in other cases, with scarcity related to the use of land by the cable system infrastructure. In both cases, government intervention in allocating frequencies, controlling cable operators and their contractual relations with station owners, and even controlling some content was deemed justified on anti-monopolistic grounds (Sunstein 1995) and on other monopoly-related grounds (*Turner Broadcasting Sys. Inc.,* 114 S. C. 2445). Extensive government regulation of broadcasting stems from the scarcity of available frequencies, and this medium's 'invasive' nature. As courts already acknowledged in the mid-Nineties, this type of scarcity is no longer present in Cyberspace *(ACLU,* 929 F. Supp. 824, pp. 868–869).

The information environment does not create the same type of scarcity. It is virtual and thus, non-rivalrous. In other words, the use of any informational product by one does not detract from the ability of others to use it (Landes and Posner 1989, p. 335). This feature further diminishes the monopoly problem resulting from scarcity and the need to create deliberate monopolies.

There is no scarcity in communication channels. The Internet is decentralized. It allows every user who complies with the standard protocols to connect to the network and use it. Technically, anyone connected to the Net can post content on the Internet and make it available to a massive number of people. Indeed, online communication is multi-channeled. Information in digital networks is a series of electric pulses transmitted in small packets and distributed simultaneously. Therefore, online use does not create the same allocation challenge posed by traditional communication technologies. When everyone is able to efficiently communicate simultaneously, it is no longer necessary to choose the single, most efficient use of the communication channel. There is no need to dedicate communication channels for each transmission of information, be it a personal conversation or mass distribution.

Consider the following example. IRC (Internet Relay Chat) is an Internet service outside the WWW (World Wide Web). It allows online users from around the world to communicate in real time with one another. IRC consists of various separate networks (or 'nets') of IRC servers. Any user of IRC can form a new channel and become its Operator. Operators ('Ops') control the channel by choosing who may join (by 'banning' some users), who must leave (by 'kicking' them out), and even who may speak (by making the channel 'moderated'). They can declare the channel open to invitees only and regulate its communications in various ways.

When users join an existing channel they are subject to its operators. In general, one must follow the current lead of the channel operators. If a user antagonizes them, he or she may be 'kicked out' of the channel forcibly and possibly 'banned' from returning. If this happens, or if someone on a channel is harassing a user, one possible solution is to replace a nick, thus changing one's identity. The other efficient remedy is to quit the channel and to start an alternative one, thus becoming an operator and inviting one's friends to join the new channel.

The easy option of forming an alternative IRC channel when one is kicked out or when the original channel is taken over by hostile invaders (such events do occur from time to time), illustrates the lack of scarcity and the simplicity with which users can take advantage of the new technological frontiers. The difference from traditional means of communication is especially striking when compared to the non-virtual equivalence of a violent takeover of a radio or television station. Consider, for instance, a takeover of a traditional television station by revolutionary forces. Such an act is likely to have consequences totally different from the hostile use of an IRC channel, owing, among other things, to the monopolistic power of the traditional television channel. While a hostile takeover of an IRC channel is likely to cause users to form an alternative channel, a takeover of a television channel is likely to have a widespread impact, and would first require the removal of the invaders before it goes back on the air. The diminishing scarcity problem thus weakens the invasiveness of online activities. In contrast to a universal medium like television, which centrally manages production and broadcast of content, the online environment facilitates the proliferation of competing distribution channels.

Finally, by creating distribution channels alternative to television, the effect of Cyberspace might easily slip over to non-virtual broadcasting as well, weakening its dominant power (Gibbons 1997, pp. 478–481).

The lack of scarcity, therefore, allows for a better match to consumers' preferences. Content created and distributed on a small scale can be tailored to meet the preferences of very small communities or specific users, almost on an individual basis. The fragmentation of Cyberspace into small communities further weakens dominance in Cyber-markets and indeed in traditional markets. It also has important political consequences that will be further discussed in Part Three. These observations regarding scarcity suggest that less regulatory intervention in Cyberspace is justified.

Having said this, Cyberspace introduces a new type of scarcity – in users' attention. The proliferation of communication channels for distributing information and the availability of means for distribution and production of information, lead to an information overload (Shenk 1997). These stacks of information challenge human cognitive capacity. Consequently, even though vast information is available on the Net, only a limited number of clips, news items, or music titles could be noticed. The bulk of available information causes an attention deficit. Vast volumes of information are competing for the scarce attention of the audience, and users' attention becomes a valuable asset.

That is where search engines come into play as intermediaries that allow users to define which information or informational goods are relevant to their needs, and identify where to find them on the Net. Information that is undetectable, or otherwise unlisted on the search results, is almost nonexistent on the Web. Access to information in Cyberspace is enabled by search engines, and controlling such enablers and their use could determine what information is actually made available. Consequently, search engines are also becoming a focal point of control. Whoever controls the search engines may filter some information, or make sites or informational goods more visible on the search results and, therefore, more accessible. This distinctive aspect of the information environment, and its ramifications, are further discussed in Chapter 6.

1.5 Summary

The features of Cyberspace mentioned above – entry and fixed costs, the size of the market and scarcity – point to a significant decline in the market failure of monopolistic powers, which indicates less justification for central intervention in the market. Within the context of each of these traditional sources of monopolistic problems, however, we mentioned new and unique phenomena that may create new monopolies. In addition, other features of

Cyberspace may operate in an opposite direction, increasing monopolistic power and introducing new types of monopoly problems that call for innovative solutions. We turn now to these new types of monopoly problems.

2. NEW MONOPOLISTIC EFFECTS AND ANTICOMPETITIVE MARKET BEHAVIOR

Several characteristics, typical of the information environment, challenge the premise of perfect competition. These features facilitate concentration of economic power by a few, and often by a single dominant market player. Standard economic analysis, especially of the Chicago School of Law and Economics, strictly focuses on the ability to unilaterally control the level of supply or demand unrestrained by price mechanisms. It defines a monopoly only within a well defined market, and identifies threats to competition in conducts that result either in higher prices or in reduced output or quality. Thus, standard economic analysis fails to detect impediments to competition of a monopolistic nature, which stem from the idiosyncratic nature of information. The information environment is elastic in the sense that it can be easily changed, and dynamic in the sense that it is subject to frequent transformations. It is an end product that can be measured by its functional or esthetic value, and at the same time a major resource for creating more information.

Above all, however, information and informational goods are context-dependent. They become valuable only within a cultural and a technological context. While tangible resources, such as land and water, may have a stand-alone value, informational goods derive their meaning and thus their economic value from their communicative capacity. In this sense, information and informational goods would only become useful within a technological context using compatible features that allow interaction and exchange. These phenomena can be analyzed in the framework of monopolistic problems that are not visible within the traditional economic analysis.

2.1 Connectivity and Interoperability

A major feature of Cyberspace, which could lead to monopolistic consequences, has to do with connectivity and interoperability. The use of any network, especially a global network that consists of a large number of independent networks, heavily relies on the use of shared standards that facilitate interoperability. Interoperability, as defined by Band and Katoh (1995, p. 6), refers to connectivity that is, 'the degree to which a product can participate in a joint activity without requiring other connected products to alter their mode of operation.' Just as our ability to communicate with one another depends on the use of shared standards, so does the exchange of signals between different systems. Operating systems must be compatible with microprocessors to enable the operation of computer hardware. Application programs must be compatible with operating systems to effectively function. Applications must be compatible with each other so they can communicate, allowing their users to exchange information and process signals created by other applications. Compatibility is, of course, mandated in a network environment.

The Internet runs due to the ability of different products and technologies used on it to communicate with one another, to process input created by other products, and to create an output that is processable by other online products. This is made possible by interface standards, with which all compatible products must comply. The operation of the Internet depends on the use of shared protocols. The TCP/IP protocol (1983) allows the interconnection of independent and incompatible computers and information systems. The introduction of TCP/IP protocol followed by the World Wide Web (1990), and Mosaic (1993), the first graphics-based Web browser, allowed open access in the sense that they were based on standards opened and available to all. These shared technological standards constitute the necessary interface for creating a network made of different technologies.

Standards in the online environment refer to the technical specifications that are required so that a technology can function online. Standards are neither intrinsically anticompetitive nor do they always advance competition. Standards can encourage competition by facilitating interoperability among competing technologies. At the same time, whoever controls a standard may exercise such control to block competitors and threaten competition.

The pro-competition aspect of standards relates to its role in establishing interoperability. Industry standards may nurture competition by facilitating interoperability among competing technologies, thus allowing end users to switch between technologies of different brands and encouraging vendors to compete for quality and price. Standards could further enhance efficiency by increasing certainty and thereby reducing the risk and cost associated with the early stages of design. By complying with the industry standard, manufacturers are able to guarantee that their technologies, no matter how innovative, can connect and interoperate with existing systems.

Standardization could further encourage specialization and competition among vendors of supplementary products such as replacement parts and compatible accessories. For instance, if the 'streaming' of all audio and video from Internet media sources would use the same standard, developers could compete in producing various media players. If video games could be played on any standard platforms, such as personal computers, and players were not limited to a single video game console (such as Sony Playstation), competition among manufacturers of game consoles would be encouraged. Standardization may further benefit consumers, lowering the cost of switching from one product to another. If, for instance, all browsers used similar standards, switching between products would involve the very low cost of learning and adapting to the new product. If European and American electrical plugs and sockets were the same, American tourists traveling to Europe could avoid the cost of electric adapters.

In the early days of Cyberspace, the dominant forces behind its creation and development came from academia. There, the major goal was to create shared standards that would enable individual users of different computers to communicate with one another. These standards were placed in the public domain. Internet standards were kept in the public domain largely as a result of the policies of standard-setting organizations such as the Internet Engineering Task Force ('IETF'). The IETF had a long-standing policy that denied proprietary standards. This policy was modified during the early 2000s.

Internet Standards are defined by the Internet Engineering Task Force (IETF) as 'a specification that is stable and well understood, is technically competent, has multiple, independent and interoperable implementations with substantial operational experience, enjoys significant public support, and is recognizably useful in some or all parts of the Internet' (Network Working Group 1996). Connecting to the Internet required merely adopting Internet standards, which were neither governed by the state, nor subject to any proprietary rights.

In recent years, Cyberspace has been gradually, but steadily, captured by economic enterprises. Firms seek to create unique standards, which will bind users of their products to other products of the same firm, thus preventing competition. Consequently, although new technologies introduced into Cyberspace must be compatible with the specifications of existing technologies, these standards are often held by private parties as trade secrets, patents, or other types of intellectual property, and are therefore not accessible (Lemley and McGowan 1998).

Indeed, standards could pose an impediment to competition. The most serious standard-related danger derives from their capacity to serve as nodes of control. The presence of standards provides a key point of control. Anyone who wishes to develop a new product must comply with the standard, and when the standard is not opened, a license is required. Whoever controls the standard has discretion in determining how the standard technology will be implemented and by whom. If the standard is equally accessible to all, and everyone is free to adopt it, it is more likely to facilitate competition.

The anticompetitive effect of standards would, therefore, depend on their nature – whether they are 'opened' or 'closed' standards (Lemley 2002, pp. 1901–1903). A standard is 'opened' when it is not subject to exclusive rights such as intellectual property rights. A standard is 'closed' when its use is exclusively controlled, and a license is required before the standard can be used to achieve compatibility. When a standard is propertized, for instance, by copyright or patent law, its owner enjoys certain exclusive rights regarding its use. Owners of standards may exclude potential developers, prohibit the development of certain technologies, or condition the grant of a license to use a standard upon compliance with restrictive terms. Intellectual property rights in standards limit the ability of potential users to switch between different technologies, thereby increasing the control exercised by standard owners over access and pricing.

One bold example in recent years for accumulating monopolistic power gained through technology standards is the Microsoft case, which was litigated in *United States of America v. Microsoft Corporation* (364 U.S. App. D.C. 330) (hereinafter – the 'Microsoft Case'). Microsoft controls the operating systems market of most personal computers that are connected to the Internet. It owns the intellectual property rights in those technologies essential for anyone who wishes to develop a product that will be accessible to Internet users. The antitrust legal action brought against Microsoft during early 2000 alleged that Microsoft had incorporated its Web browser (Internet Explorer) into its operating system, thus attempting improperly to drive the Netscape Web browser and others out of the market. The major concern was the leveraging of monopoly power from the Intel-compatible PC operating system market into the Internet browsers market.

At the same time it launched an antitrust prosecution against Microsoft, the United States administration was engaged in enacting and enforcing legislation that itself facilitates the accumulation of monopolistic powers vis-à-vis standards. That is the anti-circumvention legislation in the Digital Millennium Copyright Act ('DMCA'). This legislation, enacted in 1998, allows copyright owners to prevent the circumvention of any technological measures used to control access to their work, and to prevent the manufacturing and distribution of any tools and technologies used for circumvention.

Several vendors invoked their copyrights as protected under the DMCA to deter the development of compatible devices. A typical example is a legal suit brought by Lexmark, one of the largest printer vendors in the world. Vendors in the printer toner aftermarket must make sure that their toner cartridges comply with Lexmark's specifications. Lexmark sought to eliminate the printer toner aftermarket that offers toner cartridges at lower prices. To do so, Lexmark installed 'authentication routines' between its cartridges and printers, so that its printers will identify an original Lexmark toner cartridge. These routines were reverse engineered by Static Control Component, with the introduction of the 'Smartek' chip, which enables any cartridge to work in Lexmark printers. In *Lexmark international Inc.* (253 F. Supp. 2d, 943), Lexmark successfully invoked the DMCA to prevent the technological development that allows compatibility with its printers.

Similarly, the DMCA was invoked by Sony to prevent vendors from developing emulators that would enable the use of video games intended for the Sony Playstation Console, on any PC *(Sony Computer Entertainment, Inc.,*

203 F.3d 596). Sony further used technological standards to divide the world and its worldwide distribution into regions, so that games sold in one region would not be compatible with Playstation consoles purchased in other regions Sony sued the manufacturers of 'mod chips', which modify the Playstation consoles to permit the use of games purchased in other geographical regions (*Sony Computer Entertainment America Inc.*, 87 F. Supp. 2nd 976). A similar suit was brought in Australia under an equivalent legislation (*Kabushiki Kaisha Sony Computer Entertainment*, FCA 906).

Proprietary rights in standards may not always lead to an anticompetitive outcome (Lemley 2002). Consider for instance the use of intellectual property rights by Sun Microsystems Inc. ('Sun'). Sun is the owner of the proprietary rights in the Java technology, a programming language that is platform independent, allowing developers to write programs that can run on any operating system. If a widespread operating system creates a 'lock' on competition, the 'middleware' that allows developers to write a single program that can run on all operating systems, is a 'key'. It unlocks the technological catch. 'Middleware' is necessary to facilitate compatibility across operating systems and enables software developers to write software that can operate on different types of operating systems. The court in the *Sun v. Microsoft* (*Sun Microsystems Inc.*, 333 F.3d 517, p. 522) case explains:

> Because operating systems vary, such that applications software developers have to tailor their software to each separate operating system, middleware has been conceived for placement between applications software and the various operating systems with the ultimate idea, in part, of creating cross-compatibility in applications software for the various operating systems.

Sun developed Java to permit software applications to run on various operating systems. Such middleware is likely to encourage competition, as this would enable computer program developers to write applications that are likely to run on popular platforms. Microsoft has a monopoly in the PC operating systems market. Therefore, programmers tend to prefer writing applications programs that are compatible with the Windows operating system. Sun's middleware has the potential of encouraging developers, who were otherwise reluctant to write application programs for the non-Windows environment, to do so. Sun intended that its cross-platform application would eliminate the requirement to tailor computer programs to particular operating systems, thereby lifting a significant barrier to application software entry in the market.

To preserve Java's cross-platform capabilities, Sun required in its licenses that all implementations of Java be compatible with the core Java platform. Nonetheless, Microsoft adjusted the open standard of Java, to create its own proprietary version of Java, called 'Java Compatible' or Microsoft Java Virtual Machine ('MSJVM'). MSJVM is required for writing programs that run on Microsoft's operating system.

Sun sued Microsoft in an attempt to prevent the capturing of the open standard of Java, and turning it into a closed standard. While Sun failed to establish any antitrust claim, it was granted a preliminary injunction based on copyright infringement. The court accepted Sun's claim that Microsoft violated its copyrights in Java by violating the limited license to use Java. Accordingly, the court granted a preliminary injunction prohibiting Microsoft from distributing Java products unless certain incompatibilities were eliminated (*Sun Microsystems, Inc.,* 333 F.3d 517).

The example of Sun demonstrates that not all proprietary measures in standards are anti-competitive. In this case the intellectual property rights (or the monopolistic right) were used to maintain a competitive market, rather than to limit competition. The few examples we mentioned demonstrate the shortcomings of the traditional monopoly analysis to the new technological environment. New modeling of the monopoly problem is required.

2.2 Network Externalities

A related feature of Cyberspace that may increase monopoly effects concerns network externalities. Network externalities emerge when the use of one product is more beneficial to a particular user when more people use it. For instance, the more widespread the use of a word processor becomes, the more beneficial it becomes to the user. If we all use the same word processor, we may save the time involved in converting files, the costs of correcting errors, and even the costs caused by the inability to process digital files created by another program.

Network externalities are typical of a network environment such as Cyberspace, since it is based on connectivity and compatibility. The Internet is a network of networks, which becomes more beneficial to users – either as a marketplace or as a public forum – with the connection of each additional user. Furthermore, products that are operated in an online environment should be interoperable to increase connectivity. Once an online product becomes widespread, it gains value not merely owing to its technological superiority but also, and sometimes only, owing to its prevalence. Network externalities may limit competition by increasing the costs of entry. They provide a significant advantage to first comers, who may establish their products as the standard for future goods (Lemley and McGowan 1998).

Once again, Microsoft provides a good example. Software developers will have strong incentives to write computer programs that are compatible with Microsoft operating systems. A large number of application programs will strengthen the attractiveness of Microsoft's operating system to the consumers. This 'tipping' effect (Katz and Shapiro 1994) is, of course, anticompetitive and will make it more difficult for competitors to enter the market.

Network effects may sometimes lead to an inefficient outcome and make it difficult to replace an inferior standard with a more efficient one. Standards could be particularly advantageous in network markets, where the benefit derived by any individual user increases with the growth in the overall number of users. Therefore, even though the standard initially adapted is inferior, it would be difficult to switch to a more efficient standard. The paradigmatic example is the QWERTY typewriter keyboard. This standard keyboard was adapted despite the fact that it did not offer the most efficient way of typing. This standard keyboard still prevails today due to the lock-in effect caused by learning cost.

Network effects are, of course, typical of the online environment. The more people using the Internet, the more beneficial it becomes to each individual user. Cyberspace is a sophisticated technological infrastructure used by consumers without any intermediaries. Every new product that users must operate involves costs of learning and adapting to new work methods. Consequently, the costs of switching to a new technology may be prohibitively high. This may further increase entry costs and have a restraining effect on competition.

3. THE LIMITS OF STANDARD COMPETITION ANALYSIS AND ANTITRUST LAW

Sun v. Microsoft can serve as a useful case study for identifying the limits of the traditional paradigm. Sun Microsystems, Inc. and Microsoft Corporation are definitely two of the most important market players in the software industry, and their legal dispute touches upon problems of compatibility, innovation, network environment and technological standards. Therefore, the case provides an opportunity to examine standard economic analysis of competition law in concrete circumstances.

The dispute, as we elaborated above, concerned Java, a middleware product developed by Sun, which allows developers to write an application that runs on various operating systems, instead of according to the specifications of a particular operating system. Since Microsoft monopolizes the operating systems market for personal computers connected to the Internet, and the company's proprietary operating system, Windows, is a de facto standard in that market, a middleware such as Java has obvious pro-competition advantages. For the same reason, Microsoft perceived Java as a threat to its monopoly status that would erode a significant entry barrier: the need to tailor applications to Windows.

Sun argued that Microsoft responded to this threat with an 'embrace and extend' strategy (*Sun Microsystems, Inc,* 87 F. Supp. 2d. 992, p. 995):

> First, Microsoft "embraced" the Java technology by licensing from Sun the right to use its Java Technology to develop and distribute compatible Products. Second,

Microsoft "extended" the Java platform by developing strategic incompatibilities into its Java runtime and development tools products. According to Sun, these incompatibilities tied applications using Microsoft's Java development tools to Microsoft's virtual machine and the Windows platform. Third, Microsoft used its distribution channels to flood the market with its version of the Java Technology in [what Sun characterized as] an attempt to "hijack the Java Technology and transform it into a Microsoft proprietary programming and runtime environment."

Later Sun and Microsoft reached an agreement whereby Sun licensed Microsoft to make and distribute Java-based products, requiring that the Java platform would meet compatibility standards set by Sun. Sun argued that the Microsoft Java Virtual Machine ('MSJVM') eventually developed by Microsoft was incompatible with Sun's Java platform. Microsoft further released a programming product containing Microsoft's own middleware (the '.Net platform') that competes with the Java platform.

The district court found a serious risk that the middleware market would tip to Microsoft's .Net product in the future. The court was concerned that the vast number of Windows users would prompt software developers to write software based applications on Microsoft's middleware. This tipping effect (also referred to by the court as 'feedback effect'), namely, a product's increased attractiveness to consumers, and the subsequent rise in the number of users, would make it very difficult to compete with Microsoft's middleware.

The court granted a 'must carry' preliminary injunction. It ordered Microsoft to incorporate in and distribute with every Windows operating system and Web browser a copy of Sun Java to operate as middleman (intermediate) software and to facilitate the use of a variety of computer programs. The 'must carry' metaphor was borrowed from the regulatory regime, which applies to monopolistic cable companies, requiring them to carry content of the broadcasters, their main competitors. While acknowledging that this type of 'must carry' injunction is unprecedented, the District Court found it necessary in the extraordinary circumstances of the case.

The Court of Appeals reversed the 'must carry' injunction. On appeal, Sun was granted a preliminary injunction prohibiting Microsoft from distributing MSJVM and any product that infringe Sun's copyright without a license. The Court of Appeals denied a relief based on the anti-competition claims.

The Court of Appeals applied standard competition analysis, finding that the future harm of market tipping in favor of .Net is too speculative. It ruled that there is no market distortion in the absence of a strict market definition, as a prerequisite to identifying any market distortion is a clear definition of the relevant market. The Court held that while Sun was asking for a preliminary injunction in the emerging market of middleware, it is only able to establish that Microsoft monopolizes another market, which is the market for worldwide licensing of Intel-compatible personal computer operating systems, 'a market that by definition does not involve middleware' (*Sun Microsystems Inc.*, 333 F.3d 517, p. 532).

The leveraging theory was employed by the District Court to prevent Microsoft from taking advantage of its past antitrust violations. It prohibited Microsoft from leveraging its monopoly in the operating systems market, and expanding into the market for Internet enabled platforms. The Court of Appeals held that this theory has not received general acceptance, and applied it very narrowly to conclude that Microsoft was not involved in any monopoly leveraging.

This fascinating legal dispute between Sun and Microsoft demonstrates the anticompetitive forces that are at play in the information environment, and their innovative tactics. The two distinct legal opinions of the District Court and the Court of Appeals reflect the clash between traditional competition discourse and the novel considerations required in the networked information environment. The standard competition analysis applied by the Court of Appeals demonstrates the shortcomings of the traditional competition paradigm in addressing some of the threats to competition in the information environment. We will now highlight and summarize some of these issues:

First, standard economic analysis lacks a focus on technology. Impediments on competition in Cyberspace are no longer limited to dominant power over output and price. They are technologically dependent. Technology is not static but dynamic. It is changing as multiple players respond, among other things, to market signals. The competition in technological markets is not merely a contest between producers for the market share of passive consumers and end users. It is also a competition over the mindshare of developers: what will they develop, what technologies will be used, what will be useful. Advantages in these early stages of development may determine ultimately what becomes available to users. Market dominance should not be measured strictly by the ability to set the price, but also by the ability to set the technological standards.

Furthermore, when technology is concerned, the market distortion caused by anticompetitive conduct should not be measured exclusively in terms of price and quantities. Any analysis should also take into account the effects of market conduct on innovation. From this perspective, it is necessary to examine how conduct affects the types of technologies that become available: i.e., is it allowing the adoption of closed standards, such as MSJVM, or facilitating open standards such as Java. No less importantly, identifying future harm to the market requires considering the effects of market conduct on research and development i.e., which technologies are absent and which would not be developed at all.

Second, standard economic analysis underlying antitrust law lacks a focus on information as a distinctive commodity. Information is subject to strong network effects. Control over technological standards in one market may directly affect activities and control in other markets. Cyberspace is a network of users, and is therefore subject to strong network externalities. It is based on connectivity and compatibility and becomes more beneficial to its users with the connection of each additional user. Similarly, the attractiveness of an application or other informational goods to consumers increases with the number of users. The network effect is therefore present in Cyberspace at all levels, from the infrastructure, through the operating systems, the applications, and to the content. Network effects on market share cannot be simply disregarded as speculative, but must be an integral part of the analysis.

It follows that competition analysis in Cyberspace may not hold to strict market definitions. Applying such strict definitions to an environment with blurred boundaries between different platforms and products, an environment characterized by convergence of applications that require compatibility, could be blinding.

Competition analysis should take seriously leveraging effects. When Microsoft Word uses a Hebrew standard that is accessible only by Microsoft's Internet Explorer and not by the competing browser Netscape, its domination over the word processor market allows Microsoft to dominate the market for browsers in Hebrew and increase the cost of entry (or entirely prevent entry) for competing browsers. This leverage is not detected by conventional economic analysis of competition law.

4. SUMMARY

Cyberspace reduces the traditional non-virtual monopolistic problems, but it creates new ones. These special monopolistic effects are strictly related to technology and standards. The identification of such monopolistic power is different from identification of monopolies in the non-virtual world. The traditional solutions of price and quantity control, on the one hand, and preventing mergers or breaking up firms, on the other hand, may not be efficacious to remedy these new phenomena. Breaking up Microsoft, for example, might not be the right economic response to its monopolistic power, which expresses itself by technological dependency. The shape and type of legal intervention that may be justifiable cannot derive from the traditional market analysis of supply and demand. The new monopolies of Cyberspace, therefore, require fresh economic thinking.

5. Public Goods

This chapter explores the second market failure of the four major types of failures identified by the neo-classical school of the economic approach towards law, which might justify central intervention in the market. As in the previous chapter on monopolies, we will briefly sketch the traditional parameters for identifying and remedying public good failure of the market, and subsequently examine the application of traditional analysis to Cyberspace.

The public good market failure is central for Cyberspace, in which almost everything boils down to information, considered by traditional analysis as a public good. Emails and online chats are, in fact, interactive exchanges of informational signals; surfing the Internet is data mining, and commercial activities such as downloading software and charging a credit are no more than information processing. The main commodities exchanged in Cyberspace are informational goods such as texts, music, data, or computer programs. The rich human interactive environment we experience when we surf the Internet is merely the creation, procession, and transmission of information. Information is perceived by standard economic analysis as a public good, and therefore, in Cyberspace, the share of public goods of all goods is far greater than in the real world.

This chapter focuses on information as a public good. After briefly introducing the standard analysis of public goods, we examine its application to the information environment. We then explore some of the challenges posed by the digital networked environment to the fundamental assumptions of this paradigm. We discuss alternative modes of production of informational goods, and probe some difficulties raised by the interface between proprietary and non-proprietary systems regulating the production and distribution of informational goods.

1. INFORMATION AS A PUBLIC GOOD AND THE INCENTIVES PARADIGM

1.1 What are Public Goods?

A public good is a commodity with two distinctive, but related characteristics: non-excludability and non-rivalry. Non-excludability occurs when it is either impossible to exclude non-payers (free-riders) from using the goods or service, or the costs for such exclusion are so high that no profit-maximizing firm is willing to produce the good. Non-rivalry means that the use of such resources by one user does not detract from the ability of others to use them. Tangibles, as well as real estate, are usually subject to rivalry, i.e. their use by one person precludes others from using them.

Public goods are not likely to be produced and supplied by the market, and if they are privately provided, they are likely to be under-supplied. Thus, government intervention is necessary to guarantee the optimal supply of public goods, either by subsidizing their private provision or by producing them itself.

1.2 Non-Excludability of Information and the Traditional Remedies to Correct the Market Failure of Public Goods

Standard economic analysis considers information as a public good. Its consumption is non-rivalrous and the use of information cannot be efficiently excluded (Landes and Posner 1989; Mennel 1987, 1989). The non-excludable characteristic of informational goods derives from the virtual nature of information. Information has no physical boundaries, and its duplication and distribution involve relatively low costs. The marginal costs of exclusion are often greater than the marginal costs of provision, so it is inefficient to spend resources to exclude non-payers. Free-riding of non-payers reduces incentives for investment in generating new information, and without government intervention information tends to be under-supplied.

Take book publishing as an example. The publisher will invest the necessary resources to cover the author's fee and expenses in preparing the manuscript. He will design a cover, and pay the graphic and editorial expenses. Bearing the marginal cost of producing a large number of copies of the printed book, the publisher will also distribute it via various channels. Once the book is released in the market, a second comer could easily copy it, bearing only the marginal (relatively low) costs of creating additional copies, and avoiding the substantial cost of producing the manuscript. Thus, the second comer, who made no investment in creating the work, can easily distribute copies for a lower price, driving the original publisher from the market. Publishers would, therefore, lack incentives to invest in the production of informational goods, such as books.

Government may intervene to remedy this failure by supplying informational goods itself, either through covering the cost of creation by government funds or by subsidizing private investments. Government intervention to secure incentives for investment in new creations may also take the form of regulation, which allows the commodification of informational goods. Intellectual property laws seek to secure incentives by providing creators with a set of carefully tailored legal rights to exclude others from using the work. These rights allow the creators to trade their works and inventions. In fact, the proprietary regime can be perceived as public subsidy of enforcement costs, as it allows creators to use public enforcement to prevent some unauthorized uses, and subjects potential free-riders to legal remedies.

For instance, distributing copies of copyrighted music files by email, without authorization, will infringe on the exclusive rights of copyright owners to reproduce and publicly distribute the work. The copyright owner can prevent such unauthorized use of the work by filing for an injunction or collecting damages. By legally excluding non-payers, the law facilitates the creators' ability to reap a return on their investments through the collection of fees for the use of their works.

1.3 Information as Non-Rivalry Goods and its Economic Consequences

Non-rivalry is the second feature of information as a public good. Information is not consumed by its use. It cannot be used up. If you hear a symphony by Mozart, you do not prevent others from enjoying it. If you read a book, you don't deprive others from reading it, even though a number of users may not be able to read the same copy of the book simultaneously. The tangible media, in which works are embodied, such as printed books and plastic CDs, are not a public good. They would be subject to the rivalry suffered by other scarce resources. But this does not apply to the information contained in them. Consequently, unlike tangibles, information does not raise any allocation problem. Everyone can benefit from it without depriving others, and it is unnecessary to allocate resources to the most efficient user.

The non-rivalrous nature of information suggests that the use of information, once created, should be maximized. Yet, if we give copyright owners a monopoly over their works, they can set the price as they please. Owners will usually set the price that maximizes their profits, rather than one that equals their marginal costs of production. This would lead to deadweight losses: potential users who value the informational product at its marginal cost, but not at its monopoly price, would fail to purchase a license. Consequently, works will be underused.

These losses are particularly significant in the informational goods market, as these goods are the primary resource for further creation. Technological innovations are built on each other. Artistic works refer to one another, and use symbols, metaphors, characters and often citations from other works. The skills of human capital – the author and other inventors of informational goods – depend on access to previous works. Exposure to the books of the past, to modern art, or to available computer programs, may all become necessary for writing a new novel, or developing a new word processor. Human capital requires training and knowledge of the current state of the art. A stronger proprietary regime will increase the price of future works, and may prevent their creation altogether.

Consequently, information policy that attempts to remedy the public goods failure pulls in conflicting directions. On the one hand, the need for incentives renders a strong proprietary regime with robust monopoly rights. Intellectual property laws induce production of information by allowing non-payers to be excluded and information to be marketed at a monopoly price. On the other hand, strong property rights establish monopolistic powers that would lead to deadweight losses caused by the propertization.

Intellectual property laws aim to reflect these conflicting concerns by achieving a balance between incentives through proprietary rights, on one hand, and the need to secure unimpeded access to works and innovations, on the other hand. Copyright laws and patent laws provide incentives through monopoly rights while keeping this monopoly limited in order to minimize deadweight losses. This balance is achieved primarily by limiting the duration of the protection for patents and copyrighted works. A balance is further achieved by protecting only certain aspects of works (i.e., *expressions* are protected by copyright but not *ideas*), and by defining some privileged uses (i.e., fair use under copyright law).

1.4 Challenges to the Traditional Economic Analysis of Information

The perception of information as a public good and the *incentives paradigm* (Lunney 1996) described above, still dominate public debates over copyright protection of information, such as the controversy over the legitimacy of Napster and other online music files exchange systems, or the debate over the proper scope of protection for computer programs (Abramson 2002; Kwong 2003). But within the incentive paradigm of the economic approach, there are recent calls that dispute the balance currently struck by IP laws, and especially the limited duration of their protection. Thus, the non-rivalrous nature of informational goods was recently challenged by Landes and Posner (2003). They argued that in the absence of property rights, intangible works that fall into the public domain may be inefficiently used, and therefore advocated indefinite renewal rights.

Nevertheless, the incentives paradigm is not the only economic justification for a proprietary regime in information (Lemley 1997). Some believe that a proprietary regime in informational goods is necessary for regulating the consumption and use of goods (Kitch 1977, Easterbrook 1996, Landes and Posner 2003). Assigning property rights in informational goods is required, they argue, to guarantee the efficient use of works by allowing their commercialization.

The underlying assumption of this path of argument is that informational goods can be overused. This concern was best drafted by Hardin's *Tragedy of the Commons*, a widely cited justification for a property regime in tangible resources (Hardin 1968). Useful resources that are held in common, subject to no exclusive rights and freely usable by anyone are treated with suspicion by standard economic analysis. The main concern is that freedom to use the common goods would eventually destroy the common resources. When too many individuals are legally privileged to use a resource, such as a lake, they will tend to overuse it. This is because each individual bears only the benefits of consuming the resource (such as maximizing fishing), but will not assume the full cost of such use (namely exhausting the fishery). Since users do not internalize the negative consequences of their consumption on the resource, individuals acting separately may bring about the collective over-consumption of the resource.

Yet, while the tragedy of the commons may occur in the case of fisheries or overgrazed natural pasture (Landes and Posner 2003), it does not take place in the case of information. As long as information is non-rivalrous, it cannot be overused (Heller and Eisenberg 1998, Elkin-Koren 1998, Dam 1999a, Lessig 2001). It is simply unnecessary to encourage users of informational goods to take into account the cost imposed by their use on others. That is because the use of informational goods imposes no costs, except for transaction costs borne by the user (such as the time spent on watching a movie, or resources used to search for an academic article).

Indeed, the view that informational goods should be subject to property rights assumes that information is rivalrous, and that its value decreases with use. This challenge to the traditional public goods analysis of information was recently raised by Landes and Posner (2003), drawing an analogy between the dilution of famous brands as a result of overuse, and the potential decrease in value of copyrighted works. There is a value, they argue, in non-confusing duplication of trademarks. If the same trademark is freely used to identify goods of different origin and of various qualities, the trademark loses its distinctive value.

While this is the mainstream view of trademark law, which is an offspring of unfair competition law, Landes and Posner believe that it is also applicable to copyright law. Copyrightable works, they argue, raise a problem of 'overgrazing' (Landes and Posner 2003, pp. 487–488):

> A book or other copyrightable property is, as we noted earlier, a public good; its use by one consumer does not interfere with its use by any other. This point cannot be decisive, however; a celebrity's name or likeness has public good characteristics as well, yet unlimited reproduction of the name or the likeness could prematurely exhaust the celebrity's commercial value, just as unlimited drilling from a common pool of oil or gas would deplete the pool prematurely. The same could be true of a novel or a movie or a comic-book character or a piece of music or painting, particularly with regard to copyrights on components of completed works rather than on the completed works themselves. If because copyright had expired anyone were free to incorporate the Mickey Mouse character in a book, movie, song, etc., the value

for the character might plummet. Not only would the public rapidly tire of Mickey Mouse, but his image would be blurred as some authors portrayed him as a Casanova, others as Catmeat, others as an animal-rights advocate, still others as the henpecked husband of Minnie.

[...] We do not wish to press the argument too far. While examples can be given of even works of elite culture that have been debased by unlimited reproduction (the *Mona Lisa*, the opening of Beethoven's *Fifth Symphony,* and several of Van Gogh's most popular paintings come immediately to mind), there were counterexamples, such as the works of Shakespeare, which seem undiminished by the proliferation of performances and derivative works, some of them kitsch, such as Shakespeare T-shirts and the movie Shakespeare in Love.

Landes and Posner are concerned with a diminishing value that would result from over propertization of works, until the commercial value for Disney's Mickey would become zero. Indeed, they seek to qualify their argument, implying a rather vague distinction between Disney's products and some 'works of elite culture', but yet insisting that some elite works could be debased by unlimited reproduction. These examples demonstrate the central weakness in Landes' and Posner's analysis. A proprietary system tailored to remedy a public good failure must avoid as much as possible making any substantive out-of-market judgments regarding the intrinsic value of works. The argument that derivatives based on Van Gogh's work debased its value, while *Shakespeare in Love* did not detract from Shakespeare's works is a profound judgment, heavily loaded with values, and unsound by any objective criteria. The basis for a proprietary system in informational goods must undertake a more neutral goal, such as optimizing the investment in creation, or diversifying the types of creators. In fact, this is conceived to be a major advantage of the proprietary system as a mechanism for securing incentives vis-à-vis central sponsorship of creation by government. In the proprietary system, the market functions as a collective choice mechanism, providing the higher level of incentives to the most popular works.

A further weakness of Landes' and Posner's analysis lies in confusing the *commercial value* of informational works and their total *economic value*. The commercial value of informational goods is strictly measured by one's ability to extract profits from certain goods or services. This rather narrow perspective does not capture the entire value of information. It would focus merely on the ability of, say, Albert Einstein, who had an innovative idea, to charge money for it, or otherwise generate a financial return from it. This commercial value has nothing to do with the economic value of Einstein's innovation, which turned the science of physics upside down, opened new theoretical frontiers, and enabled new technologies. These developments obviously had significant economic value. This value does not diminish with use. In fact, the more you use it, the more beneficial it becomes. There is no need to reinvent these scientific breakthroughs or to avoid using them simply for the sake of securing a commercial value. The only reason to secure the commercial value of informational goods under the incentives paradigm is the need to secure incentives to induce creation. This, however, does not mean that the value of informational goods decreases with their use, and it implies nothing about the economic character of the use of information.

Information is developed incrementally. Scientific knowledge is accumulated and developed in what Thomas Kuhn refers to as *normal science*, where 'research [is] firmly based upon one or more past scientific achievements, achievements that some particular scientific community acknowledges for a time as supplying the foundation for its further practice' (Kuhn 1962). Scientific research relies upon exchange. Innovative ideas evolve through interplay with prior research, discoveries, and theoretical steps achieved by earlier generations in various disciplines. The use of previous theses, for either ratifying a theory or rejecting it, is an integral component of scientific methodology. In this sense, the scientific project is fundamentally communal and interactive, even though it is often executed by individuals and competing teams.

Exchange and discussion are also essential for the realm of creativity and are very much alive in the artistic world. Artists often refer to one another, rely on each other's images and symbolic references, or seek to subvert dominant meanings. Existing information stimulates the creation of more information and, therefore, its extensive use may increase the likelihood of further development.

As in the case of scientific and technological innovations, there is no need to avoid the use of works of great art simply to secure their commercial value. This is particularly unjustifiable when the commercial value is tied to a specific business model, such as artificially creating scarcity to increase the demand for a particular artifact. The economic desirability of such business tactics should not be measured exclusively by their effect on the revenue streams of owners, but also in light of the social cost inflicted on further creation and optimal use.

2. APPLYING PUBLIC GOOD ANALYSIS TO CYBERSPACE

2.1 Reducing the Cost of Copying

An initial application of the public good analysis to information in Cyberspace can lead to the conclusion that Cyberspace enhances market failure of public goods because of the significantly reduced costs of copying. The digital-networked-environment fundamentally changes the way information is distributed. It is much easier to copy informational works in a digital form. One needs neither a printing press nor a copy machine to reproduce works. The same workstation that is used for creating text, music, and clips, is also capable of producing masses of copies at no cost. The fact that it is much cheaper to reproduce works in digital format makes it more tempting for free-riders to take advantage of the initial investment made by the creators.

The Net further transforms the deliverability of works. Disseminating informational works may not involve any distribution of copies; instead, it involves providing access to works. Informational works shared online, such as recorded music, textbooks, or video-clips, are no longer embodied in physical objects such as paper or CDs. They are transmitted through the Net without any physical medium, by processing of electronic signals. One has no longer to distribute or sell copies of the work, but instead simply to make the work available on the Net so users can access it. Making works available on a Web site would allow any surfer to access such materials, by directing the browser to the server (thus creating temporal copies) and often downloading files (Elkin-Koren 1996, pp. 250–254).

In addition, the cost of communication on digital networks is relatively low, since digital bits travel in small packets and transmission does not require dedicating any communication channel for exclusive use. Thus, the costs of making an informational work available online and of retrieving remote information are low. Yet, as we further discuss in Chapter 6, distributing informational works in an environment that suffers from information overflow involves new types of costs associated with scarcity of attention and intensive competition over the rather limited capability of users to process all available information.

How does the reduced cost of copying affect the economic analysis of information as a public good? The first impression is that Cyberspace tends to convert certain types of information, which are private goods in the non-virtual world, into public goods in Cyberspace. The low cost of copying and distributing information on the Net and the de-materialization of information, suggest that we should expect a growing manifestation of free-riding, which characterizes public goods. Indeed, it seems that this sort of analysis brought the Working Group on Intellectual Property Rights of the US Department of Commerce Information Infrastructure Task Force to emphasize, in its final report, the threat introduced by the Internet to the interests of copyright holders, and to recommend the expansion of the rights granted to owners to on-line distribution (Information Infrastructure Task Force 1995).

The remedies for the public good failure in the form of proprietary rights are also questioned. These observations actually inspired John Perry Barlow in 1994 to proclaim the end of copyright law in his influential paper, *The Economy of Ideas* (Barlow 1994). The Internet, which frees information from its physical containers, and creates a purely virtual environment, is simply impossible to control. Information in its virtual form can no longer be excluded by legal rights. Information 'wants to be free' and it is therefore inevitable, he argued, that the current system of intellectual property law would collapse.

2.2 Excludability in Cyberspace and the Changing Nature of Information

A more careful analysis reveals that notwithstanding the reduced costs of copying, several features of Cyberspace might, in fact, significantly reduce the market failure of public goods. The major feature is that technology in Cyberspace enhances the ability to exclude and control the distribution of information to the extent that makes it no longer a public good. The nature of information in Cyberspace allows the application of cost-effective self-help technical measures to control the consumption and use of information. Such means allow information that used to be non-excludable in the non-virtual world to be excludable in Cyberspace. Indeed, the creation of digital copies involves very low costs. Yet distribution of copies is no longer the sole way of generating profits. Instead of selling copies, one can charge for access.

The new technical frontiers enable collecting a fee for access to a Web site and charging per-use for the information provided. They allow temporary entrance permits and restriction of usage of information to online individual use, blocking the possibilities of copying information or forwarding it, and more (Bell 1998; Dam 1998). A Web site, for instance, may only enable access to some music files after payments are made. A computer program may prevent the creation of copies or disable unauthorized copies, or may notify the software vendor every time an unlicensed copy logs into the Net.

A second feature, which is connected to excludability, is the nature of digital transmission. Since every communication in Cyberspace can be reduced to a discernible form (Gibbons 1997), digital transmission is more tangible than oral communication. The digital environment is not purely transient. Informational works cannot be experienced unintermediated. Digital bits saved as files must be processed on a computer in order to become a melody or a text. Every such processing act, operation etc is documented. Any action in a digital web leaves 'digital tracks'. The routine operations of sending electronic mail, surfing, sending and downloading files constitute data processing and are recorded in various files of the PC and the servers involved in the communications. These digital footprints make it easier to trace unauthorized uses. While monitoring infringements in the world of books and CDs involve high transaction costs, electronic monitoring reduces these costs dramatically. It allows copyright owners to replace manpower with automated crawlers and powerful software that is capable of automatically monitoring uses around the world.

Copyright management systems allow owners to monitor and manage the use of their respective works, and to license specific uses, while restricting others. The terms of the license are not merely drafted in a license agreement, but are technically embedded in the code embodying the work. The same system that provides the service (such as the computer program that facilitates access to a Web site) also defines the terms of use, namely, preventing some uses such as copying, and permitting others such as browsing. Consider, for instance, the Adobe Acrobat eBook platform. This system enables originators of content to distribute text in a digital form, but at the same time to restrict certain operations related to the files, such as editing, copying, printing or annotating.

This further facilitates alternative business models for generating profits from informational works. One shift is from selling copies to charging for access, for instance, collecting a fee for access to a Web site and charging per-use for the information provided. The new technical frontiers thus turn informational works, which were non-excludable in the non-virtual world, into excludable artifacts.

2.3 Circumvention of Excludability Technologies

The result of this analysis seems to be ideal: on the one hand, Cyberspace is causing a significant decrease in the costs of producing and distributing informational works, and therefore an increase in their production and distribution. On the other hand, information can no longer be regarded as suffering from the public good deficiencies. Thus, government intervention is not required or desirable. This analysis, however, is overlooking a key factor – technological stability. The development of exclusion measures is likely to encourage users to develop counter technology of code-breaking and hacking tools. For every protection measure, there is always a counter-technology to crack it.

For example, once the Adobe Acrobat eBook was released in 2001, a decrypting program (AEBPR) was developed. Dmitry Sklyarov, an assistant professor at Moscow Technical University, originally wrote this decrypting program as a practical application of his dissertation. It was later released by his employer, Elcomsoft Co. LTD on its Website. Files decrypted with the AEBPR program were no longer protected by encryption, and could therefore be copied and annotated as any other digital file.

The efficacy of technological protection of copyrighted works, therefore, depends on the absence of circumvention means. The development of such means, in turn, will lead to further sophistication of the exclusion tools and a continuous technological race between the two sorts of devices. Central intervention is arguably required to halt the technological race between exclusion tools and their counter technologies and prevent what is considered economic waste by some economists. Such a race, they argue, may divert funds that might otherwise be invested in more productive directions (Dam 1998).

Recognizing that enforcement by technology can be violated by counter coding technology, led intellectual property owners to call for government intervention. This was the underlying rationale of anti-circumvention legislation of the late 1990s. The US Digital Millennium Copyright Act (DMCA) 1998 and the comparable EU Directive on the Harmonization of Certain Aspects of Copyright and Related Rights in the Information Society (2001) sought to implement the anti-circumvention provision in the 1996 Geneva Internet Treaty (WIPO Copyright Treaty 1996). These statutes basically prohibit unauthorized access by circumvention, as well as the manufacturing and distribution of technological means designed to circumvent measures that either control access or effectively protect the rights of copyright owners.

The anti-circumvention legislation allowed, for instance, producers and distributors of films, television programs and home videos to win a suit against distributors of a decrypting algorithm (DeCSS). When the motion picture industry launched its digital distribution in DVD (Digital Versatile Disk), it encrypted the copies with an encryption-based security system called CSS (Content Scrambling System), designed to prevent copying of the DVD. The CSS is decrypted by an algorithm, installed (subject to a license) on standard DVD players or personal computers' operating systems. The decrypting program, DeCSS, emulated the 'key' to CSS and thus enabled users to play a DVD even in the absence of an authorized 'key'. The court held that CSS is a technological measure limiting the users' ability to make unauthorized copies of DVDs, and therefore distributors of DeCSS are liable for distributing circumventing devices *(Universal City Studios Inc.,* 273 F.3d 429).

Anti-circumvention legislation as a remedy to public good failure is very different from an intellectual property regime in which investors are assigned exclusive rights in their respective creations. Here, the government is not called upon to provide the public good or the legal means to enable its production by profit maximizing firms. Central intervention provides a privileged status to restrictions on access to information that were defined unilaterally by information providers. Indeed, what enables restrictions on the use of informational works is not the legal rule, but the availability of encryption and other protective technologies. Had it been legal to develop and distribute circumventing technologies, the market effect could have mitigated the power of content owners. A rule that prevents the development of circumventing measures assigns a privileged status to such self-made regulation.

The anti-circumvention legislation has, however, more profound consequences. As we further discuss in Chapter 8, this type of direct intervention in research and development bears direct influence on types of technologies that become available by simply raising the cost related to their development or implementation. The legal exposure created by anti-circumvention rules deters potential investments in circumvention technologies. Impediments on technologies that enable the circumvention of self-help technological locks used by content providers are very broad. Scientific research and technological innovation assume a body of knowledge, which is essentially a web of interconnected disciplines, where new conceptual paradigms facilitate novel discoveries, and mathematical breakthroughs enable cutting-edge technological inventions. Government restrictions of R&D are robust measures, threatening to throw out the baby with the bath water. Anti-circumvention restrictions inevitably cover large chunks of encryption research and other research fields in computer science. Restrictions on such research projects may thus impede, rather than induce, technological development.

3. THE INCENTIVES PARADIGM CHALLENGED: ARE INCENTIVES STILL NECESSARY?

The standard economic justification for a proprietary regime in informational works is the perception of information as a public good, and the 'incentive paradigm', which assumes that intellectual property laws are necessary to secure incentives for further investment in creation. While a passionate poet is likely to write her poems even if she lacks financial incentives, the book and music publishing industry would undersupply works. Without these industries, the passionate creators would fail to disseminate their artifacts to the public. The publishing industry sells copies of the work to create its revenue stream, and copyright law is designed to protect this business model. Cyberspace challenges some of the fundamental assumptions of the incentives paradigm, and renders notions such as 'just compensation' and 'pirating' irrelevant. Alongside the proprietary regime protected by copyright, patent and trademark laws, Cyberspace introduces new modes of production and distribution of information. It enables a non-proprietary regime where content is developed through collaborative efforts without any claim for exclusive rights in it.

Take software as an example. Microsoft Windows was written by employees of Microsoft, and Microsoft's investment was protected by copyright, patents and trademark laws, which prohibited unauthorized copying, redistribution and modification of the software. Linux, on the other hand, was created by a community of users, who volunteered to make a contribution to a grand project. Open source projects, such as Linux, are comprised of the contributions of thousands of unorganized developers, located in different places around the globe, who voluntarily contribute to a common project without direct compensation. GNU/Linux operating system and Apache server software, which were developed in a common non-proprietary regime, are increasingly gaining popularity and are considered more stable than comparable commercial programs (Gillen, Kusnetzky and Mclarnon 2003).

The extraordinary success of colossal collaborative projects such as Linux and Apache demonstrated that a complex system on a large scale could be designed and maintained by a sizeable group of unorganized collaborators in a non-proprietary setting. The development of such powerful software, which is non-rival and non-excludable, without any apparent monetary compensation and any guaranteed return for financial investment is challenging the incentives paradigm. Indeed, Mark Smith and Peter Kollock (1999, p. 230) called Linux 'the impossible public good'.

But software is by no means the only example of the new mode of production. Other online phenomena have similar attributes. Compare, for instance, the production of news by corporate employees of CNN, and news generated by subscribers of a newsgroup, in which individuals contribute news items that are rated by their peers over time for credibility and reliability. Another example is the creation of categories for classifying online Web pages. While Yahoo! is a commercial directory in which categories are created by paid employees, the Open Directory is run by volunteers, each editing a sub-category. The contributions of all individual editors are merged into an Open Source directory that everyone is free to use, and is indeed used by some of the major search engines, including Google. As argued by Benkler (2002), the digital networked environment opens up opportunities for new modes of production and distribution of information. The information economy, he argues, introduces a new, radically decentralized type of production mode, which is the *commons-based peer-production* of information.

What motivates thousands of volunteers around the world to spend their time and contribute their talent to create free online information on their Homepage, write computer programs, or report the news, in the absence of monetary compensation secured by the proprietary system? Few explanations were offered by the emerging literature. Some explanations stick to ordinary economic reasoning, arguing that even though there is no direct monetary reward in contributing to the Linux project or similar endeavors, there are side benefits. These include showing off or building a reputation, as well as learning and gaining experience that will later be cashed in, in the job market (Lerner and Tirole 2000, pp. 26–28). Others emphasize social motivations such as adhering to cultural norms connected to positive network externalities. This may be related to software (Weber 2000), to hacker culture (Raymond 1999), or to gaining status in a 'gift culture' (Veltman 2002). Indeed, the online environment revives some old schemes of creating cultural objects of human workmanship, such as folklore dances, melodies, legends and artifacts prior to the introduction of mass-produced culture. It spreads norms of collaborative research that were previously prevalent only in intimate academic settings, to the general public.

Yet, above all, peer-produced content reveals another basic motivation behind creative efforts: the human creative drive and the pleasure derived from creation (Moglen 2002). The availability of unmediated communication, and the assertion of individual expression satisfies natural needs for self-expression, sharing information with others, and a sense of belonging when collaborating within a creative community. In fact, we understand our own creative drives in terms that are disassociated from market exchanges. Furthermore, studies that explore creative motivation distinguish between external rewards (i.e., money) and inherent rewards such as pleasure, curiosity and positive experiences of autonomy and competence. Indeed, a large number of studies show that intrinsic motivation is often undermined by extrinsic rewards and people may become less creative when they are offered monetary rewards (Deci, Koestner, and Ryan 1999).

The complexity of human motivations is often overlooked in the economic literature. In fact, the passion that motivates individual human beings was absolutely irrelevant for the analysis of incentives schemes in the content industries. What makes it relevant in the context of Cyberspace is the potential comeback of individuals as major players in producing meaningful informational works. This is a major shift from mass production by industries, to decentralized production by individuals and communities. Benkler (2002) offers a more profound explanation for what he predicts will become an increasing share of peer-produced information in the overall creative activity. Production of information, knowledge and culture, he argues, no longer requires management by the hierarchy of firms, or the price signals of the market. When projects are modular in the sense that they can be divided into small independently produced components, they can rely on non-monetary motivation of individuals. Large-scale collaborations will be possible as long as diverse motivations can be pooled and merged into a single effort. The low cost of communicating and processing information makes such coordination and integration cost-effective in a way that was unavailable prior to Cyberspace. Benkler concludes that these characteristics of the information economy make it possible for individuals, nonprofit organizations, and community groups to play a significant role in producing informational works.

In economic language, the atomization of efforts can shift activities that are regarded in the physical world as work, to activities that in Cyberspace are regarded by those performing them as leisure. Many of the above examples would not have been possible had individuals been required to travel to a factory or other work place and to invest a significant amount of time to contributing their share. Many of us might have been interested in participating in a car manufacturing project had we been asked to screw one pin at home. Current technology does not enable such manufacturing of a car. It does enable the production of informational goods in Cyberspace. This is the result of two central attributes: low cost of communication, and the non-rivalry nature of information resources. Cyberspace thus transforms the notion of work and its organization, affecting also Coase's analysis of the theory of the firm. We return to this theme when we discuss transaction costs in Chapter 8 and neo-institutional law and economics in Chapter 9. In the latter, we also debate Benkler's insight that this new mode of production is outside the realm of the market.

Decentralization is not only made possible with respect to creation, but also with regard to distribution. Online dissemination of informational works of all sorts is made directly by individuals, using their personal computers to convey their ideas or share informational works with other individuals using the same protocols. Users of Gnutella-based file-sharing systems are capable of making files available for downloading by other users, by simply placing files at a designated directory on their personal computers. Electronic delivery of information involves low costs, and does not require any large investment in the production of copies and the establishment of distribution channels. Distribution of copies in Cyberspace is performed routinely by all users from all workstations connected to the Net and does not involve any substantial costs. The low costs of distribution enable direct communication among individuals, weakening the role of mass media and equivalent mass distributors.

Even if decentralized modes of production and distribution of informational works were common in the academic world and the pre-industrial age, the digital networked environment makes them more prevalent. The rise of common-based production, and of creation by individuals rather than industries, reduces the need to secure monetary incentives for investment in creation. This implies a shift in the balance mandated by the pubic goods equation. While in the non-virtual world governed by content industries, monetary incentives were a must, opportunities for alternative modes of producing content suggest that other considerations should come into play. These include the non-rivalrous nature of informational works, which supports the maximization of their use.

The proprietary regime, which was designed to secure incentives, can, in fact, impede production of content by individuals and communities. That is because informational works are necessary resources for producing new works. The use of existing works protected by intellectual property is costly: works are priced above marginal cost, and transaction costs of licensing are often high. The high cost of licensing may reduce, and sometimes prevent new creation by peers collaborating in non-commercial settings. Furthermore, as suggested by Benkler, unilateral appropriation of the common project by any individual contributor could reduce intrinsic benefits of participation and reduce motivation of other contributors. Attempts to dominate the common project to reflect one's values or advance one's private gains could alienate others. Defection in the form of excluding others from the fruits of their joint effort, or abuse of the common project to benefit a single participant could weaken the will of others to contribute (Benkler 2002).

An innovative solution implemented in the Linux project demonstrates one attempt to address these threats. The Free Software Foundation advocated the release of source codes so that software could be shared, and facilitate an 'innovative commons' (Lessig 2001, pp. 19–23). Software is a special example, of course: restrictions regarding modifying and redistributing the software are not protected solely by intellectual property rights, but are also secured by non-disclosing the source code and releasing the software in object code only. The Free Software Foundation created a legal framework that would guarantee that software remains free, that is free as in freedom, and not necessarily free as in 'free beer'. As described by Moglen (2002, p. 119):

> In Stallman's phrase, free software would be a matter of freedom, not of price. Anyone could freely modify and redistribute such software, or sell it, subject only to the restriction that he not try to reduce the rights of others to whom he passed it along. In this way free software could become a self-organizing project, in which no innovation would be lost through proprietary exercises of rights.

The innovative legal framework used for this purpose was based on contracts. Free software is protected by copyright, but is subject to a license called General Public License (GPL). The GPL basically licenses the unlimited copying, redistribution and modification of the software. The license is a 'Viral Contract', meaning an attempt to make commitments run with the digital code, and apply to future users (Radin 2000). It includes a viral provision, which requires that any derivative work that contains free software or derives from it, will be subject to the same license. This subversive use of copyright law does not utilize the proprietary regime for securing incentives, but for creating an alternative non-proprietary regime, often referred to as *copyleft*.

4. SUMMARY

The extent to which information in Cyberspace is a public good is not clear-cut. It depends, among other factors, on the technological state of the art. The technologies available in Cyberspace are changing at a rapid pace. Consequently, the public good analysis may not be conclusive in determining when government intervention is necessary. Technological development and innovation is an outcome of a complex interaction between knowledge and social institutions such as laws and markets. Technological developments should not be perceived as external to market process as they are perceived by the traditional law and economics analysis. As in the case of monopolies, we believe, therefore, that the tools of the traditional economic theories with regard to public goods are not sufficient for the analysis of Cyberspace.

6. Imperfect Information

In this chapter we analyze the third type of market failure, identified by the Chicago School of Law and Economics, that may justify central intervention in the conduct of markets. We examine whether imperfect information exists in Cyberspace and whether the application of the traditional models to Cyberspace, in this regard, is viable.

The hypothesis about competitive markets, which result in optimal production and distribution, is contingent upon the assumption of full information. In this book we use the term *information* in the broadest sense, to describe such informational goods as books and movies, symbols, inventions, ideas or simply data. In the strictly economic sense, however, *information* refers to knowledge of preferences, prices and quality. Lack of such information, and more specifically asymmetry in information, are likely to lead the market to a failure.

In traditional economic markets, the seller usually knows more about the quality of her product than the buyer. A second hand car salesman, for example, knows the mechanical state of the car much better than its potential buyer. Central intervention is thus required. Government may remedy such lack of information or asymmetry of information. To do this, it can either produce the necessary information by itself, or intervene in the voluntary market exchange, by imposing duties of disclosure or holding transactions voidable when relevant information is not disclosed. This chapter examines how Cyberspace affects lack of information or asymmetrical information and the possible consequences for introducing central intervention, in both economic and political markets, in this context.

1. CYBERSPACE REDUCES COST OF INFORMATION

Cyberspace is a virtual information environment. It is almost all about information. The sophisticated engines of the Internet make huge amounts of information available to us. Difficult and costly to obtain prior to the digital networked environment, information is now collected, accumulated, stored, and produced more efficiently. When a rational person plans to purchase goods in the non-virtual market, a necessary preparatory activity will involve inquires at shops and suppliers about prices and other terms of the transaction. This is not an easy task. It is time consuming and often costly. A rational person will, therefore, make such inquires only as long as the marginal benefits from further inquiries equal the marginal cost of such activity.

The equivalent picture in Cyberspace is very different. The same type of information that requires labor in the real world can be easily obtained in the digital environment. With the touch of a finger the Cyber-customer can run various computer programs, which are able to compare prices, quality, contractual clauses and other aspects of the transaction. Likewise, as the production and distribution of information are easier and cheaper in Cyberspace than in the non-virtual world, customers who are dissatisfied with a product (or those who are satisfied) can easily make their discontent common knowledge. Consequently, there is not only more information in terms of quantity, but also a different type of information, originated by a wide range of diversified sources. Although these activities of information exchange are not totally costless in Cyberspace, they involve a considerably lower cost. In the same time frame, one can obtain significantly more information for a much smaller investment.

These quantitative differences, we believe, amount to qualitative differences. One theoretical way to view this matter follows: Game theory analysis distinguishes between games that are played once and repeated games. Many one-round games tend to result in an inefficient solution, as defection is likely to occur. Most repeated games, by contrast, tend to have efficient outcomes, as players will opt to cooperate (Baird, Gertner and Picker 1994). This general and simplified statement can distinguish cases where central intervention is not desirable or not effective (repeated games) from situations in which central intervention is required (one-shot games). The flow of information in Cyberspace can turn typical one-round games into repeated games, thus eliminating, or at least significantly reducing, the need for central intervention in the market.

Consider, for example, a tourist who is planning a journey in which she will stay one night in every city she visits. She considers which hotels to book. Since she is staying only one night in each hotel, her contractual relations can be characterized as a one-round game. Her travel agent shows her pictures and short descriptions of possible hotels. She might be shown several options and select from them. If the hotel does not meet her expectations or its description turns out to be inaccurate, but not to such a degree that our tourist would consider a lawsuit, the game is over. Other potential tourists will not benefit from this information. They will be engaged in separate games, ending similarly. Hotels might take advantage of this situation. The law intervenes in various ways. It sets minimum standards for various utilities in hotels. It provides an official grading of hotels – from one to five stars, etc.

Booking a hotel through the Internet is a different story. The tourist can examine and compare more options. The details provided on the hotels are more comprehensive, including a variety of pictures, maps, etc. These details are provided by several sources, such as travel agencies, hotels themselves, independent tourist bureaus and the general public. Many sites on the Web allow tourists to read unedited opinions of former guests, which are more likely to be independent and impartial. When tourists run a Google search on a hotel, they are likely to find not only the official Web site of the hotel describing its services, but also other sites with some independent opinions and reviews on the hotel and its services. Of course, this type of information differs from that provided by the hotel itself or even by tourist guides.

The instant availability of information from diverse sources tends to shift the booking contract from a one-off game to a repeated game, in which the collective body of tourists can be considered as a player. Under such circumstances, some central intervention due to lack of information or asymmetric information would not be justified. In our example, Cyberspace, for example, may eradicate the justification for official grading systems of hotels.

It should be noted that the effect of Cyberspace on central intervention resulting from lack of information is not confined to transactions negotiated and completed within Cyberspace. It also affects transactions that are executed outside the Internet, and even those negotiated in the non-virtual world. In this sense, new analysis is required to reform various legal rules of disclosure, standards traditionally set by courts in applying contract law, and also the extent to which production and distribution of information by central government is justified.

2. NEW MARKET IMPERFECTIONS

While some information-related costs, such as its collection and communication, are reduced in Cyberspace, other information costs may increase and new types may appear. Cyberspace is characterized by a proliferation of information. Information previously unavailable due to its non cost-effective distribution may become obtainable in the online environment. The mechanisms of providing and distributing information in Cyberspace are decentralized and allow every user to become an information provider. Technically everyone can post information and make it accessible to millions of users around the world at low cost.

The ability to communicate directly at low cost reduces the need for intermediaries, such as publishers and broadcasters, for distributing information. Therefore, Cyberspace does not create the same bottleneck effect that characterizes traditional methods of communicating information. The vast volume of available information provided by a wide variety of sources creates new challenges. The first is how one establishes trustworthiness of information in the absence of intermediaries, and ascertaining the costs associated with determining the reliability of information distributed in Cyberspace. The second issue is how one deals with the proliferation of information: how to turn data into useful information, distinguish between information and noise, find relevant information, and define relevancy. We will now discuss these new challenges.

2.1 The Reliability of Information

The decentralized nature of the Internet was considered one of the most significant characteristics that promised to make it an alternative to existing content markets. The network infrastructure, it was thought, would replace centralized distribution methods employed by broadcasters and publishers with a potentially more decentralized flow of information. Technically, everyone connected to the Net can post their content and make it available through various channels. Entry barriers in the online information market are presumably low. Not only is the cost of distribution significantly low, but the cost of production is also going down.

As a matter of fact, the production of content still involves the high cost of human skills, but the means of production are cheaper than they used to be, and are decreasing rapidly. Furthermore, unlike broadcasters, online providers are not required to get a license before posting on the Net or setting up a distribution channel. Hence, bureaucratic hurdles for publishing are removed, making the provision of information even easier and cheaper.

Decentralized sources of information create, however, a problem of ascertaining the reliability of such information. Distribution of information in the physical world includes clues that indicate reliability. If one reads an article published by *The New York Times,* one can assume that writers took steps to certify the reported facts. If one reads news about flying cows in a tabloid, one is less likely to assume that this really happened. How can we know whether things we read on the Internet are reliable? To some extent, one may use the truth traits one uses in the non-virtual world. Thus, if one reads an article on the NYT Web site, one may rely on it, at least if the site is indeed operated by the NYT.

Some information may, however, become available from other, often unknown, sources. In the real world we often identify the source of information by relying on physical clues, such as assets, geographical locations, identifying actual people and names that are protected by trademarks and trade addresses. Authentication in Cyberspace cannot rely on such agencies. It is technically easy to disguise sources so they become unidentifiable or misleading.

The Net allows anonymity and disguise. A child can pretend to be a lawyer providing legal advice, a man can present himself as a woman, an amateur as a professional, a crook as a well-established business representative. This was captured by an old cartoon by Peter Steiner published in *The New Yorker* early in the '90s. In the cartoon, a dog sitting in front of the computer says to his fellow dog, who looks at him wondering: 'On the Internet, nobody knows you're a dog' (Steiner, 1993).

Anonymity is often celebrated as liberating: it opens new venues for asserting various aspects of one's identity, manifests diversified and more authentic preferences, and facilitates a more participatory environment for testing new ideas. On the other hand, anonymity releases the speaker, the source of information, from any accountability. The source does not have to bear the social cost and economic loss associated with misleading information, and could therefore encourage deceitful behavior.

Technical clues can assist in identifying online parties. Such are Domain Names and Internet Protocol (IP) Numbers. IP numbers indicate the 'location' of the server ('host'), which is connected to the Net. Since numbers are long and therefore hard to remember, they have been replaced by names. Domain names may often help identify an online business similar to the way it is identified outside the Net. Furthermore, cookies,[1] Spyware, and other data collection programs may enhance the ability of businesses to identify their customers. These programs, however, identify the computer from which online activity was initiated and not the actual user of that computer. No one can know who sits behind the computer, and whether a legal entity, crook or respectable business operates a fancy-looking Web site. Identifying the individual behind the computer screen requires more sophisticated identification methods, which raise questions of privacy.

To establish reliability one must both authenticate the source and validate the integrity of the document. Digital media is malleable and information that is presented digitally is very easy to modify. While a printed document represents information in fixed format, digitized information may be easily manipulated. Thus, if one reads a court decision on the Internet, one should check whether any changes were inserted to the original text. Technical solutions, such as encryption, could assist in validating the transacting party, the origin of a document or its integrity. Yet, once again, these solutions are costly.

If we return to the tourist example, a potential traveler can not easily determine whether information posted on behalf of guests is indeed authentic, or whether it was originated or altered by the hotel agents. This may cause users to confirm information with other sources, a phenomenon that does not exist in the non-virtual world, and is likely to increase the costs involved in information seeking.

---

1 A cookie is information for future use that is stored by the server on the client side of a client/server communication. The main purpose of cookies is to identify users and possibly prepare customized Web pages for them.

These changes in the availability of information and the costs of information suggest that government intervention might be desirable after all. But it should assume a different nature in correcting new kinds of market failures. For instance, rather than imposing disclosure duties, it may be necessary to standardize authentication means on the Net, or facilitate name registries, document identification means, etc.

2.2 Information Overflow

Lack of information (in the old sense) can no longer be considered a market failure in the Cyberian world and indeed outside it. Quite the contrary, in the information environment there is proliferation of information. While in the past individuals suffered from lack of information that was necessary to perform their transactions or exercise their political rights, Cyberspace creates an information overflow. The networked environment, which increases the availability of information, requires us to shift our attention from a traditional lack of information to a flood of it.

The lack of useful information is no longer an issue that characterizes markets, and should be addressed by intervention in market mechanisms. Rather, failures connected to information in the new digital environment reside in the individual realm, and highlight the limits of human cognition. The traditional market model may prove insufficient for addressing the new types of information problems emerging in Cyberspace.

The proliferation of information introduces new challenges for market players and indeed for community members who want to take part in social decision-making processes. For sellers, or for politicians or individuals who are interested in promoting an issue, the challenge is how to capture users' attention. While posting on the Web may be inexpensive and easy, making your content noticeable and detectable by users has become extremely competitive.

In the past, marketing strategists could rely on the advertising media for capturing the audience's attention. The media's hegemony over mass dissemination of information enabled them to determine which information would be distributed, and how. The media provided edited content, thus dominating control over such elements as the timing and sequence in which information was introduced, the context in which it was placed and the presence of competing or contradicting information. The media were, therefore, a focal point for gaining enhanced exposure, by placing ads in the front pages or running commercials on primetime. They also served to highlight issues for debate, placing them in specific context, emphasize or rather obfuscate them.

This is no longer feasible on the Internet, where users are navigating the Web independently. Information is no longer pushed at users. Users must define their own needs and seek the necessary information online, following links and searching via search engines. All the information is available. It is the user, however, who controls the context and the sequence, and subsequently determines what will become available to her. Since available content on the Web can no longer be restricted, information providers persistently explore new ways to directly control users' attention.

The proliferation of information in the digital environment also challenges buyers, commercially or politically, on the Net. The low cost of obtaining information and connectivity provides the average user with gigantic libraries of information. Data smog, a term coined by David Shenk (1997), describes the human experience under circumstances of information overload. For many users, the sheer volume of information is overwhelming. Rather than optimizing their performance, it impairs their ability to make decisions and to take actions. The bulk of information available for users causes an attention deficit. As stated by Herbert Simon (1971, pp. 40–41):

> Wealth of information creates a poverty of attention and a need to allocate that attention efficiently among the overabundance of information sources that might consume it.

Consequently, users become increasingly dependent on technical means that can assist them in retrieving and selecting relevant information from the large bulk of available data. Search engines were developed to serve this function. Indeed, when the problem turns out to be information overload, rather than access, the real value rests in locating and filtering information relevant to users.

2.3 Search Engines – New Intermediaries

Search engines are becoming the new virtual gatekeepers of Cyberspace. Information that is undetectable, or otherwise remains unlisted on search results, is almost nonexistent on the Web. Search engines cannot keep out undesired materials, but they can effectively control access to information. If you are not listed in the search results, you are almost out of the Web. Sometimes we look for a particular vendor or a certain Web site, and in fact, the more specific the query gets (such as a particular URL – Uniform Resource Locator, which is a standard way of specifying the location of an object, typically a Web page on the Internet), the less it is necessary to use a search engine. In the majority of cases, however, we navigate with no particular destination, and we are often unaware of the URL we seek.

Search engines are often thought of as devices that allow users to find information they value and avoid the rest. This description is somewhat simplistic and naive. It assumes that users already know what information they want and value prior to the search. More often, however, users do not know what information they need. In fact, to a great extent, what users consider valuable may be highly dependent on the search results themselves. Search results do not simply locate materials. They construct meaning. These results affect the organization and significance of information. Structuring categories in response to users' queries, they have the capacity of creating concepts for grasping the world.

By defining which information becomes available for each query, search engines may shape preferences, positions, beliefs and ideas. In this sense, the traditional assumption of the economic models of exogenous preferences must be reconsidered. We will return to this point when we elaborate on the effects of Cyberspace on the economic theory of the state, and again, during analysis of the economic approach as a whole in light of Cyberspace (Part Three).

Search engines thus turn out to be among the most significant players in the information economy and the information society. They can play a key role in structuring the online market for goods and services by granting prominence to some brands while avoiding others. Search engines can locate goods offered by a particular vendor, while systematically avoiding offers made by competitors, or pushing them to the bottom of the search results. These results can determine which products and services provided online are in fact available to users, and users would make their choices from this selection.

Likewise, search engines can affect the political, social and cultural agendas and the way discourse, deliberation and collective action are shaped, exerting real influence over public decision-making. By effectively constructing meaning and shaping choices, search engines can be politically significant to social relations and the shaping of public opinion (Introna and Nissenbaum 2000). Search results may affect concepts, which are fundamental units of thought, and organize objects, events and relations in our physical and mental world.

Consider for instance an elementary school student who is searching the Web for materials on 'Jews.' The three top results retrieved by Excite were: The Christian Jew Foundation (a messianic missionary organization which presents the gospel to Jewish people), Jew Watch (a hate site allegedly reporting Jewish monopoly, banking, and media control worldwide), HAIKUS FOR JEWS, (amusing haikus combining ancient Zen wisdom with timeless Jewish humor). A different response is provided by the search results retrieved by HotBot. The top three results were: Judaism 101 (an encyclopedia on information about Judaism and Jewish practices), Jewishnet (a global Jewish information network), and, as in Excite, HAIKUS FOR JEWS. A student having no significant previous knowledge on the subject would end up forming different concepts based on the different and sorely inadequate search experiences (Elkin-Koren 2001).

Search engines are computer programs that search the Internet for relevant Web sites based on various search algorithms. These computerized locating tools allow users to track down resources posted on the Internet that match their query. The first search engine, Archie, was developed by a student at McGill University, Alan Emtage, in 1990, before the World Wide Web was created. Since then the search engines market has been developing rapidly and dynamically. Search engines that were popular two years ago, have been largely abandoned. New ones, introduced recently, have captured the attention of users and are now being used by millions of surfers.

There are various ways to classify search engines. While some search engines are general, such as AOL, Yahoo! or Google, others focus on selective subjects. For instance, FindLaw searches for legal materials, while Searchnt specializes in resources for Windows NT. Each search engine works differently. Some search engines collect listings independently, while others rely on information submitted by Web site administrators during the registration process.

Search engines differ further in the way data is organized. Some search engines use directories and list Web site addresses under headings and subheadings. Other search engines (e.g. Infoseek, Lycos, Webcrawler, Northern Light) create a database by sending out spiders (also called 'crawler' or 'bot') – computer programs that continuously search the Web by following links on existing pages, to fetch as many documents as possible. The spider is programmed to search for keywords within the text of the Web page instead of simply looking at the page title, description, or meta-tags. The output is then indexed, creating a database that is used when an actual query is submitted. Other engines are simply directories (such as Yahoo!), organizing Web sites and materials according to categories and subcategories.

The main difference between search engines is in their classification and editorial analysis, which determine what counts, and ranks, as most relevant. These indexing and retrieval schemes are treated as proprietary information and are usually not disclosed. Disclosing the search algorithm could help competitors gain a competitive edge. It could further allow intervention, or, rather, manipulation by Web site owners who are seeking to promote their sites.

Weight may be given to words in the title, the frequency in which a keyword appears on the page or is listed in the HTML Meta-tags. The number of links is often used as an indicator for quality, thus giving a higher rank to Web pages that are connected by many links (Butler 2000). Other algorithms (such as Google's algorithms) analyze the links and consider their origin (once again, giving more weight to links from sites that are more heavily linked). Most spiders would skip a Web page that lacks any links from any other Web pages.

The high dependency on links gives prominence to pages on topics of mass interest, such as sports and sex, rather than to less popular sites that may sometimes be more relevant to a particular query. This type of ranking is further biased toward commercial Web sites that would often be pointed at from many sites due to business alliances. Commercial Web sites further enjoy an obvious advantage in promoting themselves by advertising on the Net, television and radio as well as in newspapers.

Businesses and activists who are competing for the attention of users and want to convince the masses to buy their products or adhere to their political agenda, may adopt various tactics to increase their rating on the search results. When the search algorithm is disclosed, Web site owners can more easily manipulate it to gain a higher ranking. This concern was raised in the legal dispute between Google and SearchKing (*Search King Inc.*, F. Supp. 2d, W.D.Okla).

The defendant in this case – Google – became one of the symbols of the new information environment, and encompasses many of its promises and risks. It is probably the most efficient general search engine, and definitely one of the most popular ones. Google's PageRank system is arguably based on peer production ranking. It ranks the importance of the site based on the number of links pointing to it. Pages that are heavily linked-to, count as more important than others. Google's PageRank system thus compiles the judgments of many individual Web-designers (and their employers) and turns it into a functional relevance algorithm. This unique algorithm is owned by Google, and was not disclosed. The system can, of course, be biased toward large businesses, linked by widespread commercial partnerships. It can also be distorted by networks of Link Exchanges, or Link Farms, which attempt to artificially increase the PageRank on the Google system.

The plaintiff – SearchKing – is a broker service, which places ads on clients' Web pages on Web sites ranked highly by Google. Not approving of this business model, Google argued that it undermines the integrity of its ranking system. After Google intentionally reduced the PageRank it assigned to SearchKing's site, SearchKing filed a complaint alleging tortuous interference with contractual relations. The court dismissed, holding that Google's PageRank is speech protected under the First Amendment. The court further dismissed SearchKing's request to disclose the source code of Google's PageRank system.

The Court ruling in favor of Google can assist in preventing manipulation by interested parties, but from the point of view of a market failure of information, the ruling is problematic. After all, different search engines may themselves have commercial or political agendas, which, with the assistance of the courts, is hidden from the public eye. The method of ranking is essential information for commercial and political market players, and the court's ruling paves the way for keeping this information hidden from the public.

Bias in the information provided by search engine results may also stem from a particular business model. Search engines typically rely on three sources of income: fees collected from users, advertisers or other third parties, and, increasingly, commission collected from Web sites. Search engines can apply either one of these business models or any combination thereof.

Currently, most search engines provide their services free of charge, thereby enhancing the number of users who visit their service and increasing exposure for advertiser-supported links. Revenues often come from selling banners to advertisers or selling information collected on users' behavior to third parties. Advertising space sold to advertisers is often associated with search queries, allowing advertisers to discerningly tailor ads to individual users.

Another source of income is commission collected from site owners. Some spiders collect payments from sites for a larger, boldface look in the search results. Others collect fees from Web sites for the mere right to be included in their listings. Another model is a paid-inclusion system. Under such a payment scheme, Web sites are charged for a more extensive indexing, thus increasing their chances of being included in the search results (Sullivan 2000, Sullivan 2001). Several search engines have developed a pay-for-placement model, under which Web sites pay to acquire a premier placement in the search results. It is assumed that most users review only the top results, and seldom check bottom links. Consequently, even when a site is listed, it could be buried at the bottom of the list. Under another scheme, common among bargain finders, an engine charges sellers a certain percentage of any sales resulting from its reference.

These business practices of search engines create strong links between editorial considerations and commercial interests. Search engines whose revenues depend on Web sites that are included in their results would be inclined to assign a higher ranking to those sites that pay more. These factors raise serious concerns regarding the reliability of search results and the feasibility, objectivity and neutrality of locating information posted on the Net. Surprisingly, search engines currently cover a small portion of the information published on the Web. Researchers believe that the largest search engines index no more than 16% of the Web content posted. Consequently, search engines provide only limited and selective access to information existing on the Web, while virtually burying vast majority of the rest.

Furthermore, it becomes increasingly apparent that data-mining on the Web can no longer be considered collecting information on static Web pages and creating a static directory structure. Locating information on the Web requires an active search, which involves direct inquiries of internal searchable databases. Such searchable databases include internal pages of large sites that are dynamically created, topic databases (such as patent records, SEC corporate filing, and medical databases), auctions, classified, portals, or internal holdings of academic libraries. Information on what is referred to as the Deep Web, it is argued, does not become apparent until compiled as a response to a direct query (Bergman 2000). Researchers conclude that information on the Deep Web is not only greater than that on the Surface Web, but also tends to be of higher quality. Most information is not accessible through the search engines.

This elaborate description of the operation of search engines blurs the optimistic conclusions drawn in the previous section regarding the possible elimination or sharp decline of information-related problems as a market failure in the age of Cyberspace. It is arguable that competition among search engines could fix some of the distortions described above. After all, in a competitive market search engines will be forced to provide useful and reliable results to keep their market share, and to provide enough information on their ranking procedures. If users could choose, they would arguably abandon any search engine that provides partial or inaccurate results and prefer those that provide the most comprehensive, relevant results. Thus, competition would presumably refine existing search methods. Likewise, competition among search engines is likely to bring the price of using a search engine in equilibrium to equal the marginal cost curve, i.e. to zero.

While the latter proves to be correct – most searches are provided for free – there is a possible flaw in this market solution, which leaves the former market imperfection intact: there is no full information about the operation of search engines. In other words, there is a market failure of lack of information regarding the operation of information seeking in the Internet. Services provided by search engines are not transparent and cannot be easily compared by users. Users may appreciate the ease and friendliness of use, the speed, look and feel of the results page, or the fees charged for the use (if any), but they are not able to determine whether the search results are relevant. Introna and Nissenbaum (2000) argue that competition cannot develop in the search engine marketplace since the prerequisites of an efficient market are simply not met. Thus, they argue, users' choice to use a certain search engine cannot be said to reflect their preferences, since they lack critical information about the alternatives.

Relevancy and accuracy of search results cannot be easily determined, unless users are aware of an alternative. Unless a user is looking for a particular document she knows was posted on the Web, she may never know that certain sites exist at all. Users appreciate only the results they see, and may not be aware of other results not retrieved by the search engine. Furthermore, while some results can be more easily comprehended (such as a list of sites offering products at different prices), the usefulness and trustworthiness of other types of results may not be as easily analyzed and appreciated. This applies to information-seeking for the sake of forming views, or participation in collective decision-making.

It is arguable, however, that a well-functioning market would address some information deficiencies. Competitors are likely to discover information and inform users of the limits of rival search engines. Newcomers who wished to enter the search engine market would have sufficient incentives to reveal inadequacies in existing technologies and to demonstrate the shortcomings of established search engines to highlight the advantages of their own technology.

In other words, competition itself can increase transparency and stimulate users' demand for better search engines.

The search engines market is concentrated and centralized, and dominated by around five major engines, which in January 2003 included Google, Yahoo!, MSN, AOL and AJ. These search engines are further powered (i.e., receive their search results) by one another (Sullivan 2003).

One of the impediments to developing a competitive market in search engines is the time it takes to compare search results. The average user is unlikely to invest in the time-consuming comparison of search results of different search engines. Here, technology may drive competition. If there were different searches that any given user could conduct simultaneously, in a cost-effective way, it is likely that users would be able to compare search results provided by different engines. Search engines are themselves searchable databases, and conducting a search by sending a query simultaneously to several search engines could raise users' awareness of the limits and biases of each.

Metacrawlers allow a more efficient search by passing the user's query to several search engines simultaneously. Unlike search engines, Metacrawlers do not crawl the Web itself to build listings. These computer programs are designed to query and aggregate results from various search engines and online databases (such as Excite, Infoseek, and Yahoo!). Such search results provide the raw material for the Metacrawler's editorial processes. Metasearchers compile, modify, and edit search results in various levels, depending on the crawlers' design and users' preferences. The processed results are then blended together onto one page. Some Metacrawlers offer value-added services, such as automated searches from the text itself, or contextual searches.

Metacrawlers may thus facilitate competition in the search engines market. They can assist users in proficiently comparing the different choices available to them, and they further allow easy switching from one engine to another, thus lowering the entry barriers for new engines (Elkin-Koren 2001). It is regrettable, therefore, that courts restricted the operation of Metacrawlers, holding them liable for trespassing the servers of search engines they screen (*eBay Inc.,* 100 F.Supp. 2d 1058). As in the SearchKing case, courts seem to restrict the information available in Cyberspace, contributing themselves to a market failure.

Finally, information overflow creates dependency on new intermediaries that are technologically based. Such intermediaries by technological means are lacking transparency. They hide the business interests, as well as the political and value dependent choices, behind long lines of programming, often kept secret from the general public. Similar to the information reliability issues described above, an information failure also results from lack of transparency of the commercial and political agenda of search engines. If a person chooses to obtain her information from the *Guardian* newspaper, she knows the political colors of its editors and journalists, and the consequences of these colors for the paper's reportage. The same cannot be said regarding the usage of search engines. Their political colors are hidden, and the courts legitimized this veil of secrecy on the basis of property rights and freedom of speech. While a newspaper may have an ethical code that requires it to express both sides of a particular story and diverse opinions on various issues, a search engine is free to provide a selective view without revealing its basis for selection.

The recent case of *SearchKing v. Google*, discussed above, is an interesting illustration of some of these issues. It is a case of many contradictions, concerning the largest search engine, which relies on peer-produced content, and was challenged by a small Internet enterprise that takes advantage of its ranking system. It is a case about the dual nature of search engines, such as Google. The case points out how these engines are not only large commercial players, but also facilitators of an essential public service. The case demonstrates the sophisticated nature of online discourse facilitated by secret algorithms that are owned by private companies. It reveals the potential biases of online discourse, and its vulnerability to manipulation.

3. SUMMARY

It seems that in the age of Cyberspace, traditional market failure of lack of information cannot be regarded as a source of market imperfection, and thus as a justification for central intervention by the government for producing information or regulating its disclosure. However, an opposite market failure can be observed – an overflow of information. This overflow is the drive behind the search engines market, which itself may suffer a market failure of lack of information. Even if this market tunes itself to a competitive equilibrium, market players will still have to make more choices and thus spend more time and resources on processing information. Finally, the emergence of new powerful intermediaries in the markets for information creates new costs and distinct failures that require innovative solutions. Once again, intermediate interaction by digital means lacks transparency.

7. Externalities

This chapter explores the last market failure of the four major types of failures identified by the Neo-classical school of the economic approach towards law. According to the traditional economic analysis, the presence of externalities, in particular market situations, may justify government intervention. As we did in previous chapters on monopolies, public goods and imperfect information, we briefly sketch the traditional parameters for identifying and remedying externality type market failure, and subsequently examine the application of traditional analysis to Cyberspace. We then explore whether the notion of externality as an analytical tool is still useful, given the special characteristics of the information environment.

1. WHAT IS AN EXTERNALITY?

Externality is an effect on a specific market, the source of which is external to this particular market. In other words, it is a situation in which the welfare of a market player is influenced by other players, not through the market or through voluntary exchange. Positive externalities occur whenever an activity generates benefits for others, which the actors are unable to internalize. For example, the immunization of a segment of the population positively impacts the health of those who are not immunized, and a tenant who installs a light in the parking lot of her apartment building benefits her neighbors. In both cases, the beneficiaries were not part of a voluntary exchange in which they were charged for the value of the goods or service they received. Negative externalities occur when an activity imposes costs on others. Such is the well-known example of a polluting factory that inflicts harm on its neighbors. When there is no central intervention, the factory is not charged for the cost it imposes.

Externalities bring about a market failure because the parties involved in market activity do not internalize the precise value of their actions on others, and the value of others' actions for them. Consequently, market equilibrium does not correspond with maximization of welfare or social utility. In other words, if a market player or decision-maker does not internalize the costs or benefits associated with her actions, her actions tend to be inefficient, leading to an inefficient market solution.

A factory that pollutes the water and makes it less useful to others does not pay others for that loss. Since the polluter does not bear the cost of such contamination, it continues this activity even though it may not be efficient, i.e. the cost of pollution (to others) is higher than the benefits (to the factory). This external effect will distort not only the drinking water market, or the clean air market, but also the equilibrium in the market of the products manufactured by the polluting factory; for example, the polluting factory will produce at a level higher than optimal. In such circumstances, central intervention or regulation should facilitate internalization of the external costs or benefits involved to secure an optimal level of activity. For example, a player whose activity results in negative externalities may be taxed, or an activity that involves positive externalities may be subsidized.

These remedies – taxes and subsidies – and the general analysis of externalities can be attributed to the French economist Pigou ([1920] 1952). Coase (1960) disputed this analysis, arguing that in a world of no transaction cost, voluntary exchange will take place and market imperfections will be corrected. Thus, if the benefits to the factory from pollution are lower than the harm it inflicts on its neighbors, then they will pay the factory in order to stop it from polluting, with no need for central intervention. Likewise, central intervention will be bypassed if it is inefficient. If the factory's benefits from polluting are greater than the damages to its neighbors, the factory may buy off the right not to be polluted, if central intervention prohibits it from polluting.

However, the real world is not transaction cost-free. Therefore, central intervention might be desirable, but not necessarily along Pigou's lines. Central intervention, according to Coase, should be guided by the structure of transaction cost in a particular setting. We dedicate the next chapter (Chapter 8) to a thorough analysis of transaction costs in Cyberspace. In the current chapter we will remain in the framework of traditional externalities analysis.

Following Coase's analysis of transaction costs, Dahlman (1979) identified two contemporary models of externalities in the economics literature. According to the first model, entitled by Dahlman, 'Walrasian General Equilibrium Approach', government intervention is justified when real-world allocation of resources diverges from a Pareto optimal allocation that would be likely to result from a competitive equilibrium in a transaction cost-free world. The second model views externalities as a function of transaction costs. This model takes into account the costs of third parties associated with the removal of negative externalities. If the value placed by such parties on the removal of an externality is lower than the cost associated with its removal (transaction cost), the externality will not be removed. Thus, real-world allocation reflects an attainable optimum. Consequently, there is far less room for government intervention.

Externality as an analytic tool involves several assumptions. It relies on a dichotomy between external/internal effects, and therefore necessitates a distinction between them. To determine what effects should be considered as an externality, it is first necessary to define the relevant market (or community). Effects that fall outside the scope of a particular market or community are considered an externality.

Another assumption involved in externalities analysis and related to the above concerns the hierarchy of units and sub-units. Externalities are defined by reference to a unit in which internal and external utility (or welfare) can be measured. Such basic units may be particular markets, local communities, associations, corporations, unions, or even contracting parties. Such sub-units are part of a broader scope unit, in which total welfare is measured. It is crucial for the economic regulatory approach to externalities to determine what is the relevant social unit for measuring social welfare. Maximizing a community's welfare may have positive or negative externalities that affect the welfare of outsiders. The question then becomes what is the community and who are the outsiders.

For instance, state intervention is justified in regulating the activity of local governments when the activity of the latter imposes externalities on other local communities within the state jurisdiction. The disposal of garbage or a sewage system in one municipality may affect individuals in neighboring municipalities. Such externalities are not internalized by the decision-makers in the regulating community. This will often lead to inefficiencies when considering the total efficiency of both units. From the perspective of cumulative welfare, such a situation will lower total utility and will therefore be sub-optimal.

If we take the state as the basic unit for welfare maximization, public policy has to be informed by the total social welfare on a state level, rather than on the particular, local, or sectarian levels. If we take states as self-regarding sub-units, federations or international bodies become the relevant unit for measuring total welfare. Thus, the absence of environmental protection in one state may inflict negative effects on neighboring states. International law can be viewed as a set of rules intended to internalize externalities where the whole population of the universe is considered the unit for social utility maximization (Dunoff and Trachtman 1998).

Defining the social unit (and therefore what should count as an externality) is essential for the market analysis since it is related to questions of jurisdiction and enforcement. As Trachtman (1998, p. 578), argued: 'the role of jurisdictional rule is to internalize externalities to the extent desired or alternatively to provide clear enough allocations of jurisdiction that it may be reallocated (and externalities thereby internalized to the extent worthwhile) through transactions between states.'

It is assumed that self-regarding units will reflect their total social utility, but will not reflect the utility (positive or negative) inflicted on non-consenting parties outside the community. The same applies to particular markets within a community. Market players who inflict costs or benefits on players in other markets will not take them into consideration. Therefore, the definition of the social unit will determine which body – local or state governments, firms or unions, states or international bodies – should have the power to regulate any particular behavior. In other words, from the perspective of policy making, questions of externalities are in fact questions of jurisdiction and particularization of markets.

2. THE VIABILITY OF EXTERNALITY ANALYSIS IN THE NEW INFORMATION ENVIRONMENT

We believe that Cyberspace challenges some of the assumptions underlying the viability of externality analysis, primarily because it blurs community and market boundaries. As we have seen, externality analysis requires demarcation of boundaries between markets, jurisdictions and sub-jurisdictions. Territorial borders often define such boundaries and the territorial state is typically the unit in which total welfare is measured. Drawing markets and community boundaries in Cyberspace becomes a much more complicated task. Territorial borders may no longer serve in Cyberspace to define community or market boundaries.

Cyberspace reduces the effects of physical location (Post 1996). It creates virtual markets and communities that do not exist in any particular geographical location. Consider, for instance, an on-line community in the form of a newsgroup. Information may be stored on a server in one location or on several servers in different locations. Participants may reside in different states and be connected to equipment located at yet another location. Every message posted on a Web site may be viewed, heard, or otherwise experienced by individuals in different geographical locations simultaneously. Networks and servers are equally accessible from everywhere, regardless of their location and distance from one another.[1] Users of Peer-to-Peer systems may download the program necessary for exchange from a Web site at one location, and exchange files with masses of users of that program around the globe. Participants in online exchanges often do not even know (and sometimes cannot know) the physical location of the other party. Cyberspace is therefore 'everywhere if anywhere, and hence no place in particular' (Lessig 1996, p. 1404).

Likewise, markets in Cyberspace are global. Markets for particular products and services are not limited to geographical locations, as is the case in the non-virtual world. This is particularly true for services and products that are provided within Cyberspace. But globalization also characterizes products and services that are negotiated and sold in Cyberspace and provided in the physical world. The economy has traveled a long way, with the assistance of information technology, from ancient market squares, through the invention of printing, cable communication, and wireless communication to the current Information Age.

---

1   This is a function of the speed at which information travels, and the digital character of that information, which does not decay over time and distance (Post 1996).

In fact, the economy has become transient and detached from any particular geographical region, and correspondence between economic markets and political communities, which characterized the pre-Cyberspace world, no longer exists. By establishing a robust communication network, the information environment accelerated the pace of globalization of specific markets, creating a single worldwide universal market.

In addition, the convergence of communication and content, and the heavy reliance on connectivity and interoperability (see Chapter 4), blurs the borders between markets of different products. Products and services, which in the real world could be sharply distinguished, are offered in Cyberspace as complete packages. Information technologies introduce new types of boundaries – those that are technologically dependent. Technological dependency draws explicit and implicit associations between traditionally separated products, while drawing new boundaries within traditional markets, boundaries that are often hidden.

The borderless nature of Cyberspace can have very different implications for the analysis of externalities in the context of the traditional unit of the state and for the analysis of externalities in Cyberspace itself. In the following sections we will examine externalities analysis in both realms, beginning with the latter case, where the relevant unit of analysis is Cyberspace itself.

2.1. Externalities Analysis within Cyberspace

Cyberspace is a network of networks. It consists of overlapping online communities, such as newsgroups, Linux users, subscribers to a service provider, users of online chat, players of games on a Web site, subscribers to ICQ etc. In recent years Cyberspace has also increasingly functioned as an economic marketplace. Such communities or markets in Cyberspace may vary in the level of their members' homogeneity (Lemley 1998), the duration of membership (one-time players or long-term members), or the structure of interaction among community members (moderated or non-moderated, open and public or intimate). These factors make it difficult to define the exact market, community, or jurisdiction to identify an externality.

Furthermore, unlike the non-virtual world, Cyberspace is not hierarchical in structure. One cannot find the Cyberian equivalent of federations-states-local municipalities. The viability of externalities analysis relies on the ability to identify such a hierarchical structure. The complexity of defining the basic unit and sub-units for analysis is amplified by the low exit cost and the dynamic nature of overlapping markets and communities in Cyberspace.

Some believe that the dynamic nature of online communities in Cyberspace eliminates the need to adopt a single set of rules applicable to all. Instead, various communities may adopt different (even contradictory) sets of norms from which users may choose. Post and Johnson (1997), for instance, argue that the coexistence of communities will facilitate a market for norms. Cyberspace, they argue, allows the development of diversified regimes made of rules developed 'from the bottom up.' The rules will be shaped indirectly by way of interaction between sysops defining the terms of use, and by users choosing among their preferable systems and services (Post and Johnson 1997, p.78).

Users will join online communities in which community rules ultimately suit their preferences. For example, users who treasure privacy will opt for communities that support strong encryption. Similarly, if an ISP prohibits spam on its services, it will attract subscribers who have such a preference. Those who can tolerate spam, in return for lower fees, may switch to a different service provider. Thus, the rules applied by the ISP would reflect the collective will of the subscribers (Post 1996, p.169). This, of course, entails some serious political consequences. As Post and Johnson suggest, '[t]he great virtue of the Internet is that it allows multiple, incompatible resolutions of such policy questions by giving those who disagree with the resolution of any particular question the means to avoid contract with one another' (Post and Johnson, 1997, p.78).

Diversified communities also exist in the real world. What makes Cyber-communities different is their malleability, and the ease of switching from one online setting to another, or changing membership. Members may simulta-neously belong to a large number of online communities and indeed operate in markets governed by different rules. They may also constantly switch between communities. This is due to the low costs of 'virtual exit' (Burk 1998).

In Cyberspace, the costs of exit are relatively low compared with those associated with leaving one community and moving to another in the real world. Contrast, for example, the cost of moving to a new neighborhood, changing a club or switching jobs with that of leaving an unsatisfactory online service or migrating to a new online community. The dynamic nature of the technology and of technological markets often force such frequent switches whenever a new technology is introduced, rendering some facilities obsolete.

The low cost of exit makes communities and markets in Cyberspace so dynamic that it is difficult to treat them analytically as identifiable units. The low costs of exit suggest that externalities in Cyberspace may be substantially reduced. If one community adopts a policy that inflicts positive externalities on another, its members will join the other community as well. If a rule of community A imposes costs on community B, members of community B will move to community A. In other words, if the costs of switching from community A to communities B–Z are zero or near zero, members of community A will internalize the costs and benefits that may be imposed by their actions on outside communities.

Having said that, information technologies introduce new costs of exit when switching from one technology to another. Switching to a different operating system or search engine may impose the costs of learning and adapting to a new interface and new practices. These costs will be low when the new technology complies with old standards. Yet, providers who seek a lock-in effect could easily increase exit costs by adapting an exclusive technological standard that makes it prohibitively expensive to switch to the competitors.

We further discuss this effect in Chapter 4. But we can state here that exit costs like technological lock ups can cause externalities that are very different from those of the traditional world. These new types of externalities are more difficult to identify, and the conventional remedies of taxes and subsidies will not be useful to internalize them.

The conclusion, therefore, is that when viewed as an independent and autonomous market or a conglomerate of markets, Cyberspace does not suffer from the traditional externalities failure.

2.2. Externalities in the Traditional National Unit Affected by Cyberspace

Externalities analysis in Cyberspace could lead, however, to different consequences, when viewed in the context of traditional geographical units as the basic markets or communities to be scrutinized. In this case, the notion of externalities may remain useful. Cyberspace could create significant externalities at the interface between the online environment and traditional state institutions within national borders. In other words, in the context of the traditional state unit, Cyberspace can be held to have the opposite effect of what was discussed so far – it can be seen as increasing externalities.

Cyberspace facilitates an ongoing interaction among individuals who reside in different states. Territorial rules of such states may impose positive or negative externalities on individuals who belong to other jurisdictions. These externalities are much higher than those imposed by one community on another in the pre-Cyberian world. In addition, online activities and the rules of Cyber-markets and their decision-making procedures may impose externalities in the traditional territorial jurisdictions.[2]

Consider the following example: re-mailers are simply intermediary computers that strip identifying information from the original message (name and address). While some states allow the use of anonymous re-mailers, others do not. Finland's laws, for instance, allow re-mailers within its jurisdiction. Users who reside in other states, including those that prohibit such re-mailers by law, may use re-mailers located in Finland to send anonymous messages (Hardy 1997). Such messages may allow the users to violate the law or to engage in a harmful activity without being caught, namely by imposing an externality on their local law.

---

2   For externalities as an explanation for the rise of international law, see Dunoff and Trachtman
    (1998)

Similarly, if Internet users in China are not subject to copyright laws, they can easily make available over the Net a wide range of copyrighted materials, infringing the copyrights of owners in other jurisdictions. The effects of online conduct are, therefore, no longer linked to any particular physical location in which the conduct occurred (Post 1996, p. 3). Such effects are randomly distributed within various geographic locations, inflicting externalities that were much more difficult to exact in the pre-Cyberian world.

The re-mailers and the copyright examples are tailored to the online environment and reflect the effects of a global network for instant communication. The first example is connected to a specific rule that is itself a consequence of the creation of Cyberspace. Yet, the growing externalities problem arises in a wide range of contexts. Take, for instance, the attitudes of different communities towards neo-Nazi propaganda. In some countries, such as France and Germany, it is banned. In other countries, like the United States, it is protected on the basis of freedom of expression principles. In the physical world, countries managed, more or less, to enforce their specific arrangements regarding neo-Nazi materials, without facing any serious problems of externalities. States that restricted the distribution of Nazi propaganda did so by prohibiting the distribution and broadcast of hate speech within their borders, and by controlling import to the jurisdiction via customs. Today, the operation of a neo-Nazi Web site in the United States, where such materials are not prohibited, will directly affect other territorial jurisdictions in which the activity is prohibited. Such a site's offensive content is equally accessible to users around the world, thus creating externalities in all jurisdictions.

The classic example of this clash of community norms is the Yahoo! case. In that case, a French court issued an injunction against Yahoo!, an American Internet service provider with a US-based server, which facilitated access to Web sites where Nazi memorabilia was auctioned. The French court ordered Yahoo! to prevent French citizens from accessing those pages of Yahoo!'s Web site that sell Nazi objects (*League Against Racism and Antisemitism*, County Court, Paris). Yahoo! filed an action for declaratory judgment in the United States, claiming that complying with the French court order would require it to remove all Nazi-related materials from its servers, which would violate its First Amendment rights.

The United States court held that the French court order was impermissible content-based restriction on speech in violation of the American Constitution (*Yahoo!*, 169 F.Supp.2d, 1181). The court found no justification for enforcing the French court order on a company that resides within the United States simply on the basis that such speech is accessible via the Internet to French users. Although the United States and French courts reached conflicting conclusions, their rationale is quite similar. The two courts assumed that whatever action Yahoo! undertakes online, it should comply with the rules of the traditional, physical jurisdiction in which citizens are affected by Yahoo!'s actions.

The observation of increasing externalities in territorial states as the result of Cyberspace, particularly its implications regarding the enforceability of the laws of territorial states in Cyberspace, has led some scholars to suggest that Cyberspace should be considered an independent jurisdiction (Post and Johnson 1996, Post and Johnson 1997). The argument holds that territorial rules affecting on-line activity produce externalities that influence the welfare of individuals of other jurisdictions. To prevent such spillovers, Cyberspace should be viewed as an independent unit for which the Net defines community boundaries. Utility should be maximized within this community, and attempts to regulate it by territorial governments are no longer justified.

This argument is valid insofar as local regulation can increase externalities in Cyberspace and in other jurisdictions because of Cyberspace. It is, however, insufficient regarding externalities in traditional territorial units caused by Cyberspace. In other words, the argument may be convincing with regard to the intervention of municipal authorities in online activities and their effects on Cyber-markets and Cyber-communities. It overlooks the opposite interface – the effects of Cyberspace and traditional units through Cyberspace on traditional geographical units. Self-regulating Cyberspace, which might be justified for other reasons (such as efficiency and the narrow effect of market failures), is likely to increase externalities in physical jurisdictions.

Online communities overlap with real-world communities, and it is impossible to draw a clear distinction between them. Individuals who occupy the Net necessarily live in physical communities. People who send emails, use chat rooms, sell computer programs, and consume online music, also live in physical communities (Lessig 1996, p. 1403). Their willingness to purchase a book in the neighborhood bookstore may be affected by their visit to an online bookstore that offers books at a lower price. Their willingness to pay for a new title released by a record company depends on the availability of free music on P2P systems. A libelous message posted online may inflict harmful consequences on someone's career in the real world. Visits to pedophilic Web sites may affect users' behavior with their geographical neighbors. Users who read about their government's actions over the Net may change their views regarding their representatives. Indeed, on-line experience may affect prices and markets, social relations, community standards, and politics in real world communities.

Consequently, spillover effects necessarily occur between virtual and real world communities. Consider, for instance, a user who downloads obscene materials. Assume that such materials violate a standard of the community in which she physically lives, and are prohibited under local law. These materials may, however, conform with the values of the online community to which she belongs, and to the community standards in the place from which the materials originated.

Affiliation with an online community allows users to avoid the social bargains, as well as economic pacts, of their community. The ability to identify externalities created by Cyberspace that affect physical markets or communities does not assist us to internalize them, along the lines suggested by Pigou. This is due to two main reasons. First, the mere existence of a virtual community or market alongside traditional ones precludes us from identifying the relevant units for welfare maximization. This, in turn, will render externalities analysis useless in guiding central intervention.

Second, even if such identification of the relevant jurisdiction for welfare maximization is possible, by, for example, ignoring virtual markets and communities altogether, the remedies offered by the traditional externalities analysis, such as taxes and subsidies, will prove inefficient. One of the problems we will discuss in Chapter 9, is the difficulty for the traditional territorial unit of enforcing traditional jurisdictional rules in Cyberspace. Taxes and subsidies are the most problematic types of central intervention for virtual employment and enforcement. Hence, even if identification of externalities is possible, new methods of internalization are needed. In this respect, traditional economic analysis will prove ineffective.

3. SUMMARY

To summarize, applying the framework of externalities in the context of Cyberspace yields two very different results. Within Cyberspace, our analysis tends to conclude that externalities cannot be regarded as a market failure that justifies central intervention. With regard to traditional geographical units, the analysis tends to conclude the opposite, namely that Cyberspace increases externalities. Analysis also indicates that the conventional solution of central intervention to internalize the externalities would prove ineffective.

This conclusion should be associated with, and indeed leads to, the more general question: Are traditional economic, social and political units here to stay or does normative as well as positive analysis point to their significant weakening, and even disintegration? This issue will be treated in Chapters 9 and 10, taking positive and normative vantage points respectively.

In any case, given the diffuse and dynamic nature of communities and markets in Cyberspace, and the increased overlap among communities and markets online, it is unclear whether conventional externality analysis can continue to be a useful analytical tool. It was further suggested that as long as the cost of exit is low, the notion of externalities as an analytical tool is substantially weakened. In the absence of a clear definition of communities, the analysis does not offer a lucid identification of externalities or answer to whether the government – and which government – should intervene to correct the effects of externalities.

Globalization and the establishment of various multinational, super-national and international bodies to co-ordinate rules and regulate different segments of our economic and social life are natural responses to the challenges posed by Cyberspace and other facets of the information environment. The establishment of such decision-making forums, however, does not solve the basic question: What are the relevant units for maximizing welfare? The answer to this question is essential for kicking off any externalities analysis, in terms of both the identification of externalities and the desirable remedies to correct them. Without a clear answer, externalities analysis is likely to prove futile.

8. Transaction Costs and the Law in Cyberspace

In the previous four chapters we focused on the traditional market failures associated with 'first generation' Law and Economics, namely, the traditional micro-economic paradigm. We examined the applicability of their analysis to Cyberspace and concluded that many of the insights of the traditional analysis are no longer useful when we consider the significant changes of markets and communities brought about by the Internet revolution. The current chapter will be dedicated to the 'second generation' Law and Economics, which focuses on transaction cost, as the dominant factor for the analysis of both market and out of market human activities. Similarly to previous chapters, we will examine here the viability of transaction cost law and economics to Cyberspace.

1. TRANSACTION COST LAW AND ECONOMICS – THE COASE THEOREM AND THE ROLE OF LAW

Transaction costs were not considered in the traditional micro-economic model as a separate market failure (Mercuro and Medema 1997, pp. 147–156). Indeed, what is analyzed today under the category of 'transaction costs' overlaps with some of the traditional market failures, especially externalities and lack of information. Transaction cost analysis, therefore, can be seen as a second generation of law and economics. The focus on transaction costs within the economic approach to law emerged following Ronald Coase's seminal papers 'The Nature of the Firm' (1937) and especially 'The Problem of Social Cost' (1960). The former showed the emergence of the firm as the result of positive transaction costs, which shift contractual market activities into hierarchical non-market ones. The latter criticized the conventional theory with regard to externalities, arguing that in a world with no transaction costs, contractual negotiations between parties will eliminate externalities, and will drive the market to an efficient solution without the need for central intervention. Only when transaction costs are not zero is there a need for such intervention.

Coase's work marks a shift in the common understanding of the role of government in the market. Prior to Coase, economists believed that state action would be required to fix market imperfections such as externalities. When producers do not pay all the costs associated with production, they will not cease production even when its costs are higher than the value to consumers. Take, for instance, a factory that pollutes the environment while producing goods. Pollution imposes a cost on neighboring residential areas. The producer, however, will overlook this cost and continue production as long as the direct production costs incurred are lower than the price received for the goods.

Standard economic analysis prior to Coase perceived the law as a possible remedy for such inefficiencies. A liability rule or a Pigouvian tax, requiring the factory to pay for the pollution damage caused by production, would make the factory internalize these pollution costs. By requiring the factory to bear the cost of pollution, the law would achieve an efficient outcome.

Coase showed that the existence of externalities would not necessarily lead to inefficient results. In the absence of transaction costs, Coase argued, efficiency would be achieved by the parties through bargaining in a competitive market. Thus, if the factory has a legal right to pollute, the neighbors will pay it to reduce pollution by installing air filters as long as such preventive steps cost less than the damage caused by pollution. If, instead, the neighbors have a right to clean air, the factory will pay the residents of nearby neighborhoods for permission to pollute, as long as these sums are smaller than the gains from pollution. The initial allocation of legal rights will, therefore, be irrelevant to the means and level of use of the resources. The parties will reach the most efficient outcome through bargaining.

The ramifications of Coase's conclusion for the law were dramatic. If voluntary transactions shift the market towards efficiency regardless of the initial allocation of legal rights, the function of law should be reduced to neatly define the entitlements and make sure that exchange is feasible. Thus, the Law and Economics literature following Coase marginalized the role of law. In a Coasian world legal rights no longer really matter, writes Cooter in *The New Palgrave Dictionary of Law and Economics* (Newman 1998, pp. 270–282):

> The initial allocation of legal entitlements does not matter from an efficiency perspective so long as they can be exchanged in a perfectly competitive market.

Coase (1960, p. 19) himself acknowledged the significance of law in situations where transactions are not costless. In most cases, he argued, market transactions will be so costly as to prevent the re-arrangement of rights established by law. The law should, therefore, allocate rights as efficiently as possible. This will not only ensure that an efficient outcome is reached, but will also save the cost of reaching an efficient outcome through market transactions. In other words, Coase shifted the debate regarding the moral quality of competing rules to a rather technical consideration – the desirable rule is the one that minimizes transaction costs.

In this path-breaking work Coase referred mainly to the costs of negotiation. Calabresi and Melamed (1972) took the analysis a step further, expanding the notion of transaction costs to include also enforcement and adjudication costs. They put forward a model in which the assignment of property rights and the choice of enforcement methods are determined according to the structure of transaction costs. We apply the Calabresi-Melamed framework to Cyberspace in subsection 2.3 below.

The current paradigm of transaction costs economics is much broader. It is associated with the Neo-Institutional school, which views the transaction as the basic unit of economic analysis, and hence focuses on various factors surrounding this unit and analyzes their cost structure. These include information, enforcement, governance structures of firms, political institutions and other collective decision-making structures.

This wider framework of transaction cost economics is of great importance to Cyberspace. As we argued in previous chapters, the application of traditional market economic analysis to Cyberspace is at least incomplete, as basic assumptions of the traditional analysis, such as the existence of a defined market, and the existence of central government with various intervention powers and enforcement abilities, cannot be applied to Cyberspace unimpeded. The markets of Cyberspace, its communities, and their governance differ substantially from their counterparts in the territorial state.

The new transaction cost economics recognizes that all these factors cannot be exogenous to the economic analysis and must be taken as integral components of the discussion. Thus, when applied to Cyber-markets, transaction cost economics is bound to result in different solutions than when applied to traditional markets. In Chapter 9 we analyze the tenets of the Neo-Institutional Law and Economics approach in view of the information environment.

Through the example of the polluting factory, we emphasized the analytical connection between externalities and transaction costs. However, such a connection also exists between the traditional market failure of lack of information and transaction costs. Although the concept of information costs is not identical to the concept of transaction costs, it was argued that full information would bring about zero-transaction costs (Eggertsson 1990, p. 15). In this sense, our conclusions with regard to information in Cyber-markets have an important bearing on the transaction-cost analysis that follows.

2. APPLYING TRANSACTION COST ANALYSIS TO CYBERSPACE

2.1 Cyberspace as a Perfect Coasian World

The effect of Cyberspace on transaction costs is controversial. Some writers hold that transaction costs in Cyberspace are lower than in the non-virtual world (for example, Sunstein 1995; Easterbrook 1996; Trachtman 1998). Information technology, they argue, is wiping out transaction costs at an accelerating pace. They emphasize the reduced costs of searching for information, exchanging information, and the fast and efficient transmission of information. Thus, parties may efficiently search the Web for information on their counterparts and other businesses: their activity, transaction history, range of products or services or the way in which they engage, and the background of their executives. Buyers using a general-purpose search engine or a bargain finder may efficiently find out what other products or services are available, and identify the deal that meets their preferences at the lowest price.

Cyberspace is able to substantially curtail the buyers' search cost, as the first transaction cost incurred before market exchange. The Internet reduces the explicit costs of purchasing the information, traveling to the place of exchange and the cost of devoting time to the search. The decline in the search cost is not just the consumers' privilege. Cyberspace may, to some degree, reduce sellers' search costs regarding consumers' preference. Thus sellers can specifically target advertising and promotions of certain products/services to a particular clientele. For example, Amazon.com has started using automatically collated online information to run more specific advertisements (Heling and Hayden, 2002).

Lower transaction costs entail price cuts. Indeed, some empirical data point to this direction. For example, Brown and Goolsbee (2002) found a 10% increase in the share of individuals using the Internet for purchasing insurance, which reduces average insurance prices for this group by as much as 5%. These results suggest that growth of the Internet has reduced term life prices by 8%–15% and increased consumer surplus by $115–215 million per year and perhaps more. However, at least one study points to an opposite direction: Bailey and Brynjolfsson (1997) suggests that prices on the Internet are generally higher than prices of identical products sold by retailers with physical stores, and that price variance is higher for Internet retailers. The study was conducted on Amazon and Barnes & Noble bookstores.

An interesting context for examining the effect of reduced transaction cost in Cyber-markets is the case of standard form contracts. Standard form contracts are offered on a 'take it or leave it' basis, often upon the assumption that the terms will not be read at all. The traditional economic justification for the enforceability of standard form contracts is that they facilitate a dramatic reduction in transaction costs. That is because standardization saves the costs of drafting documents and negotiating on the part of suppliers, and of repeatedly reading the terms on the part of consumers.

Furthermore, some contractual terms have network externalities. For instance, some restrictions on the use of information may become valuable only when applicable to all the users who can gain access to informational work. Standardization in contractual schemes also saves costs at the institutional level, allowing multinational corporations to define the authorities of their agents in a standardized predictable environment (Rackoff 1983).

If Cyberspace reduces transaction costs, we are likely to see more competition regarding the terms of transactions. Low transaction costs will allow suppliers to collect information about consumers' preferences and tailor contract terms accordingly. Lower search costs will allow consumers to seek and compare various contract terms for the same goods or services. If in the real world consumers lack incentive to bargain over the terms of a contract as a result of prohibitively high negotiation costs, automated protocols in Cyberspace may create demands for new contract terms. In Cyberspace, electronic agents can even conduct some negotiations, most likely making them easier and cheaper. It is, therefore, predicted that we will see more tailor-made contracts and more diversity in contract terms.

Moreover, if transaction costs in Cyberspace are lower, the economic justification for the enforceability of standard form contracts is weakened. Such contracts may lack the efficiency attributed to transactions concluded between assenting parties in the non-virtual world. Transaction costs for those contracts that in the real world justify standard form contracts, may be so low that they eliminate the need for standard form contracts. This will enhance equality and just distribution (Gibbons 1997, p. 530).

2.2 Cyberspace, Cognitive Transaction Costs and Standard Form Contracts

But this is not the full picture. While the costs of retrieving information in Cyberspace may be reduced, the costs associated with individuals' choices are not likely to be affected. If they are affected, these costs might actually increase. Faced with a vast number of opportunities, even if efficiently selected by automated means, individuals still have ultimate responsibility for making a choice. The individual engaged in various transactions must be alert, pay attention, study the different options, define her preferences, prioritize and finally choose. In addition, Cyber-markets do not have a clear advantage in informational accuracy. On the contrary, for non-standardized goods and services, which may contain hidden information, online information may be less accurate and even insufficient (Heling and Hayden 2002).

The human (cognitive) costs of engaging in a transaction are likely to remain the same, and might even increase. In fact, if the volume of transactions increases due to the decrease of transaction costs of the first type, transaction costs of the second type are bound to rise (Trachtman 1998). This is something many of us experience on a daily basis. Processing the vast volume of information instantly available from various sources: print, radio, television, telephone, cell-phone, email, and of course the Web, requires an increasing portion of our time.

The second (cognitive) type of transaction costs might also decrease in the future, with the increasing availability of technological means that undertake some of these functions. New technologies increasingly perform some of these 'cognitive' tasks automatically, such as sorting information, comparing options, and reflecting preferences in choices (Allen and Widdison 1996). Nevertheless, even if such technological developments materialize, users' attention will still be necessary for defining preferences for automated agents, providing them with enough information, and monitoring their output.

Take, for example, the Platform for Privacy Preferences Project (P3P) developed by the World Wide Web Consortium (W3C). This platform was developed to create an automated standardized scheme for online privacy policy. The collection of information online and the ease of creating profound databases and consumer profiles are threatening the privacy of online consumers. Different Web sites use various strategies and techniques for collecting online information; some are more invasive of privacy, while others are attentive to consumers' privacy needs.

Individuals may have different preferences regarding the use of their personal information. Some individuals would object to the insertion of cookies that identify their computer every time they log into a Web site, and would be annoyed when Web sites use their personal name or refer to their surfing habits. Other users would treat all information-gathering practices as a minor hassle. They would happily provide full information on their family status or shopping habits, especially in return for free access to the Internet or free software.

The collection of information is performed at various levels using different technical schemes. Therefore, privacy policies that detail what information is gathered and how it is processed tend to be long and often unintelligible to the average lay user. Reading every privacy policy prior to the use of any Web site, and shopping for those Web sites that fit consumers' preferences is time consuming, prohibitively expensive and simply unrealistic. P3P provides a platform for automatically searching and comparing privacy policies, and identifying the policies that fit the preferences of the individual user. P3P enables Web sites to define their privacy policies in a machine-readable standardized format that is readable by browsers. Users can set privacy preferences on their browsers, which automatically compare the Web site's definitions to the user's privacy preferences. Only those Web sites that meet the user's privacy expectations will be accessed.

The P3P demonstrates what it takes to enable users more choice in the information environment. Conventional wisdom suggests that if we wish to enable consumer choice regarding privacy, providers must make their privacy policies transparent. In fact, it is predicted that if there is a demand for different types of privacy policies, a market for privacy will emerge, providing sufficient incentives for online providers to create numerous privacy packages tailored to satisfy all consumers' tastes. One of the reasons that such a market failed to develop was the non-comprehensive nature of privacy terms.

Furthermore, consumers may derive a relatively small marginal benefit from each transaction, namely, avoiding being subject to information gathering practices of a Web site that might be intrusive of their privacy. Consequently, consumers may often find the high transaction costs unjustifiable when weighed against the expected benefit. The high transaction costs that prevented the evolution of a market for privacy were related to the limits of human cognition and the difficulty to read, and comprehend sophisticated definitions and legal terms. P3P is one example of how software can assist in lowering such costs by creating a standardized platform. Yet, one should bear in mind that automated solutions that encode human preferences may suffer from serious limitations. This type of solution is always highly dependent on standards, and therefore reduces people's preferences into narrowly defined universal schemes that often do not capture the wealth of human diversity and sophistication of choice.

In summary, so far there is no clear empirical evidence for a decrease in transaction costs in Cyberspace, despite the theoretical analysis in this direction. If transaction costs in Cyberspace are lower, the virtual environment is likely to facilitate more transactions, reduce prices, and minimize the justification for central intervention under standard contract law analysis.

2.3 The Calabresi-Melamed Model in Cyberspace

The Calabresi-Melamed (1972) framework focuses on the structure of transaction costs as determining the efficient method of protecting entitlements. More specifically, it considers the protection of entitlements by property rules versus such protection by liability rules. For example, the entitlement to clean air can be protected by property rules that prohibit polluting, or by liability rules that do not ban such defiling, but entitle the victim to sue for compensation. Which of the two remedies is more desirable?

According to Calabresi and Melamed, property rules should be preferred when negotiation costs are lower than the administrative costs of an enforcement agency or a court determining the value of the entitlement. In such a case, central intervention ought to be minimal, as following the construction of the legal rule, the parties are likely to negotiate for the efficient end result, adhering to or bypassing the rule. Entitlements will change hands through a voluntary exchange in the market, where the state's sole function will be to prevent bypassing of the market through injunctions and criminal law. The persons who hold the entitlement are protected by a property rule, granting them a right for injunction, which prohibits the injurer from causing them any harm. Thus, the injurers can cause damage only if they buy off the victim.

Liability rules should be preferred when the cost of establishing the value of an initial entitlement by negotiation is higher than that of determining this value by an enforcement mechanism. In addition, liability rules might be preferred in order to avoid bargaining costs. Lack of information or uncertainty as to the cheapest avoider of costs is likely to point us, according to Calabresi and Melamed, in the direction of liability rule as well. Liability rules involve additional central intervention by a state organ deciding on the objective value of the entitlement. In this case, if the victim has the entitlement, he has the right to be compensated, but he cannot prohibit the injurer from causing harm.

Cyberspace has two important features, which are relevant in the context of the Calabresi-Melamed model. First, negotiation costs, which include the costs of identifying the parties with whom one has to negotiate, information costs, the costs of getting together with the relevant party, and the costs of the bargaining process, are significantly lower than in the non-virtual world. This is true for markets that have products and services provided in Cyberspace itself. It is also true for markets in which the negotiation process and entering a contract are conducted within Cyberspace, but the product or service is provided in the physical world.

Second, enforcement can be made effective without the involvement of police, courts or other central institutions, especially for products and services provided in Cyberspace itself. Effective enforcement can be achieved through codes of access (Lessig 1996, p. 1408; Reidenberg 1998). Software vendors, for example, may distribute an encrypted version of their product, providing a personal decrypting means to paying customers only. Instead of seeking an injunction against trespassers, an online provider may simply control access by implementing a system of passwords. Rather than trying to enforce rules of behavior, one can use software, which defines the terms upon which one gains access. The PICS software, for example, enables individuals to build self-design censorship on materials they receive (Reidenberg 1998, pp. 558–559).

The new available means for effective enforcement by the code point, under the Calabresi-Melamed paradigm, to a robust preference for a property regime rather than liability rules. In fact, it seems that enforcement of liability rules in Cyberspace by conventional courts is much less effective than in the non-virtual world, as infringers can always cross geographical boundaries and disguise their physical identity. The traditional territorial-based jurisdictional rules face a major challenge when applied to online activities. These activities are almost always multi-jurisdictional, and market players are often unaware of the physical location of their counterparts, or where the bits that translate their activity in Cyberspace pass. Courts might be so ineffective that the idea of Virtual Magistrates, who are likely to be much more familiar with Cyberspace practices, has been put forward (Hardy 1997).

This rather straightforward application of the Calabresi-Melamed model may lead to the conclusion that in Cyberspace there will be a strong preference for property rules over liability rules. Since these property rules can be self-enforced by technological means, no central intervention would be required, possibly save the protection of technological enforcement. This is an interesting conclusion, as it means that even when transaction costs are not zero, central intervention may not be desirable. Support for this conclusion can be found from a different direction – the transaction costs of exit. Post and Johnson (1996, p. 45) argue that these costs are so low, that the regulation powers of governments and the desirability of such regulation will be decreased.

Nevertheless, applying transaction cost analysis to Cyberspace emphasizes its shortcomings. It stresses some of the flaws suffered by this paradigm, taking technology as a constant variable and disregarding the analysis of the interdependency between technology and law. The multi-layer link between law and technology is of particular importance in the context of the information environment, which is dynamic and subject to frequent fundamental technological transformations. The relationship between law and technology must be explained before one draws any serious conclusions based on this analysis regarding the information environment. We further discuss these aspects in Section 3 below.

3. REVISING THE COASIAN ANALYSIS FOR THE INFORMATION ENVIRONMENT

3.1 Technology Made Visible

The tentative conclusion from the application of transaction cost analysis and its extension by the Calabresi-Melamed model to Cyberspace is similar to the conclusions drawn from the application of the traditional market failures analysis – a significant decrease in the role and justification of central intervention. However, there is a glitch in Coase's paradigm, which might not have been significant in non-virtual markets, but is very important in the Cyber-market. The traditional Coasian transaction cost analysis takes the state of technological development as a given or as exogenous to the analysis. It does not give adequate consideration to the possibility of technological progress and, moreover, to the way technology changes in response to economic and legal environments.

Technology is actually absent from the analysis in two senses: first, as a dynamic parameter that may affect efficiency, and second, as one of the outcomes of applying legal rules. Obviously, technological advancements affect efficiency. That is because the state of technology determines the availability and cost of technological devices that are employed to reduce harmful consequences, which, in turn, establishes who would be the least cost avoider.

The technologies relevant to Coase's examples were not likely to change significantly as a result of the choice of legal rules. This is not the case with Cyberspace, where technologies are constantly evolving and the results of Coasian analysis may be different with each technological advancement. The pace of technological change is disputable and there are many ways to measure it. Some believe that the speed of the chip, which doubles every two years, is a good measure of technological change. A common assumption in the high-tech environment is that technology reinvents itself every six to twelve months, and that employees must keep up with this rapid pace. This very brief timeframe and the elasticity of technology, call for special consideration in the analysis.

The crucial shortcoming of the transaction cost analysis when applied to Cyberspace is that it takes technological development as static. It overlooks the interdependency and reciprocity between technological developments and legal rules. This multi-layered relationship between law and technology is a key factor for understanding technological innovation in the information environment. Thus, an analysis that takes the state of technology as an exogenous component suffers from a serious shortcoming when applied to an environment with rapid technological advances and innovations. The analysis also fails to consider the effect of legal rules on technological progress. We now turn to discuss each of these aspects of technology in view of Coase's analysis.

To appreciate the role of technology in Coase's analysis, let us look at one example he provided – 'Sparks from Engines', which was previously used by Pigou to demonstrate the traditional economic analysis of externalities. Steam locomotives on the railway release sparks, which occasionally cause fires at nearby farmers' fields. Under perfect conditions of competition, when transaction costs are zero, the farmers and the railway will trade the permit to release sparks, and will reach an efficient outcome no matter how the legal rights are allocated. If the farmers' damages are lower than the profits of the railway companies, and the farmers are entitled to prevent trains from setting fire to their fields, the railway companies will pay farmers for permission to discharge sparks. If the damages are higher than the profits and there is no legal rule preventing discharge of sparks, the farmers will pay the railway companies to stop releasing sparks.

The efficiency of activity by one party depends on the benefit it produces and the harm it inflicts on other parties. When analyzed along a continuous, rather than dichotomous, framework, the efficiency of increasing the speed of existing trains depends on the costs associated with this level of activity, including the damage it causes. Only when the damage resulting from sparks, causing fire to neighboring fields, is higher than expected benefits, will a higher level of activity be inefficient. Efficiency will be achieved when the marginal benefits from the increase of one unit of speed equals the marginal costs inflicted by additional fire-causing sparks.

Technology is not completely absent from Coase's analysis. In addition to the profits versus damages analysis, Coase relates to the cheapest avoider, i.e. to the party that can develop the measures to avoid the harm most cheaply. If the farmers are the lowest cost avoiders, through, for example, the construction of better fireproof fences, the parties will reach an agreement under which the railway companies will be permitted to release sparks. If the railway companies can efficiently prevent fire or avoid sparks by, for instance, changing the engine technology, the market exchange will again lead to this outcome. This will be the result regardless of the legal regime (and under the zero transaction cost assumption).

Obviously, sparks were not inevitable. They were caused by the mechanical design of 19th century steam engines. Pigou's essay, in which the trains and farmers example was first introduced, was published in 1924, when the first passenger railways were launched. Steam locomotives used at that time, were soon (in the 1940s) replaced by the diesel locomotives, and finally by the electric locomotives, which is the cleanest and most efficient form of railway power today.[1] Preventive options in the 1920s were not the same as those available today. The ability of one party to efficiently prevent harm depends on the availability and costs of preventive measures, namely technologies that may reduce or eliminate harm altogether. Yet, the availability of these technological advancements and their costs were treated by Coase as fixed variables.

Technologies are not the result of nature or the necessary sole outcome of scientific progress. Scientific progress depends on investment in R&D, which in turn is likely to hinge on the legal regime and specific legal rules regarding liability. States of technology, therefore, cannot be regarded as independent factors, and should not be exogenous to the analysis of the cheapest avoider. Indeed, the availability of certain technologies is contingent upon various socio-economic factors, of which law is one.

If we require that the steam engines of railway companies release fewer sparks, we create a demand for more effective devices. Such a demand is likely to attract more investment in research and development of better devices, and to stimulate competition among developers and producers. Large investments and high levels of competition are likely to increase innovation in spark-reducing measures and push down the prices of such devices. The ramifications of the choice of a legal rule on the likelihood that preventive technologies will emerge, is not taken into consideration by the standard Coasian analysis. The traditional Coasian transaction cost analysis views the state of technology as given. It does not take into account the possibility of changing technologies as a direct result of the legal rules chosen.

---

1   For more information see Train World Timeline at http://www.stormloader.com/ironhorse/
    timeline.html.

The availability of certain technologies is not determined by the law of nature. It is a parameter affected by various factors. Law is one of them. Whereas rights assigned by law may not affect efficiency in the absence of transaction costs, legal rules may do so by shaping the type of technologies that become available and their cost. By failing to make technology endogenous to the analysis, Coase overlooked the reciprocal relationship between legal rules and technological progress.

This glitch in Coase's analysis might not have been significant in non-virtual markets. Indeed, the technologies relevant to Coase's examples were not likely to change significantly as a result of the choice of legal rules. This oversight could be crucial, however, in Cyberspace, which is characterized by a great pace of technological change, and where technology is said to reinvent itself every few months. Information technologies are dynamic and constantly changing, and the results of Coasian analysis may be different with each technological advancement. It is more feasible in Cyberspace, therefore, than in the non-virtual world, that the choice of substantive legal rules regarding protection of entitlements would have a crucial effect on those technologies likely to be developed in the short, medium and long term.

3.2 Law, Technology and the Digital Environment

An old controversy among scholars of science and technology relates to the nature of technological change. On one hand, one can find a rather deterministic view, which perceives technological advances as provoking economic changes, and thereby transforming social institutions. This view believes in technological determinism, perceiving technological progress as inevitable, independent, governed by its own internal logic and moving ahead due to scientific breakthroughs and maturity of accumulated data.

On the other hand, one can find scholars who hold that technology does not have any meaning unto itself. Its emergence is not merely the outcome of technological plausibility, but rather depends on interplay between technological ability and other social and economic factors. Thus, mass production, for example, could be viewed as an inevitable outcome of the economy of atoms, but could also be attributed to major demographic changes during the 20th century, which led to population explosion, and created the 'masses'. The notion of the 'masses' affected both political theory, and the concept of the self, which in turn created a need for mass-produced goods. Technology addressed that need. In other words, technology not only affects new paradigms, but assumes, reflects, serves and indeed results from them.

We believe that technological developments and their social function should be understood within a historical context. Technologies do not develop in a vacuum; they are the result of ideologies and values. The main factors that shape the digital environment are technology, politics, law and markets, and their complex interrelationship. The approach we suggest here emphasizes the reciprocal relationship between technological and social processes, perceiving both as driving changes and influencing each other.

Lessig (1996) argues that the design of Cyberspace at any given moment is a manifestation of an ideology, and therefore reflects the choices made by administrators. Research and development introduce options that require developers to choose particular technologies over others, defining a research agenda and setting priorities and preferences. The fact that there are some options from which one can choose, however, and that alternative designs and architectures exist does not mean that the choice of every particular design reflects an ideology. Some aspects of the architecture design may depend on technological breakthroughs, luck, or incremental developments that have matured. In addition, designed architecture may yield unintended consequences. Thus, technological development is not entirely controlled and manipulated.

Laws shape technology that in turn forms the information environment either directly or indirectly. Laws may affect technological development and use directly, by defining which technologies are legitimate, and which technologies or technological uses will be prohibited. The most typical example of direct regulation of information technologies is the anti-circumvention legislation in the U.S. Digital Millennium Copyright Act (DMCA). The anti-circumvention legislation explicitly prohibits the manufacture and distribution of any technology designed primarily to circumvent protection afforded by a technological measure that protects the copyrights of a copyright owner or affectively controls access to a copyrighted work. This statute was used to stop a Princeton University computer sciences professor from publishing the results of his encryption research.

Professor Felten was the head of a research team that wanted to publish a scientific paper describing the defects in the proposed Secure Digital Music Initiative, a scheme initiated by the music industry to protect audio CDs. The recording industry threatened to sue Felten for violation of the DMCA, and forced him to withdraw the paper from a planned conference. Felten applied for a declaratory injunction, arguing that his right to discuss the weaknesses of a technological system that protects digital music, is protected under the First Amendment. In response, the government stated in documents filed with the court that scientists attempting to study access control technologies are not subject to the DMCA. Nevertheless, the court dismissed Felten's lawsuit.

The DMCA was also used to stop a company from making and selling computer chips that match remanufactured toner cartridges to Lexmark printers, thereby circumventing Lexmark's cartridge chip. Lexmark is a worldwide developer, manufacturer and supplier of laser printers and toner cartridges. It sells prebate cartridges, for use with its printers, at an up-front discount. A microchip, which carries the toner loading program, is attached to every toner cartridge and enables the printers to approximate the amount of toner remaining in the toner cartridge.

Static Control Components manufactures and sells components for remanufactured toner cartridges. One of its products, the 'SMARTEK' microchip, circumvents Lexmark's authentication sequence, which prevents unauthorized toner cartridges from being used with Lexmark's printers, allowing consumers to reuse refilled prebate cartridges. Lexmark sued Static Control Components. The court ruled that Lexmark's authentication sequence constitutes a 'technological measure' that 'controls access' to a copyrighted work (Lexmark toner loading program). Thus, by circumventing the authentication sequence, the court found that SMARTEK is likely to violate the anti trafficking provisions of the DMCA (*Lexmark International, Inc.*, 253 F. Supp. 2d 943).

The DMCA, therefore, explicitly prohibits the manufacturing of technologies, or their implementations. It further affects the availability of technologies by creating disincentives for developing certain technologies. Legal exposure created by the DMCA anti-circumvention legislation chills away potential investments in circumvention technologies, namely, technologies that enable the circumvention of self-help technological locks used by content providers.

In addition to rules such as the DMCA, which are constructed mainly to shape the direction of technological development, other rules exist that are not intended to shape technological changes, but which do just that. Such are rules that simply raise the costs involved in developing or implementing specific technologies, i.e., rules that regulate liability, and rules that allocate entitlements.

Indeed, laws affect technological development and use in a way that is more relevant to the Coasian analysis, by establishing the legal infrastructure of online markets in which players are free to act. A legal rule may determine what can be owned, how rights would be transferred, who may be subject to liability and under what circumstances. These rules may provide incentives for developing one type of technologies, while discouraging another.

For instance, liability imposed on intermediaries for injurious content distributed by their users, could provide incentives for the development of screening devices, or anonymous exchange systems. An interesting case study could be the ramifications of the Napster case. Napster designed and operated a system that facilitated the transmission and exchange of music files among its users. This peer-to-peer (P2P) system allowed the sharing of computer resources and services by direct exchange between the computers connected to it. This architecture distributes information in a decentralized way, and allows direct exchange of content among members of online communities without any central management and control. Peer-to-peer and file-sharing technologies considerably enhance the efficiency of online resources and became increasingly popular during the late 1990s.

Napster users were able to make MP3 music files stored on individual computer hard drives available for copying by other Napster users. Napster further allowed users to search for MP3 music files stored on other users' computers, and to transfer these files from one computer to another via the Internet. Users swapping copyrighted music without authorization may be liable for copyright infringement. However, while service providers prior to Napster that allowed the download of music files created unauthorized copies of copyrighted music, Napster did not create any unauthorized copy, or distribute any copyrighted music without authorization.

Nevertheless, Napster was sued by the Record Industry Association of America ('RIAA') for contributory and vicarious copyright infringement (*A&M Records, Inc.,* 114 F. Supp. 2d 896). The law recognizes an enforcement failure when the copyright infringement is committed by numerous individual infringers, each committing a minor infringement, while the entire infringing activity is facilitated by a single entity. In some circumstances the law will allow the copyright owner to sue the facilitator, thereby facilitating efficient enforcement. In some cases, however, it will not be efficient to impose liability on the contributor, for example, when the contributor does not know, or cannot efficiently acquire knowledge of, the infringing acts.

The District Court issued a preliminary injunction prohibiting Napster 'from engaging in, or facilitating others in copying, downloading, uploading, transmitting, or distributing plaintiffs' copyrighted musical compositions and sound recordings, protected by either federal or state law, without express permission of the rights owner' (*A&M Records, Inc.,* 114 F. Supp. 2d 896, p. 927). The Court of Appeals for the Ninth Circuit affirmed in part the District Court decision (*A&M Records, Inc.,* 239 F. 3d 1004).

The Court found sufficient evidence of contributory infringement for the purpose of preliminary injunction, holding that Napster's peer-to-peer file sharing service facilitated the direct infringement committed by its users. Indeed, the Court ruled that the 'mere existence of the Napster system, absent actual notice, and Napster's demonstrated failure to remove the offending materials, is insufficient to impose contributory liability' (*A&M Records, Inc.,* 239 F. 3d 1004, p. 1027). Yet, the Court found that Napster had actual knowledge that specific infringing materials are available using its system, and that, although it could block access to suppliers of such materials, it refused to do so.

Contributory liability under the Napster rule will only apply when a facilitator of an infringing activity (1) receives reasonable knowledge of specific infringing files containing copyrighted works, (2) knows or should know that such files are available on the system, and (3) fails to act to prevent viral distribution of the works (*A&M Records, Inc.* 239 F. 3d 1004, p. 1027). Similar suits have been filed against other exchange file services.

In the aftermath of the Napster case, new file sharing technologies emerged. Kazza, Morpheus and other file-swapping programs are based on the technology of Gnutella. While Napster operated an index of all files that were available for exchange by its users, Gnutella-based programs are decentralized. The programs enable users to search for files without recording any information on the servers of the company that distributes the software. Files of all sorts, not just music, are exchanged directly among users of the software, and no files are copied into the company's server. The software distributors exercise no control over the use of the software, and even if they cease operation, it will not interrupt users from continuing to use the programs (*Metro-Goldwyn-Mayer Studios*, 259 F. Supp. 2d 1029).

Another interesting example is Aimster, a file sharing technology in which files and exchanges are encrypted. The Aimster system consists of a computer program downloadable from Aimster's Web site free of charge, which allows users to swap files. Any user who downloads the program can exchange files with any other users of the program ('buddies') while they are online in a chat room enabled by an instant-messaging-service. Users designate a folder that includes the files they are willing to share. When another user enters the name of the file she is seeking, the Aimster server searches the computers for all connected users. Once the requested file is identified, it is directly downloaded from the computer in which it is hosted, to the recipient computer.

The Aimster server, therefore, merely processes information collected from users' computers but it does not create any copies of the swapped music files. All communication among users is encrypted, and decrypted by the recipient of the files. By using encrypted communication, Aimster was hoping to shield itself from actual knowledge of unlawful uses of its system, and thereby avoid contributory liability. In fact, when Aimster was sued by the Recording Industry, the company argued that since the files were encrypted, it lacked the necessary knowledge regarding 'infringing uses' that liability for contributory infringement requires. The Court of Appeals rejected this argument, holding that the use of encryption to avoid liability amounts to willful blindness and therefore constitutes 'knowledge' sufficient for liability (*Aimster*, 334 F.3d 643).

The Napster case and the attempts to construct a new technology bypassing the courts' rulings, such as the Aimster technology, demonstrate how technological implementations react to legal rules. The sole purpose of incorporating an encryption function was to avoid legal liability. Even though encryption may entail some other social benefits (such as enabling privacy of online exchanges), there were no indications in Aimster's promotional activities, branding efforts or actual users' habits that the encryption provided an independent functional advantage.

The case law on liability of service providers for copyright infringements of their users exemplifies the kind of dialog that takes place between the courts and the industry, legal rules and innovations, laws and technologies. Technology reacts to needs, and in many cases these needs are the byproduct of legal rules. This is especially evident in the context of information technology, which is malleable, dynamic, and in many cases easily tailored to changing requirements. Another lesson to be drawn from the Aimster case is that legal rules are powerful in that they can forcefully put a stop to technological advancements and shift progress to different directions.

4. CONCLUSION

The transaction cost analysis of law and economics extended the old Chicago School model. Its heart is the Coase theorem, in which transaction costs are the only factor that diverts the market from efficiency, so they are the sole factor to bear in mind when legal rules are considered. Under the Coase theorem, an initial inefficient allocation of rights will be corrected by the market, unless there are positive transaction costs. In this case, the law can be of importance, and must be constructed to minimize these costs.

The Coasian model of transaction costs assumes, however, a given technology that affects efficiency. The efficient outcome depends on the availability of technologies and their costs. Transaction costs analysis takes as given that one party can make use of technology that may increase the value of the resource or may lower the cost inflicted by harmful use. It does not take into account the possibility of changing technologies as a result of the legal rules themselves.

Coase did not consider the possibility that legal rules might have a direct or indirect effect on technology. In his example of straying cattle that destroy crops growing on neighboring land, this factor is indeed remote. It is not so far-fetched in the Cyberian world. Indeed, in Cyberspace, technologies are constantly changing and the analysis may be different with each technological advance. The substance of a legal rule may affect technological development. Therefore, the apparent shortcoming of the economic approach is that it takes technological development as static, and overlooks the correlation and reciprocity between technological developments and legal rules.

Our discussion demonstrated that technologies should not be taken as a given. The introduction of new technologies has a dialectic relationship with other processes. Legal rules and market processes may directly affect the types of technologies available by explicitly prohibiting the use of certain technologies by law or by providing incentives to particular technologies and not others. Technology should therefore become endogenous to the analysis, and the economic discourse should be expanded to address it.

In this and the previous chapters we have tried to examine how and whether Cyberspace modulates the traditional micro-economic analysis of the market and its implications for the economic analysis of law. Although our analysis is far from exhaustive, we believe that one main conclusion can be drawn.

Whether we view Cyberspace as the relevant market or look into the traditional geographical markets – local, national, international – and the effects of Cyberspace on them, the traditional analysis of competition, market failures, and the role of central intervention have to be significantly modified.

Cyberspace, on the one hand, is predicted to eliminate or at least notably diminish some of the common market failures. Some of these involve the traditional public goods (i.e., information) or monopolies. Others concern the non-virtual market problems of lack of information, externalities, and transaction costs. On the other hand, Cyberspace creates some market deficiencies, which are less noticeable under standard analysis. Technological standards as a source of monopolistic power, the changing nature of information that was traditionally perceived as a public good, the technological race between enforcement measures by the code and counter measures, and the costs involved in verifying information – are only a few examples.

Be that as it may, the primary inference from our discussion so far is connected to the viability of traditional market failure analysis or traditional micro-economic theory analysis when applied to law. This conventional analysis presupposes the organization of markets, their connection with territory-based communities, the nature and hierarchies of central government, and the means by which central government can intervene in market activities. The analysis of Cyberspace cannot be based on these presuppositions.

As we have indicated, Cyberspace creates communities that are not territory-based and that have different characteristics from non-virtual world communities. Central government in Cyberspace is constructed differently from traditional central government. Some of the ways in which it can intervene in the market are also distinct. These factors require the broadening of the framework and perspectives of the economic analysis of law, in such a way that it will include, as endogenous variables, the structure of community and its central government. For this purpose, other branches of economic analysis, such as Public Choice and Neo-Institutional economic analysis must be amalgamated to our discussion. They are considered in the next chapters, which discuss the changing concept of communities, states, and the law.

Part Three

CYBERSPACE AND THE ECONOMIC
THEORY OF THE STATE

9. Preliminary Thoughts about Neo-Institutional Law and Economics and Cyberspace

In the previous chapters we explored some of the challenges posed by Cyberspace to the traditional market model applied to the law. One of the major shortcomings of the traditional analysis is its underlying presupposition that regards as exogenous certain variables, which turn out to be crucial in the new information environment. Among these factors is the state of technology (the pace of technological change, and the interdependency between technology and law). The traditional models also view as exogenous other crucial factors, like the existence of states, the borders between them, their central governments, and their enforcement powers. Public Choice theory attempted to remedy part of this deficiency of traditional micro-economic theory by analyzing the emergence of the public sphere, the state, public law, and collective decision-making processes.

Neo-Institutional theory is the broadest framework of economic analysis insofar as it incorporates Public Choice analysis with the traditional microeconomics or welfare economics. In other words, accepting Coase's insights with regard to the emergence of firms and their internal structure, Neo-Institutional law and economics regard institutional structures as endogenous variables within the analysis of law. Thus, Neo-Institutional analysis views the political structure, bureaucratic structure, legal institutions, and other commercial and non-commercial entities as affecting each other. Political rules intertwine with economic rules, which intertwine with contracts.[1] There is no doubt that this is the most suitable economic framework for examining the changing world of Cyberspace and the law. Cyberspace is neither a conventional territorial entity with central government, nor a traditional economic market or nexus of markets. A division between the analysis of traditional law and economics and public choice might be found as non-viable with regard to Cyberspace even more than with regard to traditional markets. We thus have to examine the simultaneous effects of constitutional law, public

---

1 For a broad definition of Neo-Institutional law and economics, which consists of the works of Coase, Williamson, Stigler, and Buchanan and Tullock, among others, see Mercuro and Medema (1997).

law and the political features of Cyberspace with its private law characteristics. Then we must assess whether the law and economics project as a whole can be sustained in the emerging, rapidly changing and technological-driven world.

In this chapter we first discuss the variables held as exogenous in standard market analyses: law, norms, and their enforcement, and explore them in Cyberspace from the perspective of Neo-Institutional law and economics (Sections 1 and 2). We briefly examine how Cyberspace affects states as independent identifiable entities; how it affects collective action and rule-making processes; how it affects the law as an institution. Although in many respects the Neo-Institutional framework seems to capture many variables relevant to the understanding of the information environment, applying this paradigm to Cyberspace may seriously shake some of its tenets. We touch upon three major features of our organization of life in Cyberspace that significantly differ from their counterparts in the non-virtual world – the firm, the state and the individual (Section 3). This chapter, which looks at the economic and non-economic online markets mainly from a positive level of analysis, will also serve as a convenient spring board to the next chapter, dealing with the normative theory of the state or of collective action.

1. THE INSTITUTION OF LAW IN CYBERSPACE: THE SOURCE OF NORMS

The law is one of the most central institutions of the organization of collective life. The law is also one of the central institutions challenged by Cyberspace. There are two major aspects of law on which Cyberspace may impinge. The first is law as the source of norms/rules that regulate behavior and the way in which it is created. The second is law as an enforcement mechanism. Following are some thoughts on how each of these two perspectives might be significantly transformed by Cyberspace, thus affecting the institution of law as we conventionally define it. We begin with the analysis of law as a source for norms in Cyberspace.

1.1. Cyberspace and the Traditional Rule-making Process

The traditional view of law, which is reflected by Positivist legal theories, portrays *law* as a set of norms, created by a (human) authority or authorities recognized as such law originators, on the bases of some sort of a fundamental norm – 'the rule of recognition' (Hart 1961) or 'the basic norm' (Kelsen 1949). In addition, the norms comprising the law are portrayed as hierarchical and exclusive. The authority of legal norms, according to Kelsen (1949), for example, is derived from higher norms, and a system of laws is a closed set of norms that can be traced back to one unifying fundamental norm (which is outside law, because it was not created by another legal norm). Thus, norms of the same legal system cannot contradict each other.

Although this is a crude summary of the prevailing positive theory of law (rather than a normative one), there are interesting connections between this positive analysis and the normative theory of law, which culminated in the Liberal Western Democracy model. As in our analysis of Coase's theorem of private law in the previous chapter, here too, technological frontiers can be understood as an interesting link between normative and positive analysis.

Cyberspace affects the process of rule making in several ways. It allows decentralization and democratization of the rule-making process, namely it affects the way rules are formulated. It also facilitates the customization of rules, and the co-existence of competing rule systems. In addition, law in Cyberspace is not a sole deliberate and explicit creation of human beings, in the framework of traditional political theory. It is also the creation of technology.

Technology is, of course, human-made, but the main point to be emphasized here is that while direct creation of law by legislatures and courts is a deliberate, transparent and intentional endeavor, the creation of law by humans through technology is not transparent. In many instances it is not even deliberate and intentional. Consequently, Cyberspace transforms the emergence of law in two important ways: first, law is no longer exclusively generated by pre-meditated rule-making processes. Second, even those laws that are deliberately created as laws, are not the sole monopoly of the institutions of state governments.

The next chapter will be dedicated to the effects of Cyberspace on the theory of the state and on the normative analysis of law. Here we want to focus on positive analysis vis-à-vis the Neo-Institutional approach. However, in order to understand the impact of Cyberspace on Law, and in light of the interconnections between positive and normative analyses, let us at this stage briefly introduce the general normative background of the traditional concept of law.

The basic assumption of most political theories, and certainly those that can be associated with the economic approach, is that human beings are social creatures, and that collective action can benefit the well-being of all individuals. The bedrock of the liberal theory of the state has been contractual or consensual collective decision-making. Practical thinking and political theory about communal collective action acknowledged the obstacles faced in applying these principles to the daily life of communities, and the need for more efficient day-to-day collective decision-making processes.

The two solutions offered by modern democratic states are representative democracy and majority decision-making. The description of law (rather than the prescription of law) by legal Positivism is, of course, influenced by these solutions. Thus, for example, Kelsen's pyramid of norms reflects his normative endorsement for parliamentary democracy. But both solutions – representation and majority decision-making – should be seen in context of the existing technological frontiers at the time they were carved on the political theory stones. Cyberspace sets new technological frontiers, which might render these solutions unnecessary, affecting both the normative and positive theories of law.

Cyberspace significantly reduces the cost of communicating and processing individuals' preferences. It makes possible the efficient collection of information from individuals by asking them to click their preferences directly onto the screen. It reduces transaction costs involved in collecting information about preferences. Cyberspace also facilitates fast and cost effective information processing that allows real-time feedback on public preferences and choices. This, in turn, reduces the need for agencies or representatives. The reduced costs of coordination and communication diminish the extent of collective action problems. If transaction costs involved in coordination are low or non-existent, there is no need, or at least a diminished need for representatives – intermediaries – to reflect the aggregated will of their constituents. Individuals may directly communicate their preferences on each and every matter.

In addition, decreasing transaction costs may allow individuals to become organized. Cyberspace reduces the cost of identifying relevant parties, communicating, acting together, and spreading information that concerns all. This can lead to increased democratization and decentralization of rule-making processes, in whose various stages Cyberspace allows groups and individuals to participate. Legislative bodies, for example, may efficiently collect public comments on Bills posted on the Internet. The Israeli Knesset (parliament), for instance, invites the general public to take part in some of the deliberations of its committees through the Internet. In the future, the technology will enable government not only to consult with the public, but also to delegate to the public some decision-making powers, even if agencies or representatives are here to stay for a while. This may allow citizens to take a more active part in governance, and to effectively monitor government actions (see also Trachtman 1998). Hence, the effects of Cyberspace through its new technological frontiers, can transform both normative and positive analysis of law.

From the perspective of economic theory, two important problematic phenomena that exist in representative democracy, are toned down significantly in Cyberspace. The first is agency costs, which are associated with representative government (Musgrave and Musgrave 1980). These costs are the result of ineffective monitoring of representatives by their voters and the ability of the former to act in a self-interested manner without being penalized by voters. Self-interested behavior will occur when the costs of the penalties to the politician from such behavior are smaller than the political or personal gains. The easy and relatively cheap access to information and the lower costs of collective deliberation and action in Cyberspace are likely to increase the effective monitoring level and thus reduce these agency costs. This, in turn, may well decrease self-interested behavior by politicians.

The second phenomenon of representative democracy is the power of interest groups to seek rents, and acquire gains through pressure on representatives at the expense of the general public. Interest groups are able to succeed in their actions because of the costs of collective action. This allows only small groups to organize, groups whose potential gain from collective action is higher than the costs of organization (Olson 1965, and in the legal context Farber and Frickey 1991, 12–37). Cyberspace, as indicated above, tends to lower the costs of collective action, which in turn will enable broader interest groups to organize, bringing more equality to the political markets and diffusing the impact of narrow interest groups.

Some empirical data may lend support to this analysis. Cyberspace has become a resourceful infrastructure for non-government organizations (NGOs), such as the environmentalists and the anti-globalization movement. A profound example is the use of the Internet by the Zapatista rebellion in Chiapas, Mexico (Cleaver 1998). Another recent example is the extensive use of the Internet in organizing the worldwide campaign protesting the war against Iraq during 2003 (Clemeston 2003). Activist groups are increasingly using the online environment to link geographically dispersed groups around a common theme, and to coordinate and strategize, taking advantage of the low cost of communication. By sending emails, or setting up a Web site, NGOs may disseminate their message and raise public opinion to support their goals, at relatively low cost. Organizations using the Internet also recruit new activists and manage their activities around the world. The Net may enable NGOs expand their monitoring activities, by collecting information at low cost, and more effectively monitoring the behavior of organizations and governments.

The enhanced ability to organize collectively has its downside. Online transmission facilitates not only social activists, but terrorist organizations (Tzfati and Weimann 1999; Raman 1999). The online environment allows these organizations an outlet that is otherwise unavailable via traditional mass media. In fact, while a terrorist organization that seeks to transmit a message in the mass media will use acts of terror to receive media exposure, on the Internet, the terrorist organization is a speaker, and its status as speaker is identical, at least at the starting point, to that of an online journal, a commercial site, or any legitimate political organization (Birnhack and Elkin-Koren 2002). The latter can bestow terrorist propaganda with more legitimacy (Tzfati and Weimann 1999).

Overall, Cyberspace allows the decentralization and democratization of rule-making processes in that it facilitates effective participation of people in setting the rules. Rules may be increasingly created from the bottom up, therefore reflecting the need for diversified social and economic interests by increasingly complex societies (see Cooter 1997). Consequently, the description of law as a pyramid of norms, which is created by a pyramid of institutions (Kelsen 1949), no longer provides an accurate account of law.

1.2 Cyberspace and the Customization of Norms

So far we have seen how Cyberspace breaks the hierarchical concept of traditional law. A related issue is the dynamic nature of rules and the ability to customize these rules at relatively low cost. Reidenberg (1998), for instance, believes that rules in Cyberspace may be easily customized because they are reflected and implemented by the code. Customization of rules is, of course, also possible in the non-virtual world. Contracting parties may agree to deviate from a legal default rule (but not from a mandatory rule). Yet, if transaction costs in Cyberspace are indeed substantially lower, contractual agreements are likely to become prevalent. For instance, notwithstanding privacy laws, users may agree to some invasion of their privacy, surfing Web sites that collect personal information in exchange for free software. Furthermore, customization of rules in Cyberspace may be implemented not only through contractual arrangements but through product design. Web browsers may define privacy options for Internet surfers, by offering tailored options. Microsoft Explorer, for instance, offers High Privacy (blocking first and third party's cookies that use personally identifiable information without the user's explicit consent), Medium Privacy (blocking cookies that use personally identifiable information without the user's implicit consent), or an option to accept all cookies. This feature of the browser not only constructs the users' choice, but also creates a distinct technological meaning to the notion of online privacy.

To the extent that transaction costs in Cyberspace are lower, customization of rules may involve lower costs. It should be emphasized that not only the customization of Cyber-rules is easier, as argued by Reidenberg, but also traditional legal rules – local, national and international – are easier to customize because of lower costs incurred when these rules govern transactions carried on in Cyberspace. Yet, as explored in Chapter 8, although some transaction costs, such as search costs and communication costs, are lower in Cyberspace, others increase. The cognitive costs involved in studying the different options and choosing between the various alternatives are likely to increase. Furthermore, customization of rules involves other costs. Such are network externalities. As more people use them, norms become more valuable, to the extent that they cease to require a high level of coordination. Standardized rules will reduce transaction costs (search and negotiation) of providers and users. Network externalities provide inadequate incentives for innovative norms. Such costs would be identical in the non-virtual communities and in Cyberspace. Avery Katz (1996, pp. 1750–1751) argues, for example, that in such circumstances, 'even if newly invented norms would be more efficient than the status quo, there may be no way for a decentralized community to co-ordinate its implementation.' The costs of adapting to new rules are human costs that may not be avoided by sophisticated technologies.

1.3 Regulation by Code

The prevailing positivist theories of law, as we mentioned above, attribute the creation of law to human-made institutions: legislatures, courts and delegated bodies, such as the executive or administrative agencies. Most legal philosophers (e.g. Hart 1961, p. 44, Kelsen [1961] 1970, pp. 114, 119), and indeed law and economics scholars, also acknowledge custom as a source of law. Customs are patterns of behavior of unspecified segments of the population that carry normative value, or when violated, attract social sanction or condemnation. In a way, the description of how Cyberspace transforms the creation of primary legal rules (legislation) brings them closer to the way customs are formed – a process with mass participation and a diminished role of intermediaries. In this respect, it is interesting to note that a circle is completed. The process of law-making today, due to Cyberspace, resembles more and more ancient law or pre-modern law-making, which prevailed before the establishment of strong states' apparatuses, whose domination of rule-making processes have increased rapidly in the last two centuries.

Be that as it may, Cyberspace also introduces a new type of regulation by code, namely by technology. Technology has always shaped people's behavior, determining what is possible and what is not, what is allowed and what is forbidden. For instance, new communication technologies, such as the telegraph and telephone, confiscated the government monopoly over communication, enabling the distribution of subversive ideas by individuals. The emergence of mass communication technologies, such as broadcasting, allowed the instant communication of a single identical message to the masses. This technological development had profound political ramifications for the organization of social units, and for public discourse.

In the past, technology developed very slowly, and in the course of the human life cycle technology was almost fixed or predetermined. Races between different technologies that reflect different normative values and choices were rare. As we have seen, this feature brought scholars like Ronald Coase to ignore technology altogether when deliberating the desirable legal rules, and the description of law. Today, technology is constantly changing. Consequently, it plays a different quantitative role in its effects on daily conduct, social behavior and social norms, and thus, on the law.

Technology also plays a significantly different qualitative role. Information technologies are developing at an accelerating pace. Competing technologies are struggling to acquire the upper hand. Technology is much more instrumental in shaping our lives, affecting our choices and limiting them. When we discussed transaction cost law and economics (see Chapter 8), we emphasized that legal rules allocating entitlements and determining how to protect them will influence the course of technological developments. This, in turn, will affect efficiency, or total welfare. Thus, even in a world of zero transaction costs, the choice of rules matters. Here we want to emphasize the other side of the story: technology's effects on the law.

Cyberspace regulates behavior by its mere infrastructure. The computer programs, the communication design, and the network architecture that constitute Cyberspace are not neutral. They reflect a certain social order, they shape behavior and social interaction among users, and define the potential choices of actions available to users in Cyberspace. No one put it better than Lawrence Lessig (1999, p.6):

> ...the invisible hand of cyberspace is building an architecture that is quite the opposite of what was at cyberspace's birth. The invisible hand, through commerce, is constructing an architecture that perfects control – an architecture that makes possible highly efficient regulation. ... In real space we recognize how laws regulate – through constitutions, statutes, and other legal codes. In cyberspace we must understand how code regulates – how the software and hardware that make cyberspace what it is *regulate* cyberspace as it is.
>
> Code is law. This code presents the greatest threat to liberal or libertarian ideals, as well as their greatest promise. We can build, or architect, or code cyberspace to protect values that we believe are fundamental, or we can build, or architect, or code cyberspace to allow those values to disappear.

Generally speaking, digital representation is malleable and changes involve lower costs than those in other media of representation. Compare, for instance, the cost of changing a text that is posted online or on the computer screen, with that of modifying a published book. Having said this, the cost of inserting changes in digitized information may also be prohibitively high. Consider, for example, the minor modifications that were necessary to achieve Year 2000 compliance of computer programs. The wide scope of such minor changes imposes very high costs.

In addition, the cost involved in human adaptation to new rules (or technologies for that matter) may be prohibitively high. Indeed, if rules are reflected in the technology, the cost of customizing rules or switching between different rules systems depends on the cost of the technology. Some insights regarding the customization of rules also apply here. If changing the rule requires modification of a standard or infrastructure, the costs may be prohibitively high. Some changes (such as defining users' preferences) may be entered at low cost.

1.4 Cyberspace and the Plurality of Norms and Legal Regimes

Another feature of emerging law in Cyberspace is that Cyberspace does not require the same general applicability and exclusivity of rules that characterize legal regimes in the non-virtual world. This could be considered an advantage. At least since the rise of positivist theory of the law (especially Austin [1832] 1995, and Kelsen 1949), we view the law as hierarchical, territorial, and backed by the physical ability of enforcement through sanctions. Legal norms are created on the basis of the authority of strong ruling powers (Austin) or the authority of higher legal norms (Kelsen). Regulations are valid because statutes authorize their construction. Statutes are valid as long as they do not conflict with constitutional norms. The highest legal norm – the constitution – derives its power from the basic norm, which represents either force or physical power (Austin [1832] 1995, and Kelsen 1949) or social convention (Hart 1961). Legal norms claim a monopoly on power and superiority over other types of norms. The power of the state to enforce legal norms makes this superiority possible (Bentham [1789] 1948, Austin [1832] 1995). Hence the origins of the perception of law as territorial and corresponding to political regimes, which possess physical enforcement powers.

Cyberspace seems to fundamentally change this picture of law. It allows the coexistence of competing rule systems. Not only can rules be created from the bottom up, such rules may also apply simultaneously in different spaces, and may apply only to users who enter such virtual spaces. Rules must be generally applicable, but only to users who choose to enter their domain. Thus, conflicting rules may exist, with no hierarchy between them.

Post and Johnson (1997) have emphasized this aspect of Cyber-regimes. The nature of Cyberspace, they argue, no longer requires the adoption of a single set of rules. Unlike central regulatory institutions in representative democracies, Cyberspace, they believe, permits a plurality of rules. It allows the development of diversified regimes that will be shaped indirectly by way of interaction between sysops defining the terms of use, and users making choices regarding their preferred system and services. Internet service providers, search engines, list moderators, or Web site owners will adapt their rules to the users' wishes. Users who disagree with such rules will be able to leave and find an alternative regime that better serves their interests and values. The advantage of Cyberspace is that it can facilitate the coexistence of different regimes. Rules and norms may be generated by the 'invisible hand'. Post and Johnson (1996) endorse this model of a 'market of rules.' Under such a vision of idealized democracy, users of Cyberspace may directly choose the laws that apply to them.

From this perspective, Cyberspace facilitates different normative systems that may simultaneously apply to the same individuals, and their applicability depends on a choice to enter a particular virtual space. Diversified regimes would allow rules to be tailored to the special needs of different segments of the population. They would further allow dynamic and changing needs of individuals to be addressed.

The feasibility of this vision depends, however, on the ability to control exit. For instance, maintaining a protectionist regime where copyrights are protected and enforced and a copyleft regime that does not recognize copyrights depends on the ability to entirely block leakage of materials from one area to another. If materials distributed in a restrictive regime can freely travel to the liberal regime, division into regimes becomes meaningless. Authors who seek to distribute their works subject to strong copyright restrictions must make sure their works will not be disseminated in any copyleft online community (Elkin-Koren 1998).

Furthermore, for rules to be effective, it is sometimes necessary to make users accountable for their online behavior, be it an infringement of a regulatory norm or a violation of contract. Such accountability requires a mechanism of identification, which will match users' online identities represented by IP addresses or domain names to their physical identity. Virtual identities may not be easy to monitor and sanction since they may be multiple and unsteady. Some users may use different addresses for different purposes. Others may avoid responsibility for online harm by changing their IP address, thus escaping any sanction against them, such as restricting their access to an online area.

Accountability of users, therefore, requires a technical ability to link the virtual representations of users and their physical entities. Post and Johnson (1997) suggest that this problem can be solved by tying online identities to identifiable individuals. But such a central identification system may threaten users' privacy and allow service providers (registries, ISPs) a high degree of control over online activities. This potential control may threaten the civil liberties of users. Furthermore, if such mechanisms of identification and control are available, they may be used to place users' online behavior within the jurisdiction of their municipal governments. So far, the right equilibrium between freedom and accountability has not been achieved. However, one need not be a dreamer to imagine a new technology, which will be able to guarantee a satisfactory level of virtual enforcement, without invading privacy or abolishing the autonomous sphere of Cyberspace and its independence from traditional national jurisdictions.

A related issue is reliance on contractual means. What is the legal validity of such contractual norms and to what extent are they enforceable? If contractual norms are enforceable only within a particular regime, enforcing such rules will not eliminate any leakage. To enforce such contracts across online regimes requires a higher level of norms that apply to all users regardless of the legal regime they choose.

Finally, the efficiency of diversified regimes may depend on externalities inflicted among them. Since people who surf the Net and use one online community may also take part in another online community, as well as live communities, they inflict the consequences of rules adapted by one community on members of another community. An online community that prohibits hardcore pornography may suffer from other online communities that allow access to such conceivably harmful materials. An online community that allows online exchange of music files may threaten the business interests of the music industry, both in online and traditional markets.

Be that as it may, there is no question that Cyberspace transforms the traditional, hierarchical, and monolithic system of law. It opens up new frontiers for normative systems of collective action, expanding opportunities for plural normative systems, enabling the coexistence of overlapping of norms, and their dissociation from the territorial nation state. In the context of neo-institutional economic analysis of law, this means we can no longer regard the law as an exogenous variable. Both market activity analysis and non-market activity analysis have to incorporate the legal arrangements as endogenous variables. In addition and related to the latter, even the scope of the market itself (whether economic or political) cannot be regarded as pre-given and should be dealt with simultaneously with the analysis of market equilibrium.

2. THE INSTITUTION OF LAW IN CYBERSPACE: ENFORCEMENT

Another way in which Cyberspace transforms the law as an institution is related to enforcement. On the one hand, conventional enforcement (by the state apparatus) is much less effective in Cyberspace, as it is always possible to cross over territorial borders and to disguise the physical identity of the offender (Hardy 1997). On the other hand, Cyberspace introduces new methods of enforcement that challenge traditional thinking about enforcement and transform its meaning. Technology in Cyberspace allows efficient enforcement to a degree that does not exist in the non-virtual world. In this sense, Cyberspace challenges some of the assumptions of the traditional discourse of economic analysis of law (including Neo-Institutional Law and Economics). The two most important assumptions challenged by Cyberspace are that an enforcement system is provided by the state, and that individuals can choose whether or not to comply with rules provided by the legal system. Following a short discussion distinguishing between technology as a new regulating method that shapes behavior and as an enforcement mechanism of traditional laws, we turn to these two assumptions in light of enforcement mechanisms in Cyberspace.

2.1 Technology as Law and Technology as an Enforcement Apparatus

The architecture of Cyberspace is not neutral, but embodies value either implicitly or explicitly (Nissenbaum 2001). It manifests a certain social order, which shapes behavior and social interaction among users (Lessig 1999). But the technology of Cyberspace is not only a manifestation of norms and values or a source for law; it is also a sophisticated enforcement apparatus. It is important to distinguish between these two facets of technology vis-à-vis the concept of law.

Consider, for example, copyright laws. Copyright law prohibits the creation of copies without the authorization of the copyright owner. The owner could stop the unauthorized use of her work by seeking an injunction in court and the copier would be further obliged to pay the owner damages for the infringing copies she has made. In Cyberspace some programs may simply prevent the creation of uncompensated copies by using digital rights management systems (DRMs). Using encrypted platforms, owners may technically prevent the creation of digital copies, permit printed copies, or restrict any copying whatsoever. DRMs can constitute a new regulation, applying original norms that depart from the legislated copyright laws, thus substituting existing copyright laws as a normative source. But DRMs may also function merely as enforcement mechanisms for existing rules, making them more efficient. If the hardware and software adopt the legislated rules, they will prevent copying or charge for it whenever copyright protection is granted by statute, and allow it according to the exemptions specified in the law, e.g. fair use. In this case, the technologies are merely an enforcement mechanism of law enacted by traditional law-making institutions. However, if DRMs limit copying when the legislation permits it, Cyberspace both created a new legal regime and at the same time, provides means to enforce it. The distinction between the two courses is not always easy to identify and analyze, as the rules codified in the technological platforms are not explicit and not transparent as are legislated rules.

Another example is privacy. The privacy of users' correspondence, their communications on online chats, or the list of Web sites they had visited, might be protected either by the law or by the code. Laws that protect privacy define certain behaviors as illegal, such as unauthorized invasion of individuals' private mail. The law may impose liability or damages on invaders, thus inflicting negative incentives to discourage a behavior that is not socially beneficial. Similarly, invasion of privacy may be enforced by criminal law. Instead, in Cyberspace, privacy might be protected by the code, which may, for instance, allow the use of encrypted messages to protect the privacy of senders. Such means of self-help simply prevent undesirable behavior. Like the copyright example, technology can merely enhance or substitute enforcement capabilities of privacy laws enacted by legislatures, international treaties and the like, but they can also create new standards of privacy, shifting the rules enacted or making them irrelevant.

The distinction between regulation by code and enforcement by code has serious ramifications for power relations. If technology is not subject to rules of territorial states, owners of technology and technology designers are assigned (de facto) with the power to regulate. Is this justifiable under economic theory?

It is arguable that the power of code designers may be reduced by market effects and by the rules of supply and demand. Indeed, the use of self-enforcement measures is also subject to market rules. Copy protection that did not allow the making of any computer program copies turned out to be a commercial failure. Similarly, Web sites that make use of tracking systems that violate user privacy, such as spyware, proved to be unpopular, and Internet businesses that do not provide a security system will not be able to attract customers. Privacy concerns of users may explain the development of file sharing programs such as Kazaa-lite which allow users to remove the spyware. It follows that the power of code designers to develop the rules for Cyberspace is not unlimited.

Yet, regulation by the code, as any other type of private ordering, could only be efficient if it reflects the will of consenting parties. We are unlikely to hold that a party has given her consent to the terms of a contract unless she had the choice not to do so. But 'consent' requires not merely freedom of choice, i.e. the ability to freely exercise one's will, but the necessary knowledge required to act deliberately and not arbitrarily. Since regulation by code lacks transparency, it is unlikely that users will be aware of the norms reflected in it. In many cases, users will not be adequately informed regarding the norms and values embodied in any particular technology. If users inaccurately perceive the impact of the exchange on their utility, we can no longer be confident that the exchange will, in fact, render both parties better off (Cohen 1998).

Furthermore, market effects may mitigate the abuse of technological advantages only in the absence of market failures. If, for instance, a company exercises a monopoly power, its technology becomes the standard and consumers may not be able to resist restrictions on use and access by switching to a different program that reflects different rules. A decision on whether to allow competing regulation by the code should take into account this new and dynamic scheme of power relations.

Regulation by technology opens up a new realm of competing norms. It not only allows those in control of technology to exercise power, but also facilitates resistance by those who are technologically skilled. For example, an employer may use a program that monitors her employees' use of Internet resources in the workplace. In response, employees may use programs that prevent such monitoring or change its output. Employees who are often exposed to all sorts of monitoring by employers may also use computer programs that allow them to monitor their employers.

As our discussion in Chapter 4 demonstrates, power in Cyberspace is not merely political or economic. It may also be driven by technological advantage and control over standards. The exercise of such power to shape users' behavior does not necessarily reflect social utility or collective preferences because implementing technical means that enforce certain behaviors may reflect the interest of designers, and not necessarily of society as a whole. As a source for alternative power, however, Cyberspace can be seen as contributing to the doctrine of separation of powers and deepening the checks and balances mechanisms on traditional government power. In this sense, the fact that most successful innovators of modern information technology are neither political nor established economic powers can contribute to promoting the ultimate goals of liberal democracy.

2.2 Enforcement by the State and Enforcement by Technology

Under standard economic analysis, a law enforcement system is considered a public good that must be provided by the state. Enforcement by the code, or by technology, is a private good. The State normally requires a monopoly over enforcement means. In most circumstances, the state will not tolerate competing enforcement entities exercising power in a way that threatens its monopoly, especially its superiority over enforcement.

There are major differences between enforcement by the code and enforcement of laws in real-world legal regimes. One difference has to do with the point in time where intervention occurs. Whereas traditional enforcement of legal rules is ex-post, enforcement by the code is ex-ante (Lessig 1999, pp. 44–60; Reidenberg 1998). The rule embodied in the code prevents the violation from occurring in the first place. Thus, instead of suing for invasion of privacy, encryption of personal data may simply prevent such invasion.

A second difference is reliance on collective agencies. Enforcement by the code does not rely upon any law enforcement institutions such as courts and other administration of justice apparatus. It is self-executed and self-implemented through, for instance, systems that allow access to information only after payments are made (platforms that do not allow copies to be made, or computer programs that trace the use of unauthorized copies on the Web). The same system that provides the service (such as the computer program that facilitates access to a Web site) also defines the terms of access and the terms of use by preventing some uses, such as copying, and permitting others, such as browsing.

Although enforcement by physical or technological means in the non-virtual world is theoretically possible, it is less efficient than the traditional methods of enforcement by collective agencies. In Cyberspace the opposite may be true. Take, for example, the protection of property in the physical world versus protection of property in Cyberspace. In a lawless non-virtual society, or in a society that acknowledges property rights, but fails to provide efficient protection of these rights because of shortage of enforcement agents, such as police, or corruption, it is theoretically possible to achieve protection via physical self-help means – fences, alarm systems, weapons of self-defense etc. The accumulative costs of such devices, however, may be much higher than the development of efficient and honest central enforcement agencies. In Cyberspace the opposite is true. Establishing efficient central enforcement agencies might prove to be much more expensive than self-help by technological means.

Another noteworthy parameter distinguishing enforcement by technology and traditional state enforcement concerns flexibility. While enforcement by physical means in the non-virtual world cannot be fine-tuned to complex rules and various exemptions desirable by the rule makers, the new technologies of Cyberspace can achieve refinement of a greater degree than fine-tuning of legislated arrangements. In other words, while physical enforcement in the non-virtual world cannot achieve the exact intent of complex wording of rules, enforcement by the code can achieve a higher level of fine-tuning than any wording.

The differences discussed above between the two modes of enforcement point to a conclusion according to which enforcement by the code is more efficient than enforcement by the traditional legal system. It involves relatively lower costs. It does not involve the costs of identifying, seizing, and prosecuting violators, and maintaining the bodies of the legal enforcement apparatus, such as the police and the courts. This is particularly noticeable on the Internet, where the costs of enforcement by the traditional legal system may be prohibitively high, much higher than traditional enforcement in the physical world. Global access imposes increased costs of enforcing rules of the territorial state outside its jurisdiction (Post 1996). Access and on-line activities are not tied to any geographical place, and may constantly switch locations. Violators may effectively act from another jurisdiction, thereby defeating enforcement attempts. For example, Web sites with materials considered illegal in one jurisdiction may be relocated to a different jurisdiction. Globalized access may further increase the costs of enforcing rights outside the jurisdiction, the costs of resolving conflicts of laws, and uncertainty about the legal rules. In addition, technologies that allow encryption and anonymity may increase the costs of identifying and tracing law violators.

It arguable that to the extent self-enforcement is perfect, the prices of goods and services are likely to come down. Consider, for instance, the price of copyrighted works. The price has to cover not only the large investment in creating and marketing the work, but also the cost of enforcement, and the expected loss from failure to fully enforce the rights of the copyright holder. If the expected market for a music publisher is substantially reduced due to the creation of unauthorized copies, the publisher will raise the price per copy in order to cover his expenses. If enforcement by the code prevents the creation of unauthorized copies, the price of copyrighted works is bound to decrease. This argument has been often raised by advocates of recent anti-circumvention legislation.

Yet, enforcement by the code is not costless: it involves the costs of developing a technology and preserving its technological superiority, so that it would not be bypassed by counter-technology. In addition, the finance structure of the enforcement costs is different: costs of self-enforcement by the code are usually borne by users who wish for protection, whereas the burden of administrative costs of the legal enforcement system is usually distributed among all taxpayers (Samuelson 1999, Samuelson 2001, Cohen 2000).

The efficacy of enforcement by the code depends on technological superiority and market advantage. Consider, for example, technological protection of copyrighted works. Its effectiveness depends on the absence of circumvention means. For every protection measure, there is always a counter-technology to crack it. The development of Cyber-technologies is dialectic in the sense that it has always involved developing measures to bypass, remove, or disable other technological measures. In fact, the development of circumventing means is the driving force behind the hacker culture, which is an integral part of the history of Cyberspace. Consequently, perfect enforcement and full compliance depend on the resilience of the technology to circumvention means. This may change over time, and in Cyberspace it changes rather quickly.

If enforcement is left to the code, it is likely that social resources will be invested in developing restraining measures as well as counter code-breaking and hacking tools. This may contribute to technological development, in that some inventions designed solely to bypass technological enforcement may sometimes have other uses (Samuelson 1999). Some economists, however, perceive this as economic waste. To the extent that resources are redirected for the purpose of merely developing protection and defeating measures, they represent economic waste (Dam 1999). What is perceived as a wasteful technological race is comparable to the waste associated with the pre-property regime. There, every member had to exercise self-protection measures to prevent the taking of what she considered to be her property, and such measures were confronted with counter measures. Thus, arguably, the legal system should intervene to prevent such waste. Regulation is thus needed as a second-degree enforcement control. This was possibly the economic justification for the anti-circumvention prohibition in the DCMA legislation (DMCA §§1201–1205), and similar provisions in the EU Directive on the Harmonization of Certain Aspects of Copyright and Related Rights in the Information Society (2001) (Articles 5–6) that resulted from the World Intellectual Property Organization [WIPO] Copyright Treaty, signed in December 1996 (WIPO Copyright Treaty 1996). This anti-circumvention legislation prohibits the manufacturing and distribution of technological means that allow the circumvention of effective technological measures used by copyright owners. This new regulatory strategy directly regulates technologies, their manufacturing and distribution, rather than regulating the behaviors of users.

As we discussed in Chapter 5, however, attempts to regulate technologies are risky in the sense that they impede innovation. Developing counter technologies or circumvention tools may have positive spillovers on the technology advancement, which is directed to productive avenues. There are still no empirical findings as to whether the sum of the conflicting effects of anti-circumvention tools is positive or negative.

In a different direction, traditional governmental enforcement systems may use Cyberspace to monitor their citizens and thus reduce enforcement costs. Monitoring online activity for the purpose of traditional enforcement may involve lower costs than real world tracing. In Cyberspace, enforcement agencies may efficiently collect information not otherwise available to law enforcement agencies. This information is not related to specific law violations, but serves as a general database that can be used whenever the government wants to crack down on various groups, specific activities, etc. This may reduce enforcement costs outside Cyberspace. However, this tempting option (for traditional national government) may violate our right of privacy and other human rights, violations that are also not transparent and are often hidden from the general public's scrutiny. Cyberspace can serve as a tool in implementing George Orwell's 1984 vision, or rather nightmare (Birnhack and Elkin-Koren 2003).

2.3 Enforcement by Technology and the Question of Choice

As we have seen above, regulation and enforcement by the code differs from the enforcement of rules by traditional law enforcement institutions in that it entails perfect performance, subject to its technological superiority. It does not offer users the choice of going by the rule or violating it. The architecture simply prevents any undesirable behavior from occurring. Consequently, the level of enforcement and its success do not depend on the extent to which the public comprehends and internalizes the rules; they depend on technological effectiveness. This may not leave room for deliberate and conscientious objection or disobedience to the law. In the long run, this feature might impair a desirable level of individual critical approach to law and authority.

The key question in this context from a law and economics perspective is, of course, whether it is justified to talk about enforcement by the code as part of the law. Economic theory may treat technology as simply a design or an architectural constraint because the notion of regulation under economic analysis of law assumes a choice. The underlying assumption of the economic approach to rules is that rational agents are able to control their behavior. They are motivated by their wish to maximize their utility. Rules are sometimes necessary to correct an otherwise distorted set of incentives (due to market failures), and provide individuals with appropriate incentives so they will choose to act efficiently. Unlike legal norms, enforcement by code does not provide a definition of undesirable behaviors, nor does it design a matrix of incentives. Regulation by code makes it possible to prevent certain behaviors while allowing others. If a design simply prevents a certain behavior, we can no longer talk about regulations and incentives, since choice is no longer exercised. Is it justifiable to talk about code as a normative system directing behavior through incentives?

A possible reply is that enforcement by the code can be violated by technology of counter coding. If we view such technological developments as possible, and the only question about their materialization is one of cost, it is arguable that from the perspective of economic theory the differences between traditional enforcement analysis and the analysis of enforcement by the code are not as significant as they may first appear. We may regard enforcement by the code as part of a legal regime after all.

The existence of choice as a prerequisite to the definition of law is related also to information about the substance of laws. The principle according to which laws should be public assumes that the law can affect the behavior of people, so they should be aware of it *ex ante*. Enforcement by the code involves serious problems of information about rules that are embodied in the code itself. Users may not have perfect information regarding the rules that are implemented by the code. The rules, as well as the code, are not directly accessible to people.

Take, for instance, the network services provided by Microsoft when it launched its browser. The hidden rules of the Microsoft network services allowed automatic reading of users' information on their hard drive without their knowledge. Another example is filtering systems, which allow users to rate third party sites. Such filtering systems may embody different judgments regarding what should be considered an appropriate material. Such criteria are hidden from the public eye (Lemley 1998). It is very difficult to get perfect information on how the program operates and which sites it would block. Users may learn what a particular program or design does and doesn't do from the way they function. This takes time and often some expertise. It may be difficult, for instance, to find out whether Internet browsers or programs used on Web sites collect and store information on users, as they often do, and to whom this information is available.

2.4 Technology as Law – Summary

The differences discussed above between the traditional system of law and law enforcement mechanisms, on the one hand, and regulation and enforcement by code, on the other hand, raise conceptual issues regarding the notions of enforcement and regulation and the definition of law. The literature on technological self-enforcement regards the code as a type of regulation. For example, Reidenberg (1998) endorses the *Lex Informatica* embodied in the code as the new and modern version of the *Lex Mercatoria* of medieval merchants. Similarly, Trachtman (1998) refers to these approaches that endorse regulation by the code as 'new medievalists'.

The simultaneous existence of, on the one hand, rule-making by technology and self-enforcement measures in Cyberspace and, on the other hand, the traditional legal system, requires some thought about their interface. The code and the legal system overlap in that both legal regimes simultaneously apply to the same people. They may conflict with one another; they may compete with one another; they may complement one another. Should the traditional law intervene to change rules created by technology and self-help methods of enforcement? Of what nature should such intervention be? What are the implications of self-enforcing means (technological or social) for the question of when and how the (traditional) law should intervene?

The traditional role accorded to the law under standard economic analysis of law is to correct market failures. In the case of a market failure, the role of law will be to alter the payoff functions of players in the market (Basu 2000). In other words, when economic markets as well as non-economic ones, do not function efficiently due to a market failure, the law will change the incentives attached to individuals' choices of action, and will thereby affect the strategies adapted by individual players in the market. This may include imposing fines, liability rules, etc. In Cyberspace, the target of traditional regulation may become the technologies that affect users' behavior rather than the behaviors themselves. This is largely owing to the information problem discussed above.

The law may provide negative incentives to circumvent such systems to prevent the waste involved in the technological race for means of security and anti-security. Legislation may also prevent implementation of a certain technology altogether. It may, for example, prohibit a program that allows invasion of private exchanges, e.g. reading all emails from any workstation. However, the law may do nothing, and thus require individuals who wish to protect their privacy to encrypt their messages. Regulating technological development, and especially prohibiting it, may be inefficient. Even if certain technological developments look like waste at first glance, they have 'unintended consequences' and may prove an important contribution to society and its welfare. The grounds, therefore, for intervention by traditional regulation are shaky.

Cyberspace is likely to transform our understanding of law. The way in which law is created is changing, with the introduction of greater decentralization. The way in which law is enforced is also under change, with the replacement of the traditional enforcement institutions – police, courts – by enforcement by the code. Cyberspace is leading to globalization, effectively decreasing municipal regulations and territorial sovereignty. The conventional territorial jurisdiction will not continue to be the dominant law-making arena, as Cyberspace users cannot know through which jurisdiction their activity is directed. This is bound to lead to a change of jurisdiction rules and their applicability to Cyberspace (in the American context see Burk 1996). This may cause transformation not only of law, but of the framework of the national state. In the future, technological zoning will create new communities, from which different laws might emerge, but which will be in increasing competition with the non-virtual community. We will elaborate on the possible changes to the normative economic theory of the state in the next chapter.

3. INGREDIENTS OF THE ORGANIZATION OF LIFE AND THEIR TRANSFORMATION BY CYBERSPACE

As indicated in the introduction to this chapter we find the Neo-Institutional law and economics the most suitable framework for analyzing law in the information age. It is the broadest framework of economic analysis insofar as it regards institutional structures as endogenous variables within the analysis of law. It perceives political structures, bureaucratic organizations, legal institutions, and other commercial and non-commercial entities as affecting each other, thus providing a framework for studying their interdependency, which is crucial in the new information environment.

Examining Cyberspace through the prism of Neo-Institutional law and economics reveals shifts in the structure and role of key institutions such as the firm, the state, and the law. The economic background for the emergence of such institutions in their current shape is changing, requiring an extension, and sometimes revision of the theoretical explanations offered by the literature. New modes of communication and production, the changing nature of work, and the shift to an economy centered around informational products further call for reexamination of fundamental distinctions. These include the work and leisure dichotomy and the distinction between the public and the private spheres.

But even this broad approach of Neo-Institutional law and economics bases its analysis, as the broader liberal paradigm in general, on two important ingredients which are assumed to be exogenous or pre-given: rational individuals, who are the atoms of society, and collective organization units, such as states, which are artificial and instrumental creations whose sole purpose is to enhance individuals' well being. Cyberspace might alter the basic notions of these two ingredients, bringing the whole project of law and economics to a critical point. We elaborate on these two ingredients, after discussing the ramifications of Cyberspace on the other essential component of economic analysis: markets and firms.

3.1. Cyberspace, Markets and the Theory of the Firm

For economists, markets are the primary forums for human interactions. Neo-classical economics related only to markets in which economic goods and services are traded. The broader framework of the economic approach to law extended this analysis to describe all possible human interactions (Posner 2003, pp. 23–24). The market paradigm is used to analyze criminal activities, children for adoption, legal rules and the like. The Neo-classical school describes the interaction between individuals and firms in the market, whereas firms are portrayed as individuals, or unitary units, which are geared to achieve a single ultimate goal by their market activity: maximizing profits. Neo-Institutional economics relaxes this simplifying assumption and portrays firms as complex organizations, comprised of various groups of individuals (shareholders or owners, managers and employees), each with a different type of utility function. The organizational structure of firms is thus understood as affecting their market behavior, and is therefore taken into consideration in the market analysis. With the extension of economic analysis to include non-financial deals, collective organizations such as government are also taken on board as players in various markets.

Ronald Coase can be regarded as the pioneer of the extension of Neo-Institutional economics. His emphasis on transaction cost was the cradle of the economic analysis of legal rules and their effects on market equilibrium (Coase 1960). Yet, transaction cost analysis was instrumental not only for the analysis of law, but also for explaining the emergence of the firm as a hierarchical organization that substitutes market transactions (Coase 1937). Coase's simplified argument was that in a world of zero transaction costs, there will be no firms at all, as the production of goods and services by joint efforts of various individuals will be achieved through contractual relations, i.e. in the general framework of markets, where individuals are the only players. Only positive transaction cost shifts activities from markets to organizations, or from market to hierarchies. This analysis is applicable (and indeed was applied) in the context of the theory of the state and government power, which was briefly discussed in the previous sections and on which we elaborate in Chapter 10. In the next few paragraphs, though, we offer a few initial thoughts regarding the original Coasian argument in the context of traditional firms and economic markets, as essential ingredients of the organization of life in Cyberspace.

a. Cyberspace, the theory of the firm and the organization of economic behavior

Cyberspace is changing the transaction cost structure associated with collective action, thereby affecting the role of firms in the organization of production and the use of resources. Two major aspects should be emphasized: internal and external. Internally, digital networks are reducing monitoring costs, the cost of collecting and processing information, introducing cost effective communication means and more efficient decision-making processes. The overall lower cost of organization is likely to change the internal structures of firms and the way they operate. Firms and rule-makers are already deliberating the possibility of conducting virtual shareholders' meetings and electronic votes. Smoother decision-making processes and better monitoring by shareholders might affect not only the inner structure of firms, but also the extent of government intervention regarding the protection of shareholders and the regulation of corporate structures and procedures. In this respect, there are many similarities between our analysis of the structure of government vis-à-vis Cyberspace in the previous sections and the structure of the firm.

Externally, under Coase's analysis, firms are likely to emerge when it is more efficient to organize economic activity through firms than through markets. The potential reduction in the organizational cost of firms would arguably turn them into a more efficient option for conducting economic activity. Yet, the reduction in transaction costs of collective action is also evident in markets. As we elaborated in Chapter 8, Cyberspace reduces the costs incurred by market players, allowing more direct exchange among them. Cyberspace reduces the search cost associated with identifying a suitable transaction and transacting parties, and the costs of negotiating, drafting and entering a bargain. Thus, externally, the balance between firms and markets is likely to change. If firms were conceived as the outcome of high transaction cost in markets, Cyberspace is bound, as we elaborated in Chapter 8, to shift activities back from firms to markets. In other words, lower transaction costs in Cyberspace may transform some production activities conducted currently within the framework of firms back into markets. This forecast also has similarities to our discussion regarding the extent of governments and states.

The combined effect of the internal and external factors is inconclusive. On the one hand, the external effects predict a shift back from firms to markets due to lower market transaction costs. On the other hand, lower transaction costs also characterize the internal operation of firms, muting the effects of the shift from firms to markets. Two examples might point toward the dominance of the external factor, as in both one can identify a shift from firms and hierarchies toward the market. The first concerns the shifts in the publishing industry; the second is a more particular example of the mapping of planet Mars.

Publishing in the non-virtual world is contingent upon excessive capital investment and a centrally managed operation of production. Printing and distribution tasks are performed by complex firms, comprising different groups of skilled employees. Publishing in Cyberspace is increasingly the result of decentralized efforts and direct interactions among individuals. While some individuals simply publish single-handedly their own writings on the Internet, others engage in collaborative efforts as writers, reviewers, and publishers of news, encyclopedias, or peer review publications, all which are outside the corporate hierarchy.

The second example, which is interesting from various perspectives (some of which we will cover in the next subsection), is the Mars experimental project launched by NASA, the U.S. aviation and space agency. In this undertaking, discussed extensively by Benkler (2002), NASA launched a challenge to Internet users to volunteer in the mapping of planet Mars. Clickworkers in this experimental project were invited to assist in mapping small portions of Mars landscape by performing tasks such as marking craters on maps of Mars or classifying marked craters. The project was designed in such a way that the volunteers were given small overlapping segments, and the accumulation of the findings corrected for possible discrepancies and mistakes. The project resulted in mapping equivalent to the work of several full time paid scientists working for a year, and yielding the same qualitative results. Like the publishing example, the Mars project proves that lower transaction costs can shift complicated work conducted by several professionals within the hierarchy of an organization to the masses operating voluntarily, on the same basis of contractual relations in the open market.

Benkler (2002) offers more radical conclusions based on these observations (though limited to the production of informational goods). He disputes the dichotomy between markets and managerial hierarchies as the only two competing models for organizing economic behavior, a dichotomy entrenched in the works of Ronald Coase followed by Oliver Williamson (1975). Benkler identifies a third institutional alternative for organizing production activity in Cyberspace. In what he describes as *commons-based peer production*, large and medium scale collaborations among individuals to produce informational goods are organized without markets or managerial hierarchies.

Several attributes of the networked information environment facilitate, according to Benkler, the emergence of this mode of production. The object of production is information, the primary production resources are, first, human creative input (which is highly diversified) and second, informational goods (which are non-rivalrous). Finally, the cost of information processing, communication and exchange dramatically declined. This third mode of production is based neither on authority and hierarchy nor on market signals. Benkler perceives markets and firms as instrumental in reducing uncertainties faced by agents in evaluating different courses of action. While markets manage individuals by attaching price signals to alternative courses of action, firms manage the use of human and other resources through central command and hierarchy. Signals originated by agents higher in the hierarchy of the firm are accorded different weights.

In the case of creative production of informational goods, the process of specification within markets or firms suffers two major deficiencies, according to Benkler. One is information loss involved in specifying the complex and diverse creative tasks and individual creative capabilities. The other is the prohibitively high transaction costs associated with specifying each individual and each resource, which force us to prefer common standards rather than perfect specification. Pricing of individual creative efforts tends to be very crude. Commons-based peer production, Benkler argues, has a substantial information advantage over alternative institutional organization for producing informational goods. The organization of work by way of self-assignment remedies the information loss associated with specifying creative tasks. Individuals know best which tasks suit them in terms of their skills and motivation. They are able to undertake tasks and perform them for complex motivational reasons, even if they are unable to neatly define or price them ex-ante. Human creativity is especially difficult to manage through contracts and managerial command, because the high diversity in talent, interest and motivation makes it difficult to specify. Consequently, if individuals can self-identify themselves for tasks and assign themselves to projects, transaction costs involved in specifying tasks and capabilities are low, and the information loss is minimized. Benkler therefore concludes that *commons-based peer-production* has certain systematic advantages over these two modes of production in identifying and allocating human creativity.

We agree with Benkler that Cyberspace transforms the production mode in the direction of decreasing the role of firms. However, we believe that Benkler's analysis of commons-based peer production can be accommodated within the market paradigm. It, indeed, highlights the limits of narrow market analysis, which equates the notion of market with a price system. But the production features identified by Benkler can be analyzed within a broader perception of the market, expanding some of its traditional assumptions to maintain its explanatory and predictive virtues. The market paradigm can incorporate a more complex view of human motivations, departing from wealth maximization as the single instructive attribute of human behavior, and acknowledging diversity and heterogeneity in motivations. Market analysis can also adapt itself for analyzing dynamic decision-making processes that cannot be neatly codified by prices.

Neo-Institutional economics allows a broader understanding of markets, which goes beyond the simple price system. In fact, economic markets existed well before the notion of money and prices emerged. Barters were conducted in the framework of economic markets. But the Neo-Institutional school goes further and portrays every collective decision mechanism – political, social or other – as a sort of market interaction. Mercuro and Medema (1997, p. 130) identify two fundamental building blocks of Neo-Institutional Economics: individuals who are rationally pursuing their self-interest, subject to constraints (rationality includes the concept of bounded rationality) and the idea of wealth maximization – the search for institutional structures that enhance society's wealth-producing capacity. The operation of individuals in the new information environment can be analyzed in terms of rational behavior, especially where the emphasis is on bounded rationality and on preferences or utility as opposed to wealth. An extension is needed, however, regarding the second building block: wealth producing capacities may not be the ultimate goal of collective action and institutional design.

It is arguable that most current economics and especially law and economics writings do not sufficiently capture the information environment and the human role in generating it. Individuals often do not aim at *producing* an informational good, but rather at drawing a painting, playing music, writing software. *Creating* cultural artifacts is not perceived by the creators as production, but rather as human innovation and self-expression. Market exchanges, transactions and competition do not adequately capture the real nature of how public discourse takes place and culture really emerges. We do not trade views and meanings, we share them. We do not trade one piece of information for another, but rather build a knowledge base. We don't consume ideas, but rather nurture and develop them through interaction.

This does not necessarily mean, however, that we must give up the market paradigm of rational actors engaging in voluntary exchanges. Awareness of the limits of codifying the value of different courses of action, as demonstrated in the context of creative processes, may suggest that some conclusions based on these simplifying assumptions would be unsound. It may, however, provide a methodology for studying the gap between the simplifying assumptions regarding the world and economic behavior. The economic science can be defined as a methodology to analyze human interaction. The methodology of economics comprises the simplification of the complicated reality to an environment modeled analytically. These models allow the study of interconnections between various variables and inference from the model's results to the more complicated reality. The soft point of the science of economics is the nature of the simplifying assumptions. In the next subsection we try to identify features of the new information environment that should bring us to change some of the underlying assumptions with regard to production in Cyberspace.

The economic behavior of programmers contributing to the Linux project or marking craters on maps of Mars can certainly be understood in terms of market exchange. For example, had a potential contributor to either project assessed that the time needed to make an appropriate contribution would bring her to a state of hunger, the contribution would not have been made. Opportunity costs are relevant to the individual decision whether to participate in such a project, and in this sense, individuals do price their contributions. Such contributions are also shaped by the exchange terms. Different individuals will reach different decisions on whether to participate in specific production efforts and how much to contribute, as a direct function of the explicit or implicit terms relevant to the final production. Acknowledgments, publicity, reputation, propertization are only few examples of the contractual terms under which a contribution decision is made.

Self-assignment of projects is certainly a shift from hierarchies and firms, but it is, in fact, the heart of market activities, which are founded on individual free will and voluntary exchange. This is further accentuated by another advantage identified by Benkler. Peer production, he argues, also has an allocation advantage, allowing individuals to freely explore informational goods and collaborating partners in search of suitable resources that fit their interests and needs. When production is organized through the firm, transaction costs associated with property and contract impede access to human resources and information goods. Property and contract make clusters of agents and resources sticky: employees will prefer to work with human and informational resources affiliated with the firm, even when it would be more efficient to use resources that happen to be in another firm. Costs involved in property and contracts may prevent an otherwise efficient use.

All this is true, but it explicates the shrinkage of firms rather than of markets. The freedom to search for the appropriate collaborating partners and suitable resources is the core of market activity. The complexity and diversity of individuals' motivation and unique capabilities makes it difficult to codify and price, but the notion of market can definitely be stretched to cover such complexities, as it can capture human creativity, and human interactions involving scientific studies, creative production of cultural artifacts, or innovating new technologies. We believe that the emerging production mode in Cyberspace can be analyzed within the market paradigm. However, it consists of new market features, which have not received enough attention from the economics literature, to which we turn in the next subsection.

b.   Markets, atomization, work and Cyberspace

The Mars example we discussed above is fascinating for reasons other than the institutional changes in production. The work conducted by thousands of participants in the project was done free of charge, and, as described above, resulted in output of the same quality as of specialists' paid work. This elicits three important insights. The first is connected to the definition of work in economic literature, as contrasted with leisure. The second related insight is connected to the atomization of production. The third is related to specialization and professionalism.

The economics literature distinguishes between work and leisure, although it acknowledges also a dialectical relationship between these two notions and some overlap (Gramm 1987). People are assumed to work if they are compensated for what they do, while leisure activity is usually costly, i.e. people generally pay for it. Leisure refers to activities that are largely pleasurable, relaxing, fun, recreational and spiritually or emotionally (but not financially) enriching. It is often defined as time devoted to activities that are primarily conducted for their own sake, rather than for control over financial or other resources that the activity might produce (Nock and Kingston 1989; Cottle and Lawson 1981). Work, unlike leisure, involves compulsion (Gramm 1987). The limited time available requires individuals to choose their preferred combination of work and leisure, by definition sacrificing one for the other. Every individual decides on his or her personal mixture of the two. Thus, even if leisure does not bear a direct cost (like sitting in the garden and enjoying the winter sun), it is expensive in the sense of opportunity costs. Presumably, instead of sitting in the sun, the individual could have opted for more hours of paid work.

What is interesting in the context of the Mars project is that NASA considered the activity of thousands of individuals as work, for which it did not compensate. The participants' combined efforts saved the full salary of several skilled scientists. The participating individuals, however, considered their involvement as leisure activity. The result is obviously more efficient than what would have been achieved in the traditional markets. The same output was produced at the minimal cost of constructing the software, which aggregated the individual contributions (which was much lower than the cost of full salaries to several skilled scientists). In addition, the same software can be used again for similar project at marginal cost.

The blurred distinction between work and leisure and the dual function of the same economic activity phenomenon is connected to the second insight – the atomization of production efforts. The most important factor in the success of the Mars project was the fact that the participating individuals were asked to contribute a negligible amount of time to perform their share. Had people been asked to dedicate days or even several hours to do such a task without payment, many would have declined and the project would have not been materialized. The willingness of people to engage in an activity considered work, or contribution to production, without being paid, is a function of time. Unlike most economic models, the function of the willingness to work for different pay schedules is probably not continuous.

This broken-up function might not have been of great importance in the old economy, where transaction costs would have impeded the collection of atomized work efforts, but this is not so in the new technological world. Information technologies and networking substantially reduce the cost of coordination and integration (Weber 2000; Benkler 2002). In other words, people might have been willing to dedicate several minutes of their time to the joint effort of building a car, by coming to screw a pin or place a button, but the costs of organizing such a project, mobilizing people to the car factory etc. would have made such a project non-viable. This is not the case with many production avenues in Cyberspace. Such possibilities should receive appropriate attention from economics, and from law and economics, as this avenue raises legal questions, from tax law to liability and torts, which have not been addressed so far.

The third insight is more philosophical in nature, and relates to the quality issue. It was found that the masses of clickworkers in the Mars project produced an output which was of the same quality as the work of professional scientists. This raises serious questions vis-à-vis the economic theory of specialization. If laypeople's efforts through atomization, overlapping work, and sophisticated mechanism of aggregation and integration, can produce the same quality as specialized work, some important and established features of economic analysis have to be re-visited. The common economic wisdom is that if two individuals produce two goods, a process of specialization will result, in which each individual produces one good and exchanges some of it for the other good produced solely by his counterpart. This will make both individuals and thus society, better off. If this lesson can be extended to value judgments, as opposed to quests for scientific truth, the implications are more far reaching, as they touch upon the aggregation of preferences, decision-making theories and indeed, political philosophy.

3.2 The State as a Basic Collective Organization Unit

The models of the economic approach, including the Neo-Institutional generation, assume that individuals will engage not only in individual actions (within or bypassing markets), but will benefit from collective actions. The economic approach, as liberal theories from Hobbes to Rawls, views the state as the most important collective organization or institution, and presupposes that markets correspond to states, which are basically territorial units. A social contract, or other form of collective action, is carried out by citizens of a specific territorial unit, which becomes a state or other form of a national unit.

Central government, its organs, and structure are analyzed in a territorial context. This is true even for the broad approach of Neo-Institutional law and economics. Thus, in his recent book Barzel (2002, p. 4), for example, writes:

> The state consists of (I) a set of individuals who are subject to a single ultimate third party who uses violence for enforcement and (II) a territory where these individuals reside, demarcated by the reach of the enforcer's power.

One of the most interesting features of Cyberspace is the bankruptcy of this territorial conception of community and, by derivation, of law, thus threatening the traditional concept of the state.

Cyberspace breaks the territorial units from several perspectives. First, markets in Cyberspace are global. A user sitting physically in North America can do business with another user located in Asia. For that matter, no differences exist between this transaction and a virtual transaction she conducts with a user just across the street. Second, not only business, but also community activities – discussion groups, political groups, common culture and entertainment activities, cross geographical borders, developing new common and distinct cultural and social norms that are a-territorial. In fact, Cyberians can simultaneously find themselves members of several communities that are very different.

Third, virtual activity, when translated to actual electronic bits that are transferred from one user to another, may cross many borders. Communication between two next-door neighbors may pass through several other countries. Cyberspace users cannot even know through which jurisdiction their activity is directed (Burk 1996). Finally, not only market and communal activities break territorial borders, the ability to bypass markets and inflict externalities does the same (Post and Johnson 1997a). While in the physical world externalities were a phenomenon attributed mainly to geographic neighbors, 'pollution' in Cyberspace can be inflicted by remote players, where violation of privacy and pornographic sites are just two examples.

The implication of the borderless nature of Cyberspace on economic analysis is highly significant. One can no longer take the state as the relevant framework for market activities, for decision-making calculus or for institutional analysis. This change is significant in both the normative and positive domains. Thus, while traditional normative law and economics analysis take the state as the basic maximization unit, which has implications on the definition of externalities and the analysis of other market failures, this cannot be the case in the networked information environment. Likewise, positive economic analysis is trickier, again because the identification of markets is less straightforward than in the old world.

3.3 The Individual as the Basic Unit of Economic Analysis and Cyberspace

Cyberspace transforms not only the notion of collective communities, but also that of the individual, who is the basic unit for liberal philosophy of the state and for economic analysis. In the non-virtual world the basic unit of reference – the individual – is one person with a single identity, passport or driver's license number, a specific address and distinct physical features. In Cyberspace, the atomistic unit of analysis is a username with a password and an electronic address. There is no strict correlation between the Cyberian individual and non-virtual individual, as the same physical individual can appear in Cyberspace as several entities, each with different identification features and a different character, belonging to different communities. Likewise, several physical individuals can appear in Cyberspace as one virtual entity.

While conventional economic thinking, Neo-Institutional included, perceives individual preferences in the non-virtual world as exogenous to the political process and to the economic markets, Cyberspace requires us to internalize even the analysis of individual preferences. Conventional economic analysis assumes that our basic identity, which can be framed in terms of various sets of preferences, is the result of distinguished historical, cultural, linguistic and even climatically different backgrounds (Montesquieu [1748] 1977). Those background factors are pre-given and predate any formation of markets and collective action organizations, such as states or other national units. The definitions of state boundaries, however, are very much influenced by these ancient groupings of preferences. Even if preferences change as the result of market interactions, such as successful marketing and advertising, they are initially founded upon these ancient differences, some of which are presumably almost permanent.

Cyberspace can be viewed as threatening this perception, because it blurs historical, cultural, national and even climatic boundaries. The Indian teenager who spends 10 hours a day in front of her computer has more in common with her German Cyber-counterpart, than with an Indian her age 25 years ago. The decline of some of the more physical attributes of online users is accompanied by the pervasive effect of information technologies on processes such as individuation and will-formation. The online information environment constitutes the human condition of our time. People spend a large chunk of their time using the Internet for entertainment, business, social relationships and political activities. For an increasing number of people, some real-world activities are becoming and will become marginal. Rather than going to schools and universities, paying a visit to the public library or the museum, people view art, obtain knowledge and spend their leisure time in Cyberspace. Instead of driving to the supermarket, the bank, or the social welfare borough, people click several buttons on their computer to do business, communicate with government agencies, or settle their finances.

The comprehensive character of the online environment makes individuals more vulnerable to external effects that shape their preferences. The emergence of media, communications and software multinational conglomerates, and the rise of new monopolies described in Chapter 6, not only affect economic competition in the market for ordinary goods, but also affect individual autonomy. As phrased by Barber (2000):

> The new monopolies are particularly insidious because while monopolies of the nineteenth century were in durable goods and natural resources, and exercised control over the goods of the body, new information-age monopolies of the twenty-first century are over news, entertainment, and knowledge, and exercise control over the goods of the mind and spirit.

Power exercised by private economic agents is relevant for the formation of preferences also in the public sphere. Powerful market players that control the means of producing informational goods are better positioned to express their own agendas and thereby marginalize diversity (Barber 2000; Netanel 2000).

When power accumulated in the market is used in the public sphere, it tends to distort equal participation and reduce fair access to participation means. Informational goods, such as news and data, but also photo images, music, novels, comics, or computer programs reflect an ideology, and may shape one's identity and presences (Barber 1995). Informational products affect their own demand. Consequently, centralized power in such a marketplace could be very powerful in shaping preferences and agendas and reducing plurality, as well as social and political diversity.

Individuals in the online environment are therefore cut off from their historical, cultural and geographical context, on the one hand, and widely exposed to a relatively homogenous information environment, which affects their preferences, on the other hand. Indeed, a globalized market for goods could benefit from a relatively homogenized body of consumers, consuming goods under fairly standard interoperable settings.

We are in an interim stage of Cyber-revolution. In the future, Cyberspace may cause the disappearance of diversity, which in the non-virtual world fosters the definition of the unique self, leaving us with a brave new homogenous human being. Thus, economic analysis has to internalize one of its basic foundations – the existence of atoms – individuals – whose basic features are given. A fresh way of thinking, if not a fresh paradigm of economic analysis, must emerge in which these basic presuppositions with regard to individual preferences will be internalized.

4. SUMMARY

The transformation by Cyberspace of the two basic ingredients – the state as the major collective unit of analysis and the individual as the atom of it, together with the transformation of production activity – have bearing on the changing concept of law, and on the whole project of the economic analysis of law. We will further address the internalization of preferences issue, as well as the concept of the state, in the context of next chapter's discussion of political theories so far perceived as outside the paradigm of economic analysis.

10. The Effects of Cyberspace on the Economic Theory of the State

In this chapter we will delve into political theory and examine the ramifications of Cyberspace on the theory of the state, or more precisely, on the normative economic analysis of the state, which is, in fact, one version of the liberal theory of the state. Cyberspace may affect the economic analysis of the state and its main powers and governing tools on both the normative and positive levels. In Chapter 9 we focused on positive analysis vis-à-vis the Neo-Institutional economic theory. We argued that Cyberspace might challenge the notion of states as independent identifiable entities and is likely to transform collective action and rule-making processes.

In this chapter we offer a normative analysis, launching a totally fresh line of arguments, examining collective action, rule-making processes and the organization of the public sphere. While in the previous chapter we explored the impact of Cyberspace on the concept of law via the question 'what law is', we focus here on the question 'what law ought to be'. We ask whether the new technological frontiers opened by Cyberspace have any bearing on the liberal theory of the state (or on the economic theory of the state). We enquire whether the current concept of representative democracy governed by checked and controlled majority decision-making, which is the bread and butter of liberal democracies today, can be sustained. For this purpose, we develop a detailed theoretical argument beginning from initial moral principles, and leading to a detailed account of the desirable structure of government and the collective decision-making process. It will become apparent, however, that this pure normative argument regarding the state, its institutions and its collective decision-making process, is contingent upon significant elements of positive analysis.

The Western world celebrates two centuries of liberal democracy in theory and about one century of liberal democracy in practice. Concepts such as majority decision-making, representative government, human rights, the rule of law and separation of powers have become self-evident. Our debates concerning the good state and good government take these concepts as presuppositions, which do not require additional justification or reasoning. Indeed, we live in the paradigm of Liberalism. The term 'paradigm' was coined by Thomas Kuhn, when he put forward a theory about the development of natural science (1962). But his description of the evolution of science can be extended to the way we think about normative issues, about practical laws rather than merely theoretical ones.

The current political theory discourse is conducted within the boundaries of the Liberal paradigm. The current debate is based on a set of presuppositions, which was left unchecked through the past 100 years. The paradigm of Liberalism, which is the result of the Enlightenment, as well as technological breakthroughs of the modern era (such as the invention of the printing press), has been shaken by the technological revolution of the last decade. This chapter examines whether Cyberspace requires a paradigmatic shift in our thinking about collective action, the public sphere and the state.

We begin with a brief history of economic analysis of the theory of the state, followed by mapping the normative sources of such theories. Subsequently, we construct a fresh skeleton argument for a theory of the state, based on the consensus leading normative principle, and in light of the effects Cyberspace may have on the various links in this argument.

1. ECONOMIC ANALYSIS AND THE THEORY OF THE STATE

Since the 18th century works of Borda (1781) and Condorcet ([1785] 1955) on majority decision-making, the economic approach can be viewed as having a stake in analyzing the 'state', its organs and its tools conducting and coordinating the activity in the public sphere. *Public Choice* is the major branch of economics that focuses on these issues, as it is interested in economic analysis of non-market decision-making, or in individual decision-makers as participants in a complex interaction that generates collective decision-making and political outcomes (Mercuro and Medema 1997, p. 84). Questions related to the theory of the state are also dealt with in the framework of Game Theory (Baird, Gertner and Picker 1994). Indeed, Hobbes' Leviathan ([1651] 1979) can be regarded as the first game theory-based explanation for the creation of modern states. Likewise, the main stream of Neo-Classical economics on its various branches, or the traditional *Microeconomic* paradigm, in both normative and positive levels of analysis, is also employed as a methodological tool to discuss various questions related to the theory of the state.

On a positive level of analysis, the various economic methodologies aim to explain why institutions are structured the way they are and how these structures affect the outcomes of social or collective choices. On a normative level, different theories offer an ideal model for the structure of government, the division between constitutional and post-constitutional arrangements, the desirable form of separation of powers and related questions. Some of the differences between the models are the result of different starting points with regard to the leading moral principles that ought to guide collective action. Thus, most Chicago school law and economics writings aim at wealth maximization as the ultimate normative goal, while most public choice literature is constructed upon the social contract tradition, or its economic equivalent – the Pareto principle.

The microeconomic analysis of the emergence of the state focuses on possible market failures, which justify central intervention in the market. Such central intervention requires the existence of a state and central government. More particularly, the market failure of public goods is often portrayed as the main rationale for the very establishment of the state (Buchanan 1975, pp. 35–52, on the normative level of analysis; North 1981 on the positive level). One of the major goals of such a creation is to enable economic markets to operate, thus establishing property rights and ensuring that they will not change hands, bypassing the markets. The ability to operate markets is itself a public good which needs a central pre-market intervention in the shape of political entity such as the state. The creation of property rights is also one of the focal points of the contractarian view of the state (Skogh and Stuart 1982).

In recent years Neo-Institutional law and economics is engaged in projects in which the traditional market analysis – microeconomic or welfare economics – is incorporated with the public choice paradigm.[1] The new theoretical and methodological frameworks brought about an increasing interest of the economic approach in the analysis of the public sphere, exemplified by the recent writings on constitutional law and economics (Mueller 1996, Cooter 1999, Voigt 1999). However, it is important to bear in mind that the two branches that are the sources for the new writings – microeconomics theory or the Chicago School Law and Economics, on the one hand, and Public Choice, on the other – have different historical sources and normative backgrounds. We will elaborate on these different exogenous foundations in Section 2.

2. MAPPING THE NORMATIVE SOURCES OF THE ECONOMIC THEORY OF THE STATE

Before delving into the details of the economic theory of the state, and the possible effects Cyberspace may have on it, let us sketch a thick brush map of theories of the state, and try to locate the economic theory within this map.

The oldest and still most important debate within jurisprudence (the theory of law) is the debate between Positivist theories of law and Non-Positivist

---

1   The new political economics, the new institutional economics, positive political economics and the new economics of organization, can be viewed as some of the sub-branches, or related branches of the new-institutional law and economics. See Mercuro and Medema 1997, ch. 5.

theories, prominent among which are Natural Law theories. One can point at a similar, indeed parallel, framework with regard to the theory of the state, a framework that goes back to the great Greek philosophers. Plato viewed the state, similarly to his view of the law, as a natural creation, while Aristotle viewed it as man-made. The economic theory of the state is naturally in the Aristotelian path. As the broader liberal paradigm, the economic approach originates from the 18th century Enlightenment – an intellectual and cultural movement that emphasized reason, knowledge, human interaction and progress. Indeed, one of the most important foundations of the economic approach is the presupposition of rational individuals, who are the atoms of society. It views collective organization units, such as states and governments, as artificial and instrumental creations whose purpose is to enhance individuals' well-being.

The Positivist approach to the state is also the intellectual setting for the emergence of the Social Contract theories, which are the bedrock of most modern theories of the state, among them liberal democracy, as well as the economic theory of the state. Social contract theories view the emergence of the state as the result of a contract between its future citizens. The focal point in this view is the normative justification for collective organization, decision-making and enforcement. The justification rests on the initial consent of all those who subject themselves to the state, and for the sake of this general framework it is less important to specify at this stage whether this consent is real, hypothetical, counterfactual etc.[2]

What is important to emphasize is that the consensus principle of the social contract theories closely resembles the Pareto improvement criterion of microeconomic theory. Both justify collective decision-making only if it is supported by all individuals who are affected by it. Individuals would support a decision if it enhances their well-being or leaves them indifferent in comparison to their well-being prior to the decision. Hence, consensus will bring Pareto improvement or Pareto optimality (Coleman 1988, part IV). However, there is also a significant difference between the two. While the Pareto principle was offered as second best to utility maximization, the consensus principle is the leading normative principle of the social contract theories of the state, and the economic theory that follows this tradition.

To better understand this important difference, we have to go back to the common cradle of both principles – the Enlightenment and its view of rational individuals as the center of moral philosophy or political morality. From this common origin one can point at two parallel (chronologically and substance matter) developments. One is the birth of the neo-classical economic theory; the other is the framework for public choice theory of the state.

---

2   See the interesting debate between Richard Posner (1979 & 1980) and Ronald Dworkin (1980) with regard to this point.

Many regard Adam Smith's *The Wealth of Nations* ([1776] 1961) as the birth of modern economic science. The invisible hand that brings free markets to equilibrium is still one of the bedrocks of microeconomic theory. This monumental work was published a few years before Utilitarianism – Jeremy Bentham's ([1789] 1948) new moral theory – was launched.[3] Although Adam Smith was also a moral philosopher, and Bentham was also writing on economics, no direct connection was made between Smith's economic theory and Bentham's moral philosophy. This connection was made only a generation later by the Neo-Classical economists, who adopted for their market analysis the assumptions of Utilitarianism, and advocated the market solutions as those that maximize total utility. The works of Harsanyi (1955 and 1977) can be regarded as a direct offspring of this heritage, applied to the analysis of the constitution. Under several postulates, constitutional choices, according to Harsanyi, should reflect maximization of expected individual utilities.

It is important to highlight the new paradigm within which Utilitarianism and micro-economic theory were nurtured. This paradigm assumes that individuals are rational, that they opt for choices that maximize their happiness or utility or welfare, and that there is no value in society beyond the values individuals attribute to every decision or action. These presuppositions leave room only for a limited debate as to what is the best way to aggregate or balance between individuals' well-being or individual preferences, when a collective choice is needed, and what are the optimal collective institutions and procedures to achieve this aggregate. The Utilitarian answer, which was adopted by Neo-Classical economic theory, was that maximization of the sum of individual utilities is the right normative criterion.

But economists faced a problem with the implementation of the maximization of utility as the leading normative principle. How can individual utility be measured, and how can it be compared across different individuals? When the market is fully competitive, argued the economists, there is no need for such measurement, as the invisible hand or the market powers through voluntary interactions will bring about the desirable equilibrium, which maximizes social utility. But markets are usually not fully competitive. In most markets there are market failures, which require central intervention, and then the application of utility maximization principle is problematic.[4]

The micro-economics theory of the early 20th century found two solutions to the practical difficulties with utility measurement and comparison. One

---

3 Utilitarianism challenged the traditional Natural Law moral theory, which saw good and bad as pre-given and independent of individual human well-being. Utilitarianism sees good and bad only in context of individual well-being, where the total utility of all individuals is the criterion for the good.

4 There were other difficulties with Utilitarianism on both moral and practical grounds. Who should be included in the utility calculus and what is the right time frame for such a calculus are some of these secondary questions. However, most economists were not really bothered by these crucial questions.

solution resorted to ordinal preferences – a weaker assumption that individuals can rank various options, but cannot attribute a precise utility measure to each. This solution is reflected by the Pareto principle. The other solution was put forward by welfare economics: substituting utility with wealth. Money units are measurable and comparable. It is important to emphasize that both paths view themselves as second best, while utility maximization is still the desirable ultimate normative goal. This is also the reason why Richard Posner's (1979) advocacy of wealth maximization as the leading normative principle is innovative and departs from traditional welfare economics: it views wealth maximization as the leading normative principle, rather than the second best.

The Social Choice and Public Choice literature originate from different Enlightenment scholars who shared the same presupposition about human rationality. This tradition goes back in time to encompass the social contract philosophers – Thomas Hobbes ([1651] 1979) and John Locke ([1690] 1989). It passes through the works of Borda (1781), Condorcet ([1785] 1955) and Charles Dodgson (who was none other than Lewis Carroll). Their 20th century followers include Duncan Black (1948), Kenneth Arrow (1951) and James Buchanan (1975). The incorporation of the positive analysis of social choice theorists and the normative analysis of the social contract philosophers resulted with the works of Anthony Downs (1957), James Buchanan and Gordon Tullock (1962) and John Rawls (1971). The corresponding normative analysis of the latter direction was based on unanimity rather than maximization of utility (or, later maximization of wealth).

The unanimity or consensual principle is neither teleological (consequential, like Utilitarianism) nor deontological (governed by natural law). It belongs to a set of principles that judge desirability according to the decision-making process. Majority rule belongs to this group, but majority decision-making does not have any coherent and integral normative justification. Unanimity, or consensus, does. Under the assumption that individuals are rational, no one will give his or her consent to a decision that harms her. Thus, every decision will benefit at least one person, without harming any others.

In a world of no transaction costs (or no market failures), the requirement of unanimity will lead also to utility maximization. If there is a decision that enhances the total utility, consensus would be achieved to accept it, as it will be possible to compensate all those who are harmed by the decision, while those who gain will be better off; thus everyone will vote for the decision. This principle, therefore, guarantees individual rights (set by each and every person) and is also efficient in the sense of Pareto optimality. However, in the real world, transaction costs are not zero and very few collective decisions can be reached by consensus. So, as will be elaborated below, unanimity is the base line, from which rational individuals will depart in order to enable society to handle its daily business.

As indicated above, the Public Choice-Social Choice theory of the state is structured upon the social contract theories and the consensus principle. There is, however, a secondary but not less significant debate within social contract theories, where Thomas Hobbes represents one pole and Jean Jacques Rousseau ([1762] 1998) represents the other. This debate was also the source for the major controversy of the American founding fathers: between Pluralists and Federalists, on one side, and Republicans and anti-Federalists, on the other side. This debate is important also in the context of the economic theory of the state, as this theory can be viewed as founded or as a direct continuation of Hobbes' social contract, rejecting Rousseau's analysis.

Spelled in modern economic terms, Hobbes views individuals as rational and self-interested, with a set of preferences which are exogenous to the collective decision-making process and institutions.[5] Thus, the collective sphere is principled on bringing about an improvement for some individuals without impinging on the well-being of others. Hobbes portrayed a minimal or very thin social contract, in which all people are prepared to deposit all their rights in the hand of the Leviathan in exchange for personal security. Locke had a broader view of the content of the contract, and modern legal philosophers of this tradition, e.g. Rawls (1971), have yet a broader view of the content of the social contract. This view contrasts Natural Law approaches, which hold that the good is divine or precedes human conception of it, but also contrasts 'Communitarian' social contract approaches, which assume that there is a value in society beyond the values reflected by the preferences of its individuals. Such is Jean Jacques Rousseau's theory, which views the General Will (or the general good) as distinct or separate from some kind of summing of all individuals' wills.

We are unaware of any attempt to present Rousseau's work in the framework of an economic analysis. Yet, we think that such an attempt is worth exploring, especially in the context of Cyberspace and its effect on the theory of the state. From an economic analysis perspective, one can present Rousseau's theory as differing from Hobbes and his tradition in one important assumption or presupposition. Economic analysis à la Rousseau assumes that individual preferences are not exogenous, but endogenous to the political process. In other words, the difference between the General Will and the sum of the wills of all individuals can be presented as the result of changes of preferences, from self-regarding toward more cooperative and less conflicting preferences. This change of preferences is the result of collective endeavors,

---

5   The presupposition regarding the 'good' is linked to the rationality-self interested assumption, but it ought to be emphasized that this assumption does not necessarily mean that individuals seek to maximize only wealth, as often some economic models assume with regard to the behavior of 'ordinary' individuals. It also doesn't mean that individuals seek to maximize only political power as often is assumed with regard to the behavior of politicians or other actors in the public arena. The rationality-self maximization assumption requires only that individuals are able to rank various options facing them in every juncture of decision-making, and that this ranking is complete and transitive.

such as deliberation and participation. We will return to this important theme later.

Let us examine now how, on the basis of the unanimity normative principle, a theory of the state can be derived, and how Cyberspace may affect the traditional liberal democratic notion of the state.

3. THE ECONOMIC THEORY OF THE STATE – THE SKELETON ARGUMENT

So far we have laid down the possible leading normative principles for a theory of the state. We will continue by adopting *consensus* as this leading principle, setting aside deontological theories, on the one hand, and utility or wealth maximization, on the other hand, although we will refer to those normative guidelines as well. What follows are several links in a chain construction of a theory of the state. They are based on the consensus principle, alongside analyses of the effects of Cyberspace on each link of the argument.

3.1 The Justifications for the Creation of States

The common theme of most Positivist theories (as opposed to Natural Law theories) that discuss the creation of the state is that the establishment of the collective entity called 'state' can benefit the individuals who are to become its future citizens. The meaning of 'benefit' is, of course, contingent upon the substantive-normative foundations adopted by each theory. But these foundations are not limited to a consequential (teleological) or procedural sort of morality, such as Utilitarianism, wealth maximization or Pareto optimality or consent. They are broader than the common foundations of the economic approach. This idea of transformation from a state of anarchy to a centrally governed society was put forward by Thomas Hobbes in *Leviathan* ([1651] 1979). Indeed, Hobbes can be viewed as both the founder of the social contract theory of the state and the founder of the economic theory of the state. His ideas were rephrased in economic language in the second half of the 20th century, by, among others, Downs (1957); Buchanan and Tullock (1962); Buchanan (1975); North (1986) and Mueller (1996, pp. 51–54).

There are different contemporary variations of this idea. Some theorists emphasize that the establishment of the state, or any political society, is a response to the market failure of public goods. Those goods will not be produced (or will be under-produced) in the absence of a central collective organization. Thus, the state is created, according to this rationale, because it enables the production and consumption of public goods, which are not produced or supplied in the state of nature (Buchanan 1975, pp. 35–52). Defense and justice are two of the most significant examples of such goods (the former is the sole justification for the establishment of the state according to Hobbes). The mere ability to operate markets founded on private property and voluntary transactions is another such good (John Locke justified the state as a common mechanism to protect private property).

Others theorists view the emergence of the state in a way similar to Coase's (1937) description of the emergence of the firm – a result of vertical integration. This is caused by transaction and information costs associated with contracting within markets, which force production and exchange out of the markets and into organizations such as the firm or the state (Silver 1977; Macey 1988). A related view portrays the state as a framework for providing alternative institutional arrangements to contracts in the free market, which cannot be negotiated due to high transaction costs (Tullock 1982).

These rationales focus on market failures as the justification for the creation of the state. But one must keep in mind that even in a perfect market with no failures whatsoever, a collective organization will be required to ensure that the market will not be bypassed. Markets cannot operate without the concept of private property (Easterbrook 1996, pp. 212–214), and a collective organization is required to create and protect private property. The state is also required to ensure that market transactions are followed by the parties to the transaction and by third parties. This applies even in a perfect world where there are no internal market failures impeding the conclusion of efficient transactions.

Cyberspace may have an effect on all of these rationales. For instance, Cyberspace, as we have seen in Chapter 5, can remedy some public goods failures by enabling exclusion through the usage of sophisticated technological means, thus turning some goods that were public in the non-virtual world into private goods. This is true for some public goods, which can be distributed by, or through, Cyberspace, such as education or information (these goods can easily be excluded and commodified in the online environment). It is also applicable to other goods traditionally provided by governments, such as the provision of tools of enforcement, for example of contracts or of intellectual property rights. Indeed, powerful technologies allow individuals to rely on self-help means for executing and enforcing their contracts, thereby reducing (though not diminishing) their reliance on the state's enforcement services. It is not true for other public goods such as defense and health. Having said that, since Cyberspace may also break the territorial notion of political communities, it may abridge the need for traditional defense methods, diminishing the demands for such services, while creating new security needs across territorial borders. We will touch upon this point below.

As noted above, Cyberspace challenges the territorial notion of communities and thus of the state as a collective organization that resides within specific geographical borders. The traditional social contract literature, as well as the economic theory of the state, assumed that the only sensible way for organizing communities is along territorial units, thus viewing the state as reflecting a distinct geographical unit. Montesquieu ([1748] 1977) even argued that differences in political cultures are the result of climate and geography. Indeed, the borders between existing political units are heavily influenced by geography. All this is significantly altered by Cyberspace. Geography does not play the same central role in the creation of commercial, cultural, social or political communities in Cyberspace, and Cyberian citizens face similar climatically and geographical conditions – they sit facing the computer screen in a closed room. There is no significance whatsoever to mountains and oceans that separate physical locations. In fact, communication between two next-door neighbors can pass through several continents in the same way as communication between geographically distant individuals.

Be that as it may, these changes may affect the compass of the state and the division between the public sphere and the private one. But as long as the Cyberian citizens have to walk out of their computer room to the nearby grocery, as long as they may be threatened by non-virtual burglars, these developments would not abrogate altogether the justification of the state or a similar collective entity with a direct link to some territorial considerations.

3.2. The Formation of the State

The establishment of the state is viewed by the economic approach as the result of a contract, to which all individuals who are its future citizens are parties. In political or legal terms, this contract is dubbed 'constitution'. This consensual agreement is portrayed by some scholars (e.g. Rawls 1971, Posner 1979) as a hypothetical consent, and indeed, we can hardly find historical examples for full consensus as to the content and wording of the constitution.

However, the drafters of constitutions who set the terms for their ratification in many cases make a serious attempt to obtain very wide support for the document as a condition for its adoption. This can characterize the process in which the United States Constitution was ratified (a unanimous vote of the constituent assembly and ratification by all future states' legislatures), as well as the more recent process of adopting new constitutions in the countries of Eastern and Central Europe, which have undergone a transition from communism to democracy (Salzberger and Voigt 2002). In the majority of these countries the constitution was the result of an agreement in roundtable talks including representatives of all political groups followed by referendum. The consensual mode or justification for a constitution brought many constitutional documents to reflect numerous compromises and additions of various articles in order to obtain general consent.

At any rate, conventional constitution-making is perceived as possible only through the work of agents – members of constitutional assemblies – rather than a product of the general consent of all future citizens of the emerging entity. In many cases, however, the constitution-making process was conditional upon approval by general referendum. The reason for the need of agents is high decision-making costs. In the physical world, these costs might be so high that it will be impossible to obtain consensus. In Cyberspace, these costs are significantly lower, though some costs associated with choice might be higher, as we elaborated in various previous chapters of this book (particularly Chapters 8 and 9).

Information technologies enable not merely cheap and widespread communication of individual preferences, but the employment of software that can aggregate preferences, negotiate bargains across different issues and identify resolutions and packages that enjoy consensual support. In addition, the weakening of the strict correspondence between territories and political entities, combined with the cheap exit option, enable the formation of communities or states. These entities comprise various individuals around the globe who have common or similar preferences, enabling better outcomes of collective action in terms of satisfying individual profiles. Online communities increasingly emerge instantly, organized ad-hoc, to serve an immediate, often limited, agenda.

Even if territorial entities are still needed to produce goods or services which are territorial in their nature, such as defense, the role of such entities diminishes as they co-exist alongside non-territorial collective entities. The development of worldwide threats to personal security, in the form of global terrorism, often indifferent to geographical borders, can be analyzed in the same context. The idea of governments without territorial monopoly was put forward, without special attention to Cyberspace, by Bruno Frey (2001, 2003). The ability to conduct collective debates and voting through the Net contributes to this breakdown of the territory-dominated collective organization and to the proliferation of collective entities, as it also weakens the role of intermediaries in the process of establishing collective organizations.

What should be emphasized here is that from a pure normative point of view, formation of collective entities, such as the state, can be justified only by the consent of all the members to the general framework and basic rules of these entities. Cyberspace enables us to get closer to this utopist idea, a fact that should cause us to re-think the current conventions with regard to constitution-making processes.

Thus far, we outlined the justifications for a collective decision-making mechanism, which might interfere with the private sphere. According to the leading normative principle, however, this collective mechanism ought to be founded on the basis of the contractual or consensual principle. We also saw that the new world of Cyberspace weakens this rationale and the scope for justifiable collective actions, but does not discard it altogether. It seems that we still need a collective organization based on a social contract of individuals living in the same geographical proximity. However, this agreement can exist side by side with other social contracts of individuals who do not live in the same geographical areas. In this sense, Cyberspace has an important role of breaking the monopoly of the traditional state and creating alliances across territorial borders.

3.3 The Rise of Central Government

The contract, or the constitution, should lay down the basic principles guiding the interactions of individuals – the protective role of the state – and the basic principles dealing with collective action, its productive role (Buchanan 1975, pp. 68–69). In its protective role the state serves merely as an enforcement mechanism of the various clauses in the social contract, making no 'choices' in the strict meaning of the term. In its productive role the state serves as an agency through which individuals provide themselves with – produce and allocate – 'public goods' (Gwartney and Wagner 1988).

In the old (pre-Cyberian) world, the rationale for the establishment of the state, in fact, merges into the rationale for the rise of central government, as Mueller (1996, p. 57) puts it:

> The constitutional perspective towards government sees its normative foundation as resting on the unanimous agreement of the community in the constitutional contract that creates the government, a unanimous agreement that arises because the institutions defined in the constitutional contract are designed to advance the interests of all citizens.

The unique features of Cyberspace, especially regarding enforcement (see Chapter 9, Section 2), may lead to interesting insights on these two functions of the state – its protective role and its productive one. We will also have to examine whether the combined rationale for the establishment of the state and the emergence of central government exists in Cyberspace.

The argument of the economic theory of the state justifying the construction of central government goes like this: The initial contract, obviously, cannot foresee every potential problem in both domains – the protective and productive roles of the state, especially where the constitution is designed to be in force for a very long time. According to the unanimity rationale, the solution for a new public issue would have been to gather everyone whenever a new problem arises, and to decide upon it unanimously. But such a solution would involve immense decision-making costs, or 'internal costs', in the language of Buchanan and Tullock (1962, pp. 63–84). This is the major justification, given by most scholars, for the need to have a central government in which the powers to protect and produce are deposited, or, rather, entrusted. It is intended to represent the will of the people. In contractual terminology, the establishment of central government and other state institutions is the result of uncertainties that exist in each individual's mind about the future of the society in which one lives and about the future behavior of other members of that society (Mueller 1996, p. 61).

The two solutions offered by modern democratic theory to the immense costs of maintaining unanimous decision-making in the public sphere are representative democracy and majority decision-making. Indeed, the Athenians' support for majority rule and the appointment of government personnel by lottery were intended to overcome the difficulties of consensual decision-making (although the latter remained the ultimate goal). The modern developments of representative democracy and the tools designed to overcome its fallacies (such as the separation of powers), sought to overcome the same difficulties.

Representatives acting on behalf of their constituents save the costs of frequently measuring public preferences on each and every issue and the prohibitively high costs of coordinating massive numbers of people. Cyberspace significantly reduces the costs of communicating and processing individuals' preferences. It makes it possible to efficiently collect information from individuals by asking them to click their preferences directly onto the screen. It reduces transaction costs involved in collecting information about preferences, yet increases some cost associated with individual choice (see Chapter 8).

Cyberspace also facilitates fast and cost-effective information processing that allows real-time feedback on public preferences and choices. This, in turn, lessens the need for agencies and for their scope of functions. The reduced costs of coordination and communication diminish the extent of collective action problems. If transaction costs involved in co-ordination are low or nonexistent, there is no need for representatives – intermediaries – to reflect the aggregated will of their constituents. Individuals may directly communicate their preferences on each and every matter.

Imagine that every morning we were asked to vote on several policy issues, and the various motions could pass only by consensual support or by a supermajority. This sounds like a remote dream in the non-virtual world, but it becomes increasingly feasible in the virtual world. Policy makers may efficiently collect public comments on bills posted on the Internet. The low cost of communication and information processing enables governments not only to consult the public but also to delegate to the public the actual decision-making powers. Not only can this vote be carried out swiftly and cheaply, technology offers automated negotiation tools that facilitate the ability to reach compromises on various issues, so that a consensus or near consensus can be reached. Information technologies may provide tools for diverse stakeholders to actively participate in policy making. Automated simulations, for instance, may support deliberation and debate on various public issues such as urban planning, education, environmental concerns and budget allocation.

In addition, low transaction costs allow individuals who were unable to get organized in the non-virtual world, to become organized. Connectivity, interactivity and search tools reduce the cost of identifying relevant parties, communicating, acting together, and spreading information that concerns all. The ability to collaborate with individuals outside the territorial boundaries of the state may create new interest groups that were unable to get organized in the past due to high transaction costs. This can lead to increased democratization and decentralization of rule-making processes, in whose various stages Cyberspace allows groups and individuals to participate.

From the perspective of economic theory, two important problematic phenomena which exist in representative democracy ought to be mentioned, as they are toned down significantly in Cyberspace. The first is agency costs, which are associated with representative government. These costs are the result of ineffective monitoring of representatives by their voters and the ability of the former to act in a self-interested manner without being penalized by voters (or where the costs of the penalties are smaller than the political or personal gains). Cyberspace allows citizens to take a more active part in governance, and to effectively monitor government actions. The easy and relatively cheap access to information and the lower costs of collective deliberation and action in Cyberspace are likely to increase the effective monitoring level and thus reduce these agency costs.

The second phenomenon of representative democracy is the power of interest groups to seek rents at the expense of the general public, and make gains through pressure on the representatives. Interest groups are able to succeed in their actions because of the costs of collective action. These costs allow only small groups to organize – groups whose potential gain from collective action is higher than the costs of organization (Olson 1965, and in the legal context see Farber and Frickey 1991, pp. 12–37). Cyberspace, as indicated above, tends to lower the costs of collective action, which in turn enables broader interest groups to organize, bringing more equality to the political markets and diffusing the impact of narrow interest groups.

A separate economic rationale for central government in general and representatives in particular, comes from the theory of specialization. Traditional economics assumes that specialization can contribute to total welfare. Applied to the theory of government, this rationale can imply that better collective decisions would be reached if those decisions were reached by specialized bodies – administrators or politicians, who devote their time to studying carefully the issues and possible courses of actions. Cyberspace may affect this line of argument as well. We elaborated in Chapter 9 on the NASA project to map Mars. One of the interesting findings from the experiment was that the accumulated efforts of many individuals was found equivalent (in quality as well as quantity) to the year-long work of several specialists. This finding stands in conflict with the specialization rationale. One can induce that if this is true with regard to scientific projects, it may well be applicable to decision-making which involves value judgment and scientific or professional components.

It is unrealistic to assume that, had we been asked to take part in all public decision-making, we would have researched and mastered every question we were dealing with. However, the individual decision regarding which areas to study and in which votes to take part, signals the intensity of our preferences in this area. A regular dichotomous vote does not reveal the intensity of preferences. This is one of the deficiencies of majority decision-making, in light of the consensus normative principle (and for this matter, also in the light of utilitarian morality). The participation of everyone in every decision, which is made possible in the new technological environment, will also assist in revealing intensity of preferences. This, in turn, might enable departure from a strict unanimity rule toward some qualified majority.

Parliaments in many countries are currently engaged in various projects to delegate more decision-making powers to the public at large or to incorporate the general public in the decision-making process. However, from the theoretical and normative perspective of Liberalism, it is the public at large that delegates powers to representatives. The rationales for such delegation, such as the immense decision-making costs of the public at large, are seriously impaired by the technology provided by the Internet. In other words, when legislators and other politicians talk today about more participation of the general public in their work, they speak within the current democratic paradigm, in which representative government and majority decision-making are taken as given normative truths. Yet, the opportunities for collective action in Cyberspace call for reexamination of the existing paradigm. We should rethink whether representative government, and indeed, central government is needed at all, and if so, whether it should be guided by majority decision-making.

3.4 The Republican Twist and Law and Economics

The challenge to the justification of representative government is highly significant from a Republican theorist's point of view. Some Republican theorists of the state, in contrast to Liberal theorists, emphasize that central government is needed not only to reflect the preferences of the general public in a more efficient or cheaper way, but to lead the community toward civic virtues and 'better' preferences. This idea was phrased sharply by Edmund Burke in his famous *Address to the Electors of Bristol* (1774). He said: 'Your representative owes you, not his industry only, but his judgment; and he betrays, instead of serving you, if he sacrifices it to your opinion'. Other Republican theorists emphasize the need of the desirable political community to have not only technical mechanisms of preferences aggregation through representatives, but also a more substantive content to the public sphere, which will enable real deliberation and participation by all individuals.

The Republican view rejects the notion that the democratic scene is a competitive marketplace of ideas that must be kept free so it can best reflect the aggregated choice of citizens. Political institutions, according to the Republican view, shape public discourse, and thereby affect preferences. Preferences are considered a by-product of a political process that takes place in the public sphere and are shaped by deliberation or sometimes by the inability to deliberate. The way public discourse is structured affects the way individuals develop their ideas, shape their positions, identify their interests, and set their priorities. Preferences do not exist prior to the deliberating process, but are rather the output of political processes. Institutions and processes which are based on individual participation and responsibilities, it is argued, are likely to shift self-centered individual preferences into more public-regarding preferences. This latter Republican idea is reflected by Rousseau's distinction between the general will and the sum of individual wills or preferences.

One of the major arguments of the Republican perspective of the state (as it was, for example, put forward by the anti-Madisonian or anti-Federalist group among the American founding fathers) is that civic virtues can be developed by the participation of citizens in government, their exposure to different and conflicting views and the deliberation of these views (Sunstein 1988). Participation in the public sphere is likely to shift self-centered individual preferences into more public-regarding preferences (Sen 1987). Civic virtue describes an *other-regarding* rather than a purely *self-interest* approach—a willingness to give priority to the communal interest. Civic virtue thus enables participants in their capacity as citizens to undertake responsible decisions that are informed by, and respectful of, the claims of other groups and individuals. This may also enhance the well-being of individuals by creating a sense of communal belonging and social solidarity.

We indicated before that there are hardly any attempts to incorporate Republican thinking into the economic approach.[6] In fact, one can reconcile the two, or phrase some of the Republican theorists' claims in economic terms. In economic terminology, Republicans view individuals' preferences as endogenous, rather than exogenous, to the political process. They believe that deliberation and participation may change individual preferences to be more other-regarding, thus enabling a higher sum of utilities in collective actions or an ability to reach a superior point on the Pareto frontier. This is the reason why the American Republican founding fathers (or anti-Federalists) opposed a strong federal structure for the USA, in which, according to them, individual involvement in the public sphere would be minimal, the preferences of

---

6 Farber and Frickey (1991) incorporate Republican thinking into their Public Choice and Law analysis. However, they generally conclude (p. 45) that the two theories are in conflict, and they incorporate Republican thinking into law and economics only at the positive level, showing why Republican assumptions can explain, for example, the rare occurrence of collective decision-making problems, such as cycling. They do not go as far as implementing Republican thinking as to the basic assumption of economic models regarding the origin of preferences. See also Mashaw (1988).

individuals more self-regarding, and thus, the outcome of collective action would be worse.[7]

From a Republican perspective, Cyberspace might change the conditions for achieving desirable participation and deliberation. On the one hand, the ability to deliberate and participate in Cyberspace is much less dependent upon the number of participants and especially on their geographic distance from the major collective institutions of central government. The picture of Mr. Smith from the Midwest, who is so remote from the power centers in Washington that he loses interest in the public sphere, is no longer true for Cyberspace. The ideal Athenian city-square can be achieved in Cyberspace with many more participants who do not gather physically, but virtually. The Swiss Cantons' excuse not to grant women voting rights because there is no physical place where they can join the general assembles in the main square cannot be sustained.

From the Republican perspective, the way information markets are structured is of great importance for shaping preferences since preferences are not prior and exogenous to the political process, but rather an output of that process. Processes in the *public sphere* should be given a broad understanding to include all discursive will formation processes that take place in our cultural life (Elkin-Koren 1996). Cyberspace facilitates more opportunities for individuals to undertake an active part in the public sphere. While public discourse in the pre-Cyberspace age was facilitated exclusively by the mass media, online exchange allows more individuals to directly communicate with each other. The low cost of communication provides individuals with more affordable access to news, large databases, and cultural artifacts. Yet, not everyone is hooked up to the Net, and many do not even know how to use a computer. Within the limits of the digital gap, Cyberspace is (potentially) accessible to all and significantly expands the number of potential participants in public discourse.

Digital networks further affect the quality of participation in the public sphere, enabling interactivity and facilitating more active involvement. Participation is no longer limited to passively consuming television shows and editorials of major newspapers. There are increasing opportunities to speak out and actively take part in online debates, by using talkbacks, posting one's own positions and analyses in online forums, and challenging the views of others. The low cost of producing and distributing informational goods (see Chapter 5), and the interactive nature of digital representation, allow

---

7   This is, it should be emphasized, only one interpretation of Republic thought. Whether the differences between Rousseau's General Will and the sum of individual preferences can be attributed to the shift of preferences which is the result of collective organizations attempting to convince the general public as to the best course of actions of society, is an open question. Some Republicans would probably argue that this is not a fair and full view of the Republican perception of the public sphere. We will not elaborate on this interesting philosophical point here.

individuals to participate in creating their own cultural artifacts, publish on their own Web pages, adopt fictional characters to reflect their own meaning or political agenda, participate in collaborative writing of online stories or report news to a newsgroup. Online discourse, therefore, opens up opportunities for transforming the structure of public discourse from the mass media scheme of one-to-many, to a more decentralized, and more democratic many-to-many structure.

On the other hand, Cyberspace may create new types of problems, which are relevant to the Republican view of collective organization and action. In Part II we discussed at great length the effects of Cyberspace on the information markets. We showed that Cyberspace may facilitate new types of monopolies and centralization (Chapter 4) and offer new measures of control over informational goods and cultural artifacts (Chapter 5). When production of content is centralized, few bodies determine what becomes available to the public, thus limiting the choices regarding which values, identities and positions to adapt. Accumulation of control over content through standards (Chapter 4), pervasive use of intellectual property laws to limit technological developments (Chapter 5), or impeding access to information by search engines (Chapter 6), may interfere with the opportunities for participation described above.

Another type of problem is discussed by Cass Sunstein in his book *Republic.com* (2001). Sunstein argues that the architecture of Cyberspace can encourage people to close themselves in homogeneous communities or enclaves, immune from diverse views, and thus in danger of being part of Cyber-cascades. This, according to Sunstein, will eliminate shared national experiences and the real deliberative nature of democracy will be lost. In economic terminology, Sunstein argues that Cyberspace may make people more egocentric in their preferences and less other-regarding. Thus, from the point of view of collective decision-making, the result will be worse for everyone.[8]

These claims, however, are made in the framework of the old paradigm of representative democracy and in the context of the traditional territorial conception of society. They are also made under the assumption of lack of regulative intervention in Cyberspace or against specific content of regulation. They are not made against the new technological frontiers or the development of Cyberspace as a provider of new opportunities for forming, expressing and negotiating preferences and for forming new a-territorial communities. In other words, Sunstein's argument is made in the context of the debate regarding whether Cyberspace should be regulated, and if so, how, and not in the context of examining how Cyberspace might affect our basic philosophy of the state.

---

8 In the past, Sunstein (1995, p. 1783) argued that Cyberspace, in contrast to the Madisonian vision of the state, enables large-scale substantive discussion, which brings us closer to the deliberative democracy or the Republican vision of the state. This is somehow different from his more recent arguments in *Republic.com* (2001).

We may agree with Sunstein in his conclusions as to the question of whether Cyberspace should be regulated. But this question is a false one anyway, as the architecture of Cyberspace is itself a form of such regulation (Lessig 1999), and there is no real option, therefore, of abstaining from its regulation. The only question is how to govern it (Salzberger 2002), or what is the substance of such regulation. Be that as it may, we do not share Sunstein's concerns regarding the loss of social cohesion, the alienation and isolation in homogeneous Cyberian communities. This may be true in an interim stage, but we think that even at this point, Cyberians are more exposed than those in the non-virtual world to differing views. In the long run, however, we can expect a process in which all preferences will be endogenized and even homogenized (Elkin-Koren and Salzberger 1999, pp. 579–580).

To summarize, the Republican perspective expands the traditional reasons for establishing a central government beyond a good (and cost-saving) representation of the public preferences, focusing on its role in shaping individual preferences. Many Republican theorists focus on political participation of citizens in government as a process that can produce civic virtue. From this perspective Cyberspace offers more opportunities for participation, potentially bringing participating individuals toward more cooperative and responsible preferences and choices. This, in turn, can diminish the need for central government even in Republicans' eyes. Cyberian communities managing their own affairs with no central government, it can be argued, will bring the participating individuals towards more cooperative and responsible preferences and choices. Having said this, Cyberspace may facilitate new types of monopolies and centralization in information markets (see Chapters 4 and 5), thus interfering with such opportunities for participation. In any case, adopting the Republican paradigm vis-à-vis Cyberspace ought to direct us to a significant modification of the definition and roles of traditional central government.

From both perspectives of collective action – Liberal and Republican – Cyberspace enhances opportunities for participation of individuals in setting the rules, thus facilitating decentralization and democratization of rule-making processes. Rules may be increasingly created in a bottom-up fashion, and therefore, in the absence of the failures discussed above, reflect more diversified social and economic interests in increasingly complex societies. A legal regime in which individuals are able to directly communicate their preferences has several advantages over a legislative process exercised by elected representatives. Individuals are able to reflect their preferences directly, hence more accurately. This reduces the chances of mistaken assessment of public preferences and therefore inaccurate setting of the rules. This factor should be viewed as an advantage from both Republican theory and Pluralist-Liberal vantage points.

3.5   The Shift from Consensus to Majority Decision-making

So far we touched upon one pillar of the existing liberal paradigm of the state –
representative government. We now turn to the other pillar – majoritarianism.
Regardless of the question of who should operate the state – its citizens in a
form of direct democracy or a central government representing the public in
large (according to Pluralists) or guiding it (according to Republicans) – there
is a no less important issue of the desirable daily decision-making rule. The
economic reasoning for the shift from consensus to majority rule is best
represented by the model of collective decision-making set by Buchanan and
Tullock's *Calculus of Consent* (1962). This model can be considered one of the
classical presentations of a normative analysis of collective decision-making in
the framework of the consensus principle. It is a good reference point for the
analysis of collective action in Cyberspace.

Buchanan and Tullock distinguish between external costs of collective
decision-making and internal costs. The former is the total costs to individuals
negatively affected by the collective decision. These costs diminish, as the
majority that is required for reaching a decision is larger. In unanimous
decision-making the external costs are reduced to zero, as rational individuals
will not grant their consent to decisions that harm them. A super majority
decision-making rule will, on the average, impose less external cost than a
simple majority. A dictator's rule (one dictator has the power to make the
decisions) inflicts the highest external costs on the members of his or her
community. The internal cost function reflects the costs involved in the
decision-making process itself. It is shaped in an opposite way to the external
cost function: dictatorial rule is the least expensive to operate. As the majority
required for passing a decision is greater, so are the costs involved in the
decision-making process. Consensual rule is the most expensive to operate.

The optimal decision-making rule, according to Buchanan and Tullock, is
the one that minimizes the sum of the two types of costs. Buchanan and
Tullock show that in most areas this optimal rule is a simple majority, but there
might be special types of decisions in which the optimal decision-making rule
is a qualified majority. These latter types of decisions are usually characterized
by asymmetry between the external costs and benefits inflicted on the
members of the community, e.g. decisions that touch upon basic human rights,
for which the costs to the members whose rights are violated are far greater
than the benefits to the others. The Buchanan-Tullock model is one of the few
modern justifications for majority rule.

The application of this analysis to Cyberspace is interesting. Its results
depend on the definition of the Cyberian community. If we regard the whole of
Cyberspace as the unit of analysis, we believe that the external cost function
will not change notably in comparison with the non-virtual world (subject to
the assumption that individual preferences are exogenous to the political

process), while the internal cost function – the decision-making costs – will decrease significantly. Collective decisions, as we have already discussed, are cheaper to arrive at because of lower costs of information, negotiation, and communication. If the marginal cost function of decision-making as related to the majority required for deciding is more moderately sloped, we can expect the optimal decision-making rule to be greater than a simple majority. Hence, the democratization in Cyberspace is reflected not only by weakening the dependency on representative structure and the agency costs it is associated with, but also by shifting the decision-making rule from simple majority towards unanimity, all within the framework of consensus as the leading normative principle for collective action. This can increase the total well-being of the members of the community.

So far we have referred to Cyberspace as one community. If, however, we view Cyberspace as a conglomerate of communities, a change will also occur with regard to the external-costs function. This is because of the exit option, which is much easier to opt for in virtual communities. The availability of this option is likely to decrease the external cost function in addition to the internal cost function. This might not change our conclusion regarding the optimal decision-making rule, as this conclusion is contingent upon the marginal functions of both types of costs. But this assumption will lead us to an even greater total advantage from collective action, as for every decision-making rule, the total costs – decision-making and the reduction in one's utility – will be lower than the equivalent decision-making rule in the non-virtual world.

To summarize, the new technological frontiers enabled by Cyberspace ought to make us re-think two fundamental ingredients in the current liberal democracy paradigm – the need for a central and representative government and the adoption of majority decision-making. In the traditional economic theory of the state, both are the result of immense costs that will be incurred when operating a state by direct democracy based on unanimous decision-making. We tried to show here that the new technological frontier of Cyberspace might weaken the justification for central government and majority decision-making. It may, however, not discard these two foundations altogether, but fresh thinking is needed as to the functions, decision-making process and scope of operation of central government, as well as to its structure – the next point in our analysis of the economic theory of the state.

3.6 The Organization of Government – Separation of Powers

We talked about the justifications for the state and its central government. The next link in a skeleton argument for the economic theory of the state concerns the structure of central government. This desirable structure ought to be derived from the list of functions assigned to the state. The list of these functions is embodied in the rationale for central government itself. Here we want to explore their specification and organization. The doctrine of separation of powers is the major structural principle of the economic theory of government. Separation of powers can be viewed as comprising several components: separation of functions, separation of agencies, separation of persons and a form of relations between the powers. Let us elaborate on each of these components and examine the effects Cyberspace may have on their traditional analysis.

a. Separation of functions

There are two types of separation of functions; one of them is usually overlooked. We have distinguished between the protective function of the state and its productive function. The protective function is connected mainly, but not exclusively, to the constitutional stage and the binding force it exercises upon post-constitutional collective processes. The productive function is related mainly to the post-constitutional stage (Buchanan 1975, pp. 68–70). From a theory of state point of view, this distinction should be considered as the more important grounds for separation of functions.

A second functional division of central government is between rule making, rule-application and rule-adjudication, or, as they are more commonly called, legislation, administration and adjudication. History reveals that this functional division has always existed, regardless of the era (or at least long before the doctrine of separation of powers was under discussion) or the type of regime (Montesquieu [1748] 1977, Book I, Section 3). This phenomenon also has an 'economic' logic: governing according to rules, their application and their enforcement, rather than making each decision individually and independently, is more efficient. It minimizes transaction costs from the point of view of the government or of the decision-makers, as it is cheaper to apply a rule than to deliberate every question from initial principles. It also minimizes agency costs from the viewpoint of the citizens, namely the exercise of individual control over the government, by providing certainty and predictability (Brennan and Buchanan 1985, Chapters 6–8).

Cyberspace may alter both divisions of functions. The primary division – between the protective and the productive functions – is a direct consequence of the shift from consensus in the constitutional stage to majority rule in the post-constitutional stage. This separation of functions loses its magnitude if such a shift is not needed, as described in the previous section, if at least a greater share of collective decisions can be reached by consensus rather than by majority vote even in the post-constitutional stage, or in the realm of the productive function of the state. In other words, if post-constitutional collective decisions can be reached through direct votes (rather than votes of representatives) using unanimity or super majorities, the distinction between constitutional and post-constitutional spheres loses its viability.

The secondary division (between rule-making, rule-application and rule-adjudication) is also blurred by Cyberspace. First, Cyberspace can provide technological means for enforcement that can replace some of the existing human institutions (see Chapter 9 and Elkin-Koren and Salzberger 1999, pp. 574–577). Thus the need for enforcement apparatus as a separate governmental function diminishes. Second, the regime of norms in Cyberspace is less hierarchical than in the non-virtual world. In contrast to the conventional pyramid of norms, in Cyberspace we are likely to see overlapping and contradicting norms. Individuals could have greater freedom to subject themselves to certain norms and not to others. This phenomenon blurs the distinction between general and individual norms, or between rules and their executions. This point adds to obfuscating the boundaries between the three traditional functions of central government.

b. Separation of agencies – constitutional versus post constitutional organs

There is a long way, both historically and conceptually, between mere separation of functions and the separation of agencies. The latter principle has a significant effect on the structure of government, because, according to it, not only do the three functions – legislative, executive and judicial – exist, but they should be carried out by separate institutions or branches of government. Before discussing this type of separation of agencies, however, let us spare a few words on the separation of agencies aspect of the earlier distinction between the protective and productive functions of the state.

A careful look at the role definition of the protective and the productive functions will result in the conclusion that corresponding separation of agencies is necessary due to the conflict that arises between the two functions. While the protective state is aimed at enforcing the initial contract (the constitution), the productive state is engaged in activities involving production of public goods for which the costs are shared by the individuals, and hence involve re-allocation of resources. There are, naturally, conflicting desires within the productive state, but in the non-virtual world their resolution cannot be based on unanimity (as we have explained, the optimal decision-making rule, which takes into account the excessive costs of the decision-making process, will depart from unanimity). Conflicts between the outcomes of the productive state and the initial social contract are, therefore, to be expected.

The productive state will tend to overstep the boundaries of the initial contract, aiming to reach its 'technical productive frontier' (North 1986; Eggertson 1990, pp. 319–328). This may be worsened by principal-agent problems between the government and the people, interest-group politics and rent-seeking activities (Gwartney and Wagner 1988, pp. 17–23; Eggertson 1990, pp. 350–353). The protective state will not take into account the benefits of any one alternative against its opportunity costs, and its outcomes will not necessarily be the set of results which best represent some balance of opposing interests (Buchanan 1975, pp. 68–70). Even if the productive state will be guided by utility maximization or wealth maximization, it will not compensate those who become worse-off from the decisions, because their votes will not be needed to pass decisions (unlike the case where unanimity is required for passing a decision). For these reasons, it is desirable to separate the agencies assigned to fulfill the protective and the productive functions.

Parliaments in the physical world are the main institutions of the productive state. Separating the protective and productive agencies means that parliaments should not be given constitution-making powers. The constitution is aimed at limiting the powers of the parliament, and it will not perform its tasks if it is drafted and approved or amended only by parliament.

In the post-constitutional stage, the protective function is of a judicial nature, and in most Common Law countries it is indeed assigned to the judiciary; but it is distinguishable from the role of the judiciary within the productive state. Indeed, in many Civil Law countries, the protective function is assigned to a body such as a constitutional court, which is not perceived to be part of the ordinary judiciary. This distinction between the regular court system and the constitutional court makes sense vis-à-vis the rationales for separating agencies of the productive and protective states. The constitutional court has to be independent from the post-constitutional organs of the state, but accountable to the people. The regular courts, whose main task is to adjudicate disputes between individuals, must be independent from the public, but less so from the post-constitutional organs of government.

Cyberspace, as specified above, blurs the distinction between the productive and protective states, and this should also have bearing on the need for separate agencies. Furthermore, even under the assumption that some sort of separation of functions is needed, the necessity for separating agencies diminishes. The problems with the productive state in the non-virtual world are toned down in Cyberspace, as (1) rent-seeking problems decrease, due to the low costs of collective organization and (2) agency costs are lower due to the improved technological methods of principals to monitor their agents. To this, one has to add the ability in Cyberspace to shift the decision-making rule of the productive function from simple majority towards unanimity, as well as the low exit costs of shifting from one normative regime to another.

c. Separation of agencies – Legislature, executive, judiciary

Let us return to the more familiar separation of agencies between the legislature, executive and judiciary, which can be seen as a division of powers within the productive state. The productive state can be perceived, from a microeconomics perspective, as a micro-decision unit (like a firm) or perhaps as a set of micro-decision units (like an industry), producing primarily public goods. In this context, separation of agencies is connected to the monopoly problem (Silver 1977; North 1986; Whynes and Bowles 1981). The concentration of all governing powers in the grasp of one authority creates a vertically integrated state, which has monopoly powers, or even discriminating monopoly powers. Monopolies cause inefficiency and a distorted division of wealth between the producers and the consumers, i.e. in the case of the state between the government and the citizens.

There are several possible ways to promote competition in the case of the state as a monopoly: the existence of other states, to which it would be possible to emigrate, namely the 'exit' option (Hirschman 1970), a federal structure (Tullock 1969; Posner 1987, Mueller 1996), and the separation of agencies. These forms of promoting competition can be regarded as substitute measures. Thus, a more accessible exit option can soften the need for separation of powers. Likewise, a federal state weakens the need for a rigid separation of powers. As we have noticed before, Cyberspace increases the possibility to use the exit option, at least with regard to some sort of public goods (e.g education, culture, community services). This means that in the Cyberian era, the necessity of a strict separation of agencies might be weaker than in the traditional world.

It is important to note that the rationales for separation of functions and for separation of agencies are different. Theoretically, one could devise a structure of government in which separated agencies are performing similar functions. It can be argued, however, that in the non-virtual world, de-monopolization through separation of agencies assigned to carry out the various functions (every agency performing a different function), or a vertical disintegration of the state, would be efficient, as derived from a basic rule of economics – the rule of specialization and trade. But separation of powers can also increase the production costs due to a combination of higher communication costs and reduced costs of non-optimal operation (Posner 1987, pp.11–14).

The efficacy of separation of agencies and its correspondence to the separation of functions, therefore, will also depend on the size of the society or jurisdiction (Silver 1977). It can be argued, for example, that American-style separation of powers does not suit smaller countries. This may be one explanatory factor for differences in government structures across the world. This constraint disappears when we talk about possible future Cyberian political entities. Geography does not have any importance in Cyberspace, and the number of citizens in a Cyberian community can be worked out to the optimal number more easily than in the traditional world.

In the non-virtual world separation of agencies, when vertical (within the central government), rather than horizontal (federalism), can, in fact, increase the monopolistic powers of the government vis-à-vis the general public, by diminishing the quantity of public goods produced (Brennan and Hamlin 2000). In other words, when a monopoly is broken up into several firms, each producing a different ingredient of the final product, the monopolistic exploitation of consumers rises. Only competition in the production of the same ingredients achieves desirable results. Thus, separation of agencies itself does not guarantee desirable results from the point of view of the public well-being. Only certain kinds of separation – in which the separated organs are fulfilling together some overlapping functions – will achieve the desirable results. This component will be analyzed in the last point of this skeleton argument.

Lower transaction costs in Cyberspace abolish the need for a federative structure or horizontal separation of powers, as was observed by Dennis Mueller (1996, p. 77–78), writing to justify federalism:

> In a world of zero-transaction (decision-making) costs, and in which unanimity rule is used in the national (highest) legislative level, no other level of government would be necessary. All collective decisions for all citizens could be made in a single legislative body formed of representatives from across the entire country.

Mueller's insight should be extended to vertical separation of powers. Unanimity and zero transaction costs diminish the rationale for separation of agencies. Therefore, to the extent that transaction costs in Cyberspace are lower, the justification for separation of agencies is reduced.

There is another important rationale for separation of agencies – diminishing agency costs. As we have seen above, the democratic system is a kind of a compromise or a second best option, which is the result of the need to transfer powers from the people to a central government, and at the same time place the government under the control of the people in a way that would not be too costly. In this sense, it was probably appropriate to describe democracy as the least bad system of government. The main problem of the transmission of powers to a central government, leaving only periodical control, is agency costs, which are caused by the differences between the incentives of the agents – the politicians – and the incentives of the principals – the citizens.

There are three typical categories of costs involved in a principal–agent relationship: bonding costs, monitoring costs and residual loss (Jensen and Meckling 1976). In the case of central government (agent) and citizens (principals), the residual loss is the dominant element. This loss is created by the mere fact that the rulers-politicians seek to maximize their own utility by gaining more powers (or materializing their private ideologies), instead of maximizing the population's well-being (Michelman 1980, Backhous 1979). One way to reduce these agency costs is to divide the agency into separate sub-agencies, creating different incentives for each. In that way, while legislators act to maximize their political powers and chances of re-election, administrators and judges have different incentives, as a result of different institutional arrangements. If this is the case, the reduction of agency costs would be more significant if the division of powers were not only by separation of agencies but also by assigning each agency a different governing function (Macey 1988). Here, we are getting closer to the classical idea of separation of powers.

The economic history explanation (e.g. North, 1981) of the political changes in seventeenth and eighteenth-century Europe, among them the emergence of separation of powers, is a particular example related to the theoretical explanation above. In a nutshell, this explanation focuses on the financial crises of the early nation states, which brought the rulers (the monarchs) to seek loans from the public. One of the methods to gain the confidence of lenders in the government's commitment to honor its credit was the creation of other governmental agencies, including an independent judiciary, which were assigned to enforce these contracts in an impartial manner. The emergence of representative government is also associated with this explanation.

This rationale may hold when we consider relations between different Cyberian entities. In other words, some separation of agencies to credibly commit a Cyberian community might be beneficial, and thus desirable. One sort of such separation can be separation between bodies whose major aim is economic profits and those who are not geared primarily to maximize profits. The regulation or government of Cyberspace through the code or its architecture is one of the bold examples for this insight. Cyberspace, much more than physical political forums, is regulated by its architecture, or by the code. This code was originally designed by the US army with the goal of decentralization and by university professors whose aim was to create an egalitarian, democratic, open and deliberative forum. Today, Cyberspace is captured more and more by economic powers whose interests are very different. Since the code is a significant source for the government of Cyberspace, it can be argued that there is a pressing need for some separation of agencies in the regulation and rule of Cyberspace.

This conclusion is, on the one hand, in sharp contrast to the call for traditional governments to leave Cyberspace alone to its own anarchic development. On the other hand, our conclusion does not necessarily endorse heavy regulation of the economic players in Cyberspace and their prevention from regulating through the code and technological innovation. The separation of agencies approach endorses competition between the economic forces and non-economic governing forces (which in Cyberspace can be performed by the community of all users). Regulation should, therefore, focus on enhancing technological freedom, enabling competition among different technologies, and preventing anti-competitive economic and technological strategies.

d. Separation of Persons

Separation of persons is considered the third fundamental element in the pure doctrine of separation of powers (together with separation of functions and of agencies), and the most dramatic characteristic of it (Marshall 1971, pp. 97–100). This element was, in fact, already incorporated into our analysis of separation of agencies, because economic analysis is based on individuals and their rational-personal choice. This choice (or the utility function) is crucially dependent upon exogenous circumstances. Thus, choices made by government personnel are dependent upon the branch of government in which they work. In other words, in the context of economic analysis, there is no meaning to establishments and institutions without their human operators. Likewise, there is no meaning to the analysis of individuals' behavior without examination of the institutional arrangements and incentives mechanism to which they are subject. Thus, separation of agencies is meaningless unless separation of personnel is an integral component of it. This applies equally to the separation of persons in the context of separating the constitutional and post constitutional agencies. Thus, there is no meaning for such separation, from an economic analysis point of view, if the composition of the constituent assembly is identical to the composition of a parliament, or that parliament also functions as a constituent assembly.

This does not mean that only lawyers should be part of the judiciary and only bureaucrats should work in the executive. There are legal systems (especially in Continental Europe) in which a mixture of professionals in the different branches of government is encouraged, and from our perspective this may even be more efficient. Separation of persons merely means that no one should be part of more than one branch of government at the same time. This is not a trivial requirement, as it appears at first glance. In many systems, such separation of persons does not exist, when, for example, cabinet members can and in some systems must also serve as parliament members.[9]

We noted before that separation of agencies might reduce agency costs, which are the result of the government–citizens (agent–principals) relationship. One way of achieving this is different representation structures for each of the branches, which can increase the people's control over the government and the interplay between particular and general issues on the public agenda and between short, medium and long term interests. Without separation of persons, a significant share of these advantages would fade away. The desirability of separation of persons is further derived from the optimal relationships between the powers, as will be explained below. The American system, which uses the advantages of different representation structures, is also quite strict about this

---

9   The most notable example is the Lord Chancellor in Britain, who is a member of all three branches of government.

element of separation of persons. The Vice President is the only top figure who is part of more than one branch of government.

Since we concluded that in Cyberspace the urge for separation of agencies of both types – constitutional versus post-constitutional, and legislature, executive and judiciary – is decreased because of the ability to maintain direct rule by consensus or near consensus, the need to separate persons correspondingly decreases too. In addition, when applying the argument for separation of persons to Cyberspace, we have to bear in mind that Cyberspace transforms not only the notion of collective communities, but also that of the individual, who is the basic unit for liberal philosophy of the state and for economic analysis. In the non-virtual world, the basic unit of reference – the individual – is one physical person. In Cyberspace, the individual is a username with a password and an electronic address. There is no strict correlation between the Cyberian individual and non-virtual individual, as the same physical individual can appear in Cyberspace as several entities, each with different identification features and a different character. Cyberspace allows multiple representations of the same physical individual, as well as a single virtual representation of several physical individuals. The separation of persons, which is central to the traditional theory of the state, is, therefore, significantly muted in Cyberspace.

e. The Relationships Between the Powers

The most controversial element of the desirable structure of government is the relationships between the separated powers or branches of government. There are at least two distinct, though interrelated, questions here: (1) to what degree separation of powers is advantageous (this question involves the issue of delegation of powers); and (2) what is the degree of freedom or independence that we ought to assign to each of the branches. The former question relates mainly to functional separation; the latter relates to institutional separation (separation of agencies). These questions are strongly interrelated in the sense that there could be a great deal of trade-off in different combined solutions to them.

Judicial review can serve as a good example. The conventional debate concerning judicial review is usually within the boundaries of the second question: should the legislature and the executive be controlled by the judiciary, and if so, to what extent? But this issue could also be raised in the framework of the first question. In this context we would first ask whether judicial review is part of the legislative or the judicial function. If it is seen as part of the legislative function, we will have to ask whether the allocation or delegation (Salzberger 1993) of the powers to participate in rule making to the judiciary is desirable or legitimate (Salzberger and Voigt 2002a).

The two extreme approaches to the second question are the independence approach or the pure doctrine of separation of powers, on the one hand, and the checks and balances approach, on the other hand (Yassky 1989; Vile 1967; Marshall 1971, pp. 100–103). Analytically these two approaches can refer to the functional level, which is directly related to the first question about sharing powers (or delegating powers), or to the institutional and personal levels, i.e. the accountability of agents in each branch to those in the other branches, or to both levels.

It is possible, for example, to argue that an optimal structure of separation of powers would adopt the checks and balances doctrine with respect to the functional level, and the independence doctrine with regard to the personal level. This is the underlying idea behind the American form of separation of powers: on the one hand, every collective decision of one of the branches of government is subject to approval or review by the other branches. On the other hand, it is very difficult for one branch of government to remove any of the agents in other branches. Thus, in contrast to popular perception, the checks and balances approach is adopted in the USA only on the functional level, while independence (or pure separation) is adopted on the personal level. In contrast, in most European parliamentary democracies, there is no independence on the personal level. The members of the executive are accountable to the legislature and the Prime Minister has the power to dissolve Parliament. Likewise, appointment and promotion of judges is under the power of the executive. But there is relatively more independence on the functional level. For example, the legislature cannot review appointments within the executive, and legislation is not subject to a veto by the executive.[10]

The theoretical framework for analyzing these questions is, again, transaction costs and decision-making costs on the one hand, and agency costs on the other hand. A smaller degree of independence is inclined to raise the former costs but reduce the latter ones, and the optimal level may depend on variables including the size of the jurisdiction (Silver 1977), and the representation structure of each branch. Cyberspace, as indicated before, is expected to decrease both transaction costs or decision-making costs and agency cost. Thus, while the need for different branches of government to balance and monitor each other decreases, the costs involved in such conduct also go down. The rationale for monitoring and balancing weakens, and the increased decision-making costs are just a secondary result of the non-virtual state's need to tackle agency and monopolistic costs. Therefore, one may conclude that Cyberspace should ease the need for a strict mechanism of checks and balances between the different branches of government.

As to the first question about the degree and rigor of the desirable separation, the solution might be a result of a cost-benefit analysis, or, more

---

10 In most European countries legislation is subject to judicial review, but not by the regular judiciary. The reviewing body is a special constitutional court, which cannot be identified fully with the judicial branch of government.

accurately, a comparison of cost analysis. This analysis is the second stage in a theoretical hierarchical decision-making model. Let us take, for example, the function of rule making. In the first stage of this model, we have to decide on the merits of a substantive issue – whether a certain decision is desirable at all. In the second stage, we have to decide which of the three branches of government can make the decision most cheaply. The costs include both transaction costs (the costs of the decision-making process) and agency costs (Aranson, Gellhorn and Robinson 1982, pp. 17–21). In making general rules, we may expect that the legislature would be the most expensive with respect to transaction costs, but the least expensive regarding agency costs. This might not be the case with minor, secondary or more particular rules. If it is, one can conclude that separation of powers (or, rather, separation of functions) should not be absolute. Cyberspace enables new mechanisms for creating rules and it blurs the distinction between rules and particular decisions. Hence, again, its effect on a theory of the state level points toward a less rigid separation of powers.

Another factor, connected to transaction costs of decision-making, as well as to agency costs, which should be considered when deciding the degree of separation or the degree of functional independence, is the theory of collective decision-making. The theory of Social Choice taught us that majority rule, which is usually employed by legislatures in the non-virtual world, might bear the grim results of cycling or arbitrariness. One method for ameliorating this situation is to allow additional bodies to take part in decision-making, bodies that have different decision-making processes, incentives and representation structures. The legislative veto and judicial review in the American system can be seen as performing this task (Tullock 1981; Aranson, Gellhorn and Robinson 1982; Mayton 1986; Moe 1990; Salzberger 1993), and indeed some scholars argue that they were designed for this purpose.

The conclusion drawn from this consideration is, again, the rejection of the 'pure' doctrine of separation of powers, in favor of some degree of power-sharing and functional dependency. It is important that the institutional structure and division of powers would be specified in the constitution; otherwise they would be subject to the same problems of cycling and arbitrariness and thus unstable. A constitution ought to reflect unanimous decisions, and therefore is not subject to the problems of majority rule (Eggertson 1990, pp. 70–74). But if in the new Cyberian world we can change the dominant decision-making rule (also in the post-constitutional stage) from simple majority toward unanimity, the rationale for separation of powers is moot, and the crucial debate in the traditional world with regard to the desirable relations between the powers is much less significant.

A sharp analysis of the relations between the powers of government was offered recently by Brennan and Hamlin (2000). They show how 'strategic' separation of powers (pure separation) leads to exactly the opposite results from the point of view of the population's welfare from 'competitive' (check and balances) separation of powers. While the former will reduce the quantity of the public goods supplied to increase government gains, strengthening the monopolistic powers of government and exploitation of the public, the latter will increase competition and improve the public welfare.

The interrelations between the branches of government can digress from the protective function to the productive function of the state. It is possible to advocate, for example, as some do, checks and balances within the protective state or with regard to 'ultimate power', and independence or pure separation within the productive state, or with regard to 'operational power'. In other words, it can be suggested that the checks and balances model be employed to enforce the initial contract, but within this contract each power be given full autonomy. Again, since Cyberspace is likely to blur the boundaries between the protective and the productive state, the need for co-existence of different types of separation of powers is diminished.

To summarize, separation of powers is the major tool of liberal democracies to compensate for the shift from unanimity to majoritarianism and from direct democracy to representative democracy. Cyberspace enables us to operate more direct democracy and more consensual or super majoritarian decision-making and rule-making processes. This, in turn, invalidates some of the rationales for separation of powers and diminishes the magnitude of others. As the structurally crafted and structured separation of powers in the physical world and especially, the establishment of mechanisms of checks and balances are costly themselves, the Cyberian state will need less structured separation and fewer checks and balances mechanisms. These elements will evolve naturally from the decentralized and the somehow anarchic nature of the new Cyberworld.

4. SUMMARY

We tried in this chapter to present the major difference between Liberal and Republican theories of the state as resulting from a presupposition with regard to individual preferences, and whether these are exogenous or given or internal to the collective decision-making process. Maybe Cyberspace should be a trigger for broadening the economic theory of the state, to incorporate such traditional Republican views of the state, which until now were considered as external to the economic theory of the state. This, however, requires fresh economic thinking and modeling, which is beyond the horizons of this chapter.

We still live under the governance of the Liberal Democracy paradigm. Netanel (2000, p. 407), summarizing the literature, defines Liberal Democracy as

...a political system with representative government elected by popular majority, the rule of law enshrined to protect individuals and minorities, and a significant sector of economic, associational and communicative activity that is largely autonomous from government control. It rests upon the principles of individual liberty, civic equality, popular sovereignty and government by the consent of the governed.

In this chapter we questioned this paradigmatic view. We examined what are the sources for majority decision-making and representative government, and we argued that on the basis of the new technological frontiers the same normative foundations may lead to a different concept of the state. In Netanel's framework we examined whether the principles of individual liberty, civic equality, popular sovereignty and government by the consent of the governed should direct us to a political system with representative government elected by popular majority. We argued that in the new world of Cyberspace the answer should be negative. Based on the same normative foundations, we must re-think the conventions of the existing concepts of the state.

The analysis and conclusions of this chapter can be seen as the result of the interplay between values, technology and the law. Our scientific methodology involved viewing values as fixed or pre-given, and examining, in light of these value foundations, how the changing technology affects the basic institutional arrangements regarding the state. It is important to note that the areas we overlooked are certainly suited to further research. We focused on the effects of technology on the desirable law, disregarding, for now, the opposite effect of the law (and values) on technology. This question was partly dealt with in other parts of this book (for example, the discussion of the Coase theorem in Chapter 8). We also overlooked the effects of technology on values. These are fascinating topics for a different book.

References

CASES

ACLU v. *Reno*, 929 F. Supp. 824 (1996).

A&M Records Inc. v. *Napster, Inc.*, 114 F. Supp. 2d 896 (2000).

A&M Records Inc. v. *Napster, Inc.*, 239 F. 3d 1004 (2001).

Aimster Copyright Litigation, 334 F.3d 643 (2003).

Bates v. *State Bar of Arizona*, 433 U.S. 350 (1977).

eBay Inc. v. *Bidder's Edge, Inc.*, 100 F. Supp. 2d 1058 (2000).

Metro-Goldwyn-Mayer Studios Inc. v. *Grokster Ltd.*, 259 F. Supp. 2d 1029 (2003).

League Against Racism and Antisemitism (LICRA) v. *Yahoo! Inc., Yahoo! France* (County Court, Paris, 20.11.00).

Lexmark international Inc. v. *Static Control Components Inc.*, 253 F. Supp. 2d 943 (2003).

Kabushiki Kaisha Sony Computer Entertainment v. *Stevens*, FCA 906 (2002).

Search King Inc. v. *Google Technology Inc.*, F. Supp. 2d W. D. Okla (2003).

Sony Computer Entertainment Inc. v. *Connectix Corp.*, 203 F.3d 596 (2000).

Sony Computer Entertainment America Inc. v. *Gamemasters*, 87 F. Supp. 2nd 976 (1999).

Sun Microsystems Inc. v. *Microsoft Corp.*, 87 F. Supp. 2d. 992 (2000).

Sun Microsystems Inc. v. *Microsoft Corp.*,333 F.3d 517 (2003).

Turner Broadcasting Sys. Inc. v. *F.C.C*, 114 S. Ct. 2445 (1994).

United States of America v. *Microsoft Corporation*, 364 U.S. App. D.C. 330 (2001).

Universal City Studios Inc. v. *Corely*, 273 F.3d 429 (2001).

Yahoo! Inc. v. *LICRA*, 169 F.Supp.2d 1181 (2001).

LEGISLATION

Digital Millennium Copyright Act of 1998, Pub. L. No. 105–304, 112 Stat. 2860, Codified as 17 U.S.C. §§1201–1205.

EU Directive 93/98/EEC on the Harmonization of Certain Aspects of Copyright and Related Rights in the Information Society (May 2001).

National Information Infrastructure Copyright Protection Act (NIICPA), H.R. 2441, 104th Cong., 2d Sess. 1995.

Next Generation Internet Research Act of 1998, Pub. L. No. 105–305, enacted October 28, 1998.

World Intellectual Property Organization [WIPO] Copyright Treaty signed in December 1996.

BOOKS AND ARTICLES

Abramson, B. (2002), 'Promoting Innovation in the Software Industry: A First Principles Approach to Intellectual Property Reform', *Boston University Journal of Science & Technology Law*, **8**, 75.

Allen, T. and R. Widdison (1996), 'Can Computers Make Contracts?', *Harvard Journal of Law and Technology*, **9**, 25.

Aranson, P., E. Gellhorn and G. Robinson (1982), 'The Theory of Legislative Delegation', *Cornell Law Review*, **68**, 1.

Arrow, K. (1951), *Social Choice and Individual Values*, US: J. Wiley.

Austin, J. (1832), *The Province of Jurisprudence Determined*, reprinted in W. E. Rumble (ed.) (1995), UK: Cambridge University Press.

Backhous, J. (1979), 'Constitutional Guarantees and the Distribution of Power and Wealth', *Public Choice*, **33** (3), 45.

Bagdikian, B. (1997), *The Media Monopoly*, US: Beacon Press.

Bailey, J. and E. Brynjolfsson (1997), 'In Search of "Friction-Free Markets": An Exploratory Analysis of Prices for Books, CDs and Software Sold on the Internet', Presented at the 25th Telecommunications Policy Research Conference, Alexandria, VA. 27–29 September, retrieved September 2, 2003, from http://www.tprc.org/abstracts97/bailey.html.

Baird, D., R. Gertner and R. Picker (1994), *Game Theory and the Law*, US: Harvard University Press.

Band, J. and M. Katoh (1995), *Interface on Trial, Intellectual Property and Interoperability in the Global Software Industry*, US: Westview Press.

Barber, B. R. (1995), *Jihad vs. McWorld, How Globalism and Tribalism are Reshaping the World*, A. Schulz (ed.), US: Ballantine Books.

Barber, B. R. (2000, 11 September), 'Globalizing Democracy', *The American Prospect*, **11** (20), retrieved 1 September, 2003, from http://www.prospect.org/print-friendly/print/V11/20/barber-b.html.

Barlow, J. P. (1994, March), 'The Economy of Ideas: A Framework for Patents and Copyrights in the Digital Age', *Wired*, **2.03**, retrieved 31 August, 2003, from http://www.wired.com/wired/archive/2.03/economy.ideas.html.

Barzel, Y. (2002), *A Theory of the State*, UK: Cambridge University Press.

Basu, K. (2000), *Prelude to Political Economy: A Study of the Social and Political Foundations of Economics*, UK: Oxford University Press.

Bell, T. (1998), 'Fair Use v. Fared Use: The Impact of Automated Rights Management on Copyright's Fair Use Doctrine', *North Carolina Literary Review*, **76**, 557.

Benkler, Y. (2002), 'Coase's Penguin, or, Linux and The Nature of the Firm', *Yale Law Journal*, **112**, 369.

Bentham, J. (1789), *An Introduction to the Principles of Morals and Legislation*, reprinted in Wilfrid Harrison (ed.) (1948), UK: Blackwell.

Bergman, M. (2000), 'The Deep Web: Surfacing Hidden Value', *The Journal of Electronic Publishing*, retrieved 31 August, 2003, from http://www.brightplanet.com/deepcontent/tutorials/DeepWeb/deepwebwhitepaper.pdf.

Birnhack, D. M. and N. Elkin-Koren (eds) (2002), *Fighting Terror Online: Legal Ramifications of September 11*, retrieved 8 September, 2003, from http://lawcourses.haifa.ac.il/ec_workshop/index/main_eng/pos_papers/terror_e.pdf.

Birnhack, D. M. and N. Elkin-Koren (2003), 'The Invisible Handshake: The Reemergence of the State in the Digital Environment', *Virginia Journal of Law and Technology*, **8**, 6.

Black, D. (1948), 'On the Rationale of Group Decision-Making', *Journal of Political Economy*, **56**, 23.

Borda, J.C. (1781), *Mémoire sur les élections au Scrutin. Histoire de l'Académie Royale des Sciences*, Paris.

Bouckaert, B. and G. D. Geest (eds) (2000), *Encyclopedia of Law and Economics*, UK: Edward Elgar.

Brennan, G. and J. Buchanan (1985), 'The Reason of Rules: Constitutional Political Economy', [Electronic version] in J. Buchanan, *Collected Work of James M. Buchanan*, IN: Liberty Fund, Inc.

Brennan, G. and A. Hamlin (2000), *Democratic Devices and Desires*, UK: Cambridge University Press.

Breyer, S. (1982), *Regulation and Its Reform*, US: Harvard University Press.

Brown, J. R. and A. Goolsbee (2002), 'Does the Internet Make Markets More Competitive? Evidence from the Life Insurance Industry', *Journal of Political Economy*, **110** (3), 481.

Brynjolfsson, E. and M. Smith (2000), 'Frictionless Commerce? A Comparison of Internet and Conventional Retailers', *Management Science*, **46**, 563.

Brynjolfsson, E., M. Smith and Y. Hu (2003), 'Consumer Surplus in the Digital Economy: Estimating the Value of Increased Product Variety at Online Booksellers', *MIT Sloan School of Management, Working Paper 4305–03*, retrieved 29 August, 2003, from http://papers.ssrn.com/sol3/papers.cfm?abstract_id=400940.

Buchanan, J. (1975), *The Limits of Liberty: Between Anarchy and Leviathan*, US: University of Chicago Press.

Buchanan, J. and G. Tullock (1962), *The Calculus of Consent: Logical Foundations of Constitutional Democracy*, US: University of Michigan.

Burk, D. (1996), 'Federalism in Cyberspace', *Connecticut Law Review*, **28**, 1095.

Burk D. (1998), 'Virtual Exit in the Global Information Economy', *Chicago-Kent Law Review*, **73**, 943.

Burke, E. (1774), *Address to the Electors of Bristol*.

Butler, D. (2000), 'Souped-Up Search Engines', *Nature*, **405**, 112.

Cairney, R. (1998), 'Bookstore an Online Goldmine?', [Electronic version] *See Magazine*, **255**, retrieved 29 August, 2003, from http://www.seemagazine.com/Issues/1998/1015/web.html.

Calabresi, G. (1991), 'The Pointlessness of Pareto: Carrying Coase Further', *Yale Law Journal*, **100**, 1211.

Calabresi, G. and D. Melamed (1972), 'Property Rights, Liability Rules and Inalienability: One View of the Cathedral', *Harvard Law Review*, **85**, 1089.

Cleaver, H. (1998), 'The Zapatista Effect: The Internet and the Rise of an Alternative Political Fabric', *Journal of International Affairs*, **51** (2), 621.

Clemeston, L. (January 15, 2003), 'Protest Groups Using Updated Tactics to Spread Antiwar Message', [Electronic version] *The New York Times*, Section A , Page 9 , Column 1, retrieved 8 September, 2003, from http://query.nytimes.com/gst/abstract.html?res=F50813F838550C768DDDA80894DB404482.

Coase, R. (1937), 'The Nature of the Firm', *Economica*, **4**, 386.

Coase, R. (1960), 'The Problem of Social Cost', *Journal of Law and Economics*, **3**, 1.

Coase, R. (1981), 'How Should Economists Choose?' in *Essay on Economics and Economists* (1994) 15, 27.

Cohen, J. E. (1998), 'Lochner in Cyberspace: The New Economic Orthodoxy of "Rights Management"', *Michigan Law Review*, **97**, 462.

Cohen, J. E. (2000, 23 May), 'Call it the Digital Millennium Censorship Act: Unfair Use', *The New Republic Online*, retrieved 8 September, 2003, from https://ssl.tnr.com/p/docsub.mhtml?r=sub&uri=%2Fcyberspace%2Fcohen052300.html.

Coleman, J. L. (1988), *Markets, Morals and the Law*, UK: Cambridge University Press.

Condorcet, J. N. A. (1785), *Sketch for a Historical Picture of the Progress of the Human Mind*, reprinted in J. Barraclough (trans.) (1955), UK: Weidenfeld & Nicolson.

Cooter, R. D. (1997), 'Normative Failure Theory of Law', *Cornell Law Review*, **82**, 947.

Cooter, R. D. (1999), *The Strategic Constitution*, US: Princeton University Press.

Cottle, R. L and R. S. Lawson (1981), 'Leisure as Work: A Case in Professional Sports', *Atlantic Economic Journal*, **9**, 50.

Dahlman, C. (1979), 'The Problem of Externality', *Journal of Law and Economics*, **22**, 141.

Dam, K. W. (1998), 'Who Says Who Can Access What? The Policy Crisis Over Cryptography in the Information Age', in S. U. Raymond (ed.), *Science, Technology, and the Law*, US: New York Academy of Sciences.

Dam, K. W. (1999), 'Self-help in the Digital Jungle', *Journal of Legal Studies*, **28**, 393.

Dam, K. W. (1999a), 'Intellectual Property and the Academic Enterprise', in *The Changing Character, Use and Protection of Intellectual Property*, **17**, German-American Academic Council Foundation (GAAC Bonn-Washington).

Deci, E. L., R. Koestner and R. M. Ryan (1999), 'A Meta-Analytic Review of Experiments Examining the Effects of Extrinsic Rewards on Intrinsic Motivation', *Psychological Bulletin*, **125**, 627.

Downs, A. (1957), *An Economic Theory of Democracy*, US: Harper.

Dunoff, J. and J. Trachtman (1998), 'Economic Analysis of International Law: An Invitation and a Caveat', *Yale Journal of International Law*, **24**, 1.

Dworkin, R. M. (1978), *Taking Rights Seriously*, US: Harvard University Press.

Dworkin, R. M. (1980), 'Is Wealth a Value?', *Journal of Legal Studies*, **9**, 191.

Easterbrook, F. (1996), 'Cyberspace and the Law of the Horse', *University of Chicago Legal Forum*, 207.

Eggertsson, T. (1990), *Economic Behavior and Institutions*, UK: Cambridge University Press.

Elkin-Koren, N. (1996), 'Cyberlaw and Social Change: A Democratic Approach to Copyright Law in Cyberspace', *Cardozo Arts and Entertainment Law Journal*, **14** (2), 215.

Elkin-Koren, N. (1998), 'Copyrights in Cyberspace – Rights without Law', *Chicago-Kent Law Review*, **73**, 1155.

Elkin-Koren, N. (2001), 'Let the Crawlers Crawl: On Virtual Gatekeepers and the Right to Exclude Indexing', *University of Dayton Law Review*, **26**, 179.

Elkin-Koren, N. (2003), 'Information Smog', in S. Lavi (ed.), *Technologies of Justice; Law, Science and Technology*, Tel Aviv: Ramot, pp. 223–276 (Hebrew).

Elkin-Koren, N. and E. Salzberger (1999), 'Law and Economics in Cyberspace', *International Review of Law and Economics*, **19**, 553.

Farber, D. and P. Frickey (1991), *Law and Public Choice – A Critical Introduction*, US: University of Chicago Press.

Frey, B. (2001), 'A Utopia? Government without Territorial Monopoly', *The Independent Review*, **6**, 99.

Frey, B. (2003), 'Flexible Citizenship for a Global Society', *Politics, Philosophy and Economics*, **2**, 93.

Gibbons, L. (1997), 'No Regulation, Government Regulation, or Self-Regulation: Social Enforcement or Social Contracting for Governance in Cyberspace', *Cornell Journal of Law and Public Policy*, **6**, 475.

Gibson, W. (1984), *Neuromancer*, US: Ace Books.

Gillen, A., D. Kusnetzky and S. Mclarnon (2003), 'Five Pros and Five Cons: A Look at Changing User Perceptions on Linux', *IDC study*.

Gordon, W. J. (1998), 'Intellectual Property as Price Discrimination: Implications for Contract', *Chicago-Kent Law Review*, **73**, 1367.

Gramm, W. S. (1987), 'Labor, Work, and Leisure: Human Well-being and the Optimal Allocation of Time', *Journal of Economic Issues*, **21**, 88.

Gromov, R. G. (2002), *The Roads and Crossroads of Internet History*, retrieved 8 September, 2003 from http://www.netvalley.com/intvalstat.html.

Gwartney, J. and R. Wagner (eds) (1988), *Public Choice and Constitutional Economics*, Greenwich, CT: JAI Press Inc.

Hagerty, C. L. (2000), *The Spirit of the Internet: Volume I: Speculations on the Evolution of Global Consciousness* [Electronic version], C. L. Hagerty and J. Hanna (eds), retrieved 29 August, 2003, from http://www.matrixmasters.com/spirit/html/1a/1a.html#chap1.

Hanson, J. L. (1986), *A Dictionary of Economic and Commerce*, UK: Pitman Publishing.

Hardin, G. (1968), 'The Tragedy of the Commons', *Science*, **162**, 1243.

Hardy, T. (1997), 'The Proper Legal Regime for Cyberspace', *University of Pittsburgh Law Review*, **55**, 993.

Harsanyi, J. C. (1955), 'Cardinal Welfare, Individualistic Ethics and Interpersonal Comparisons of Utility', *Journal of Political Economy*, **63**, 309.

Harsanyi, J. C. (1977), *Rational Behavior and Bargaining Equilibrium in Games and Social Situations*, UK: Cambridge University Press.

Hart, L. A. (1961), *The Concept of Law*, UK: Clarendon Press.

Hauben, M. and R. Hauben (1997), *Netizens*, US: IEEE Computer Society Press.

Heling, S. and M. Hayden (2002), 'E-commerce, Transaction Cost, and the Network of Division of Labour: a Business Perspective', Retrieved 12 September, 2003, from Monash University, Department of Economics Web site: http://rich.buseco.monash.edu.au/column/hlshi/academic/E-commerce-perspective.htm.

Heller, M. and R. S. Eisenberg (1998), 'Can Patents Deter Innovation? The Anticommons in Biomedical Research', *Science*, **280**, 698.

Hirschman, L. (1970), *Exit, Voice and Loyalty – Responses to Decline in Firms, Organizations and States*, US: Harvard University Press.

Hobbes, T. (1651), *Leviathan*, reprinted in 1979, UK: Dent.

Hunter, D. (2002), 'Philippic.com.', *California Law Review*, **90**, 611.

Information Infrastructure Task Force (1995), *Final report of the Working Group on Intellectual Property Rights: Intellectual Property and the National Information Infrastructure (White Paper)*, retrieved 31 August, 2003, from http://www.ladas.com/NII/NIITofC.html.

Introna, L. and H. Nissenbaum (2000), 'Shaping the Web: Why the Politics of Search Engines Matters', *The Information Society*, **16**, 169.

Jensen, M. and W. Meckling (1976), 'Theory of the Firm: Managerial Behavior, Agency Costs and Ownership Structure', *Journal of Financial Economics*, **3**, 305.

Katz, A. (1996), 'Taking Private Ordering Seriously', *University of Pennsylvania Law Review*, **144**, 1745.

Katz, M. and C. Shapiro (1994), 'Systems Competition and Network Effects', *Journal of Economic Perspectives*, **8**, 93.

Kelsen, H. (1949), *General Theory of Law and State*, US: Harvard University Press.

Kelsen, H. (1961), *The Pure Theory of Law*, in M. Knight (trans.) (1970), US: University of California Press.

Kitch, E. W. (1977), 'The Nature and Function of the Patent System', *Journal of Law and Economics*, **20**, 265.

Kuhn, T. (1962), *The Structure of Scientific Revolution*, US: University of Chicago Press.

Kwong, D. L. (2003), 'The Copyright Contract Intersection: SoftMan Products Co. v. Adobe Systems, Inc. & Bowers v. Baystate Technologies, Inc.', *Berkeley Technology Law Journal*, **18**, 349.

Landes, W. and R. Posner (1989), 'An Economic Analysis of Copyright Law,' *Journal of Legal Studies*, **18**, 325.

Landes, W. and R. Posner (2003), 'Indefinitely Renewable Copyright,' *University of Chicago Law Review*, **70**, 471.

Lemley, M. (1997), 'The Economics of Improvement in Intellectual Property Law', *Texas Law Review*, **75**, 989.

Lemley, M. (1998), 'The Law and Economics of Internet Norms', *Chicago-Kent Law Review*, **73**, 1257.

Lemley, M. (2002), 'Intellectual Property Rights and Standard-Setting Organizations', *California Law Review*, **90**, 1889.

Lemley, M. (2003), 'Place and Cyberspace', *California Law Review*, **91**, 521.

Lemley, M. and D. McGowan (1998), 'Legal Implications of Network Economic Effects', *California Law Review*, **86**, 479.

Lerner, J. and J. Tirole (2000), *The Simple Economics of Open Source*, retrieved 31 August, 2003, from http://www.people.hbs.edu/jlerner/simple.pdf.

Lessig, L. (1996), 'The Zones of Cyberspace', *Stanford Law Review*, **48**, 1403.

Lessig, L. (1999), *Code and other Laws of Cyberspace*, US: Basic Books.

Lessig, L. (2001), *The Future of Ideas: The Fate of the Commons in a Connected World*, US: Random House.

Linux Counter, retrieved 10 September, 2003, from http://counter.li.org/.

Locke, J. (1690), *Two Treatises of Government*, reprinted in P. Laslett (ed.) (1989), UK: Cambridge University Press.

Lunney, G. S., Jr (1996), 'Reexamining Copyright's Incentives-Access Paradigm', *Vanderbilt University Law Review*, **49**, 483.

Macey, J. (1988), 'Public Choice: The Theory of the Firm and the Theory of Market Exchange', *Cornell Law Review*, **74**, 43.

Marshall, G. (1971), *Constitutional Theory*, UK: Clarendon Press, Oxford.

Martin, M. (1996, 9 December), 'The Next Big Thing: A Bookstore?', *Fortune Magazine*, retrieved 29 August, 2003, from http://www.fortune.com/fortune/articles/ 0,15114,375337,00.html.

Mashaw, J. (1988), 'As if Republican Interpretation', *Yale Law Joutrnal*, **97**, 1685.

May, C. (2002), *The Information Society: A Skeptical View*, US: Polity Press.

Mayton, W. (1986), 'The Possibilities of Collective Choice: Arrow's Theorem, Article 1 and the Delegation of Legislative Powers to Administrative Agencies', *Duke Law Journal*, **5**, 948.

McLuhan, M. and Q. Fiore (1967), *The Medium is the Message*, US: Bantam Books.

Mennel, P. (1987), 'Tailoring Legal Protection for Computer Software', *Stanford Law Review*, **39**, 1329.

Mennel, P. (1989), 'An Analysis of the Scope of Copyright Protection for Application Programs', *Stanford Law Review*, **41**, 1045.

Mercuro, N. and S. Medema (1997), *Economics and the Law – From Posner to Post-Modernism*, US: Princeton University Press.

Michelman, F. (1980), 'Constitution, Statutes and the Theory of Efficient Adjudication', *Journal of Legal Studies*, **9**, 430.

Mishra, K. A. (2002, February), *Media Decision Models for Online Advertising*, retrieved 29 August, 2003, from State University of New York, Management Binghamton Conference on optimization in Supply Chain Management and E-Commerce, Web site: http://www.ise.ufl.edu/Scmec/mishra.pdf.

Moe, T. (1990), 'Political Institutions: The Neglected Side of the Story', *Journal of Law, Economics and Organizations* SI, **6**, 213.

Moglen, E. (2000, April 23) 'Free Software Matters: When Code Isn't Law', *LinuxUser Magazine*, retrieved 8 September, 2003, from http://moglen.law.columbia.edu/publications/lu-01.html.

Moglen, E. (2002), 'Anarchism Triumphant: Free Software and the Death of Copyright', in N. Elkin-Koren and W. N. Netanel (eds) (2002), *The Commodification of Information*, UK: Kluwer Law International.

Montesquieu, C. (1748), *The Spirit of the Laws*, D. W. Carrithers (ed. & trans.) (1977), US: University of California Press.

Mueller, D. C. (1996), *Constitutional Democracy*, US: Oxford University Press.

Musgrave, P. A. and P. B. Musgrave (1980), *Public Finance in Theory and Practice*, US: McGraw-Hill.

Netanel, N. W. (2000), 'Market Hierarchy and Copyright in Our System of Free Expression', *Vanderbilt Law Review*, **53**, 1879.

Network Working Group (1996), 'The Internet Standards Process – Revision 3', *Harvard University*, retrieved 29 August , 2003 from http://www.ietf.org/rfc/rfc2026.txt.

Newman, P. (1998), *The New Palgrave Dictionary of Economics and the Law*, UK: Macmillan.

Nissenbaum, H. (2001), 'How Computer Systems Embody Values', *IEEE Computer*, **34** (3), 120.

Nock, S. L. and P. W. Kingston (1989), 'The Division of Leisure and Work', *Social Science Quarterly*, **70**, 23.

North, D. (1981), *Structure and Change in Economic History*, US: Norton.

North, D. (1986), 'Is it Worth Making Sense of Marx?', in Elster J., *Making Sense of Marx*, UK: Cambridge University Press, pp. 57–63.

Olson, M. (1965), *The Logic of Collective Action*, US: Harvard University Press.

Pigou, A. (1920), *The Economics of Welfare*, reprinted (1952) UK: Macmillan.

Posner, R. (1979), 'Utilitarianism Economics and the Legal Theory', *Journal of Legal Studies*, **8**, 103.

Posner, R. (1980), 'The Ethical and Political Basis of the Efficiency Norm in Common Law Adjudication', *Hofstra Law Review*, **8**, 487.

Posner, R. (1987), 'The Law and Economics Movement', *The American Economic Review*, **77** (2), 1.

Posner R. (2003), *Economic Analysis of Law, 4th edition,* US: Aspen Publishers.

Post, D. (1996), 'Governing Cyberspace', *Wayne Law Review*, **43**, 155.

Post, D. and D. Johnson (1996), 'Law and Borders – The Rise of Law in Cyberspace', *Stanford Law Review*, **48**, 1367.

Post D. and D. Johnson (1997), 'And How Shall the Net Be Governed? A Meditation on the Relative Virtues of Decentralized, Emergent Law', in B. Kahin and J. Keller (eds), *Coordinating the Internet*, US: MIT Press.

Post, D. and D. Johnson (1997a), 'The New Civic Virtue of the Net: Lessons from Models of Complex Systems for the Governance of Cyberspace', *Stanford Technology Law Review*, **3**, 10.

Press, L. (2000, July 18), 'The State of the Internet: Growth and Gaps', *Internet Society*, retrieved 8 September, 2002, from http://www.isoc.org/inet2000/cdproceedings/8e/ 8e_4.htm.

Rackoff, T. (1983), 'Contracts of Adhesion: An Essay in Reconstruction', *Harvard Law Review*, **96**, 1173.

Radin, M. J. (2000), 'Humans, Computers, and Binding Commitments', *Indiana Law Journal*, **75**, 1125.

Raman, B. (1999, February), 'Psychological Warfare (Psywar) in the New Millennium', *Sapra India articles*, retrieved 8 September, 2003, from www.subcontinent.com/ sapra/nationalsecurity/img_1999_02_002.html.

Rawls, J. (1971), *A Theory of Justice*, US: Belknap Press of Harvard University Press.

Raymond, E. (1999), *The Cathedral and the Bazaar*, US: O'Reilly and Associates.

Reidenberg, J. (1998), 'Lex Informatica: the Formulation of Information Policy Rules Through Technology', *Texas Law Review*, **76**, 553.

Roberts, L. G. (1999), *Internet Growth Trends*, retrieved 8 September, 2003, from http://www.ziplink.net/~lroberts/IEEEGrowthTrends/IEEEComputer12-99.htm.

Rosenzweig, R. (1998), 'Wizards, Bureaucrats, Warriors and Hackers: Writing the History of the Internet', *American Historical Review*, **103** (5), 1530.

Rousseau, J. (1762), *The Social Contract, or Principles of Political Right*, in H. J. Tozer (trans.) (1998), US: Wordsworth Editions Ltd.

Salzberger, M. E. (1993), 'On the Normative Facet of the Economic Approach Towards Law', *Mishpatim*, **22**, 1 (Hebrew).

Salzberger, M. E. (2002), 'Cyberspace, Governance, and the New Economy: How Cyberspace Regulates Us and How Should We Regulate Cyberspace', in H. Siebert (ed.), *Economic Policy Issues of the New Economy*, US: Springer.

Salzberger, M. E. and S. Voigt (2002), 'On the Delegation of Powers: With Special Emphasis on Central and Eastern Europe', *Constitutional Political Economy*, **13**, 25.

Samuelson, P. (1999), 'Intellectual Property and the Digital Economy: Why the Anti-Circumvention Regulations Needs to be Revised', *Berkeley Technology Law Journal*, **14**, 519.

Samuelson, P. (2001), 'Anticircumvention Rules: Threat to Science', *Science*, **293**, 2028.

Sen, A. (1987), *On Ethics and Economics*, UK: Clarendon Press, US: Norton.

Shapiro, C. and H. R. Varian (1999), *Information Rules*, US: Harvard Business School Press.

Shenk, D. (1997), *Data Smog: Surviving the Information Glut*, US: Harper San Francisco.

Silver, M. (1977), 'Economic Theory of the Constitutional Separation of Powers', *Public Choice*, **29**, 95.

Simon, H. (1971), 'Designing Organizations for an Information-Rich World', in *Computers, Communications, and the Public Interest*, US: Johns Hopkins Press.

Skogh, G. and C. Stuart (1982), 'A Contractarian Theory of Property Rights and Crime', *Scandinavian Journal of Economics*, **84** (1), 27.

Smith, A. (1776), *An Inquiry into the Nature and Causes of the Wealth of Nations*, reprinted in C. Edwin (ed.) (1961), UK: Methuen.

Smith, M. A. and P. Kollock (eds) (1999), *Communities in Cyberspace*, UK: Routledge.

Steiner, P. (1993, 5 July), *The New Yorker*, **(LXIX)** (20), 61.

Sullivan, D. (2000, 3 November), 'Paid Inclusion at Search Engines Gains Ground', *The Search Engine Report*, retrieved 31 August, 2003, from http://searchengine-watch.com/sereport/article.php/2163151.

Sullivan, D. (2001, 2 July), 'The Evolution of Paid Inclusion', *The Search Engine Report*, retrieved 31 August, 2003, from http://searchenginewatch.com/sereport/article.php/2163971.

Sullivan, D. (2003, 5 May), 'Who Powers Whom? Search Providers Chart', *SearchEngineWatch.com*, retrieved 2 September, 2003, from http://www.searchengi-newatch.com/reports/article.php/2156401.

Sunstein, C. (1988), 'Beyond the Republican Revival', *Yale Law Journal*, **97**, 1539.

Sunstein, C. (1995), 'The First Amendment in Cyberspace', *Yale Law Journal*, **104**, 1757.

Sunstein, C. (2001), *Republic.com*, US: Princeton University Press.

Trachtman, J. (1998), 'Cyberspace, Sovereignty, Jurisdiction and Modernism', *Indiana Journal of Global Legal Studies*, **5** (2),561.

Tullock, G. (1969), 'Federalism: Problems of Scale', *Public Choice*, **6**, 19.

Tullock, G. (1981), 'Why So Much Stability?', *Public Choice*, **37** (2), 189.

Tullock, G. (1982), 'Welfare and the Law', *International Review of Law and Economics*, **2**, 151.

Tzfati, Y. and G. Weimann (1999), 'Terror on the Internet', *Politika*, **4**, 45 (Hebrew).

Veltman, K. (2002), *On the Links between Open Source and Culture*, retrieved 31 August, 2003, from http://erste.oekonux-konferenz.de/dokumentation/texte/veltman .html.

Vile, M. (1967), *Constitutionalism and the Separation of Powers*, UK: Liberty Fund.

Voigt, S. (1999), *Explaining Constitutional Change: A Positive Economic Approach*, Cheltenham and Northampton, MA: Edward Elgar Publishing.

Voigt, S. and E. M. Salzberger (2002), 'Choosing Not To Choose: When Politicians Choose to Delegate Powers', *KYKLOS*, **55** (2), 289.

Walker, D. (2001, May 10), 'Electronic Election', *The Guardian*, retrieved 1 September, 2003, from http://www.guardian.co.uk/online/story/0,3605,488197,0.html.

Weber, S. (2000), 'The Political Economy of Open Source Software', *BRIE* Working Paper, **140**, retrieved 31 August, 2003, from Berkeley University Web site: http://e-conomy .berkeley.edu/publications/wp/wp140.pdf.

Webster, F. (1995), *Theories of the Information Society,* UK: Routledge.

Whynes, D. and R. Bowles (1981), *The Economic Theory of the State*, US: St. Martin's Press.

Williamson, O. E. (1975), *Markets and Hierarchies: Analysis and Antitrust Implications: a Study in the Economics of Internal Organization,* US: Free Press.

Willmore, L. (2002), 'Government Policies toward Information and Communication Technologies: A Historical Perspective', *Journal of Information Science,* **28**, 89.

Wishart, A. and R. Bochsler (2003), *Leaving Reality Behind,* US: Harper Collins Publishers, Inc.

Yassky, D. A. (1989), 'Two Tiered Theory of Constitution and Separation of Powers', *Yale Law Journal,* **99**, 431.

Yen, A. C. (2003), 'Western Frontier or Feudal Society? Metaphors and Perceptions of Cyberspace', *Berkeley Technology Law Review,* **17**, 1207.

Index